Roz S. ...ran is Professor of Translational Psychology at the Institute of Child Health, University College London, and founder of the Charlie Waller Institute of Evidence-Based Psychological Treatment. Her clinical and research interests include cognitive behavioural theories and treatments for anxiety disorders, eating disorders and perfectionism. She has over 125 publications. She is an associate editor of *Behaviour Research and Therapy* and recipient of an award for Distinguished Contributions to Professional Psychology from the British Psychological Society.

Pam Myles is Director of Training at the Charlie Waller Institute of Evidence-Based Psychological Treatment, University of Reading. Her clinical and training interests include cognitive behavioural treatments for anxiety disorders and depression across the age range. Pam's research predominantly focuses on CBT training and supervision. She is editor-in-chief of *The Cognitive Behavioural Therapist* and recipient of the University of Reading Teaching and Learning Team Award. Pam also sits on the Scientific Committee for the British Association for Behavioural and Cognitive Psychotherapies.

The CBT Handbook

Pamela Myles and Roz Shafran

ROBINSON

First published in Great Britain in 2015 by Robinson

5 7 9 10 8 6 4

Important Note
This book is not intended as a substitute for medical advice or treatment.
Any person with a condition requiring medical attention should consult
a qualified medical practitioner or suitable therapist.

A CIP catalogue record for this book
is available from the British Library.

ISBN 978-1-78033-201-7

Typeset in Palatino by Initial Typesetting Services, Edinburgh
Printed and bound in Great Britain by Clays Ltd, St Ives plc

Papers used by Robinson are from well-managed forests
and other responsible sources

Robinson
An imprint of
Little, Brown Book Group
Carmelite House
50 Victoria Embankment
London EC4Y 0DZ

An Hachette UK Company
www.hachette.co.uk

www.littlebrown.co.uk

DEDICATION

Pam –
To Rob

Roz –
To Tina and Michael Shafran, and David, Matthew, Anna
and Rachel Gittleson.

ACKNOWLEDGEMENTS

We are grateful to all our mentors and those whose work this book draws upon. Special thanks to Ray Novaco for kindly allowing us to use his *Dimensions of Anger Reactions II* and to Carl Lejeuz for giving his time and advice so generously on the Behavioural Activation section. Thank you also to our patients from whom we have learnt so much.

Contents

PART 3
Staying well

1 Introduction

Is this just *another* self-help book?

Emotional problems such as depression, anxiety and anger are so common that they affect around one in four people every year. These problems range from mild to severe, but they all affect quality of life. Crucially, emotional problems don't just affect individuals, but often extend to their families, friends and colleagues. They also impact on an individual's work life, the economy and society in general.

Individual therapy can help. Cognitive behavioural therapy (CBT) is the leading evidence-based 'talking therapy'. Research shows that this form of therapy, which involves talking through negative feelings with a trained professional, is effective in changing the way people experience distress and therefore improves their quality of life. It is important to bear in mind, however, that this therapy can be difficult to access, time-consuming and may not be necessary for everyone.

The aim of this book

If you are experiencing mild to moderate depression, anxiety and/or anger problems, then this book will help you to understand and overcome your difficulties using CBT. Why *this* book? Well, for a start, other books tend to focus on one particular problem area, whereas we believe that problems don't always come in neatly labelled boxes. Furthermore, although some are very clearly written, there are many others that can be hard to understand. We have written this book to be as easy to follow as possible. We want it to give you both the skills to make changes to help your feelings of distress, and also the confidence to give it a go. After all, change can be very difficult. In fact it can be impossible if it is not clear how to make those changes, and if the benefits of those changes are not immediately and dramatically obvious. We hope that the suggestions we make in this book about how you can change contribute a real and lasting difference to your life.

Personality

We all have a personality! It is what makes us unique. A group of researchers have identified five key aspects of personality. These are called the 'Big 5 Personality Dimensions' and include neuroticism (very sensitive, obsessive and anxious), extraversion (looking outside oneself for pleasure and fulfilment, for example through interaction with other people, being active, expressive and outgoing), openness to experience, agreeableness and conscientiousness (wanting to do what is right). These different dimensions are measured using a very long questionnaire. If you would like to know about your own personality you can complete the questionnaire online (http://www.personalitytest.net/cgi-bin/q.pl).

Whatever your personality, it is important to know that you can take control. Even if you tend to be introverted and you believe you have the personality of 'a worrier', for example, it does not mean that you cannot change. Similarly, if you were brought up to see the glass half empty instead of half full, then that doesn't mean you can't change your own perspective. Being able to see things differently, and solve worries using a variety of strategies (such as examining your worrying thoughts to see if there is another way of looking at things, or problem-solving, both of which we will describe in later chapters) can be very helpful in breaking established ways of thinking and behaving.

No matter how long-standing your difficulty, it is always worth trying to see the situation differently, and trying to behave differently, to see whether this has a positive impact on your emotional health.

Is this book for you?

We have used the techniques in this book to help hundreds of individuals, and have also used them in our own lives to help when times are tough.

The questions in Table 1.1 will help you to work out whether this book is for you.

Do you:	Yes	No
1. Suffer from persistent low mood?		
2. Feel worried or anxious often?		
3. Feel angry a lot?		
4. Feel stressed a great deal of the time?		
5. Think badly of yourself (have low self-esteem)?		
6. Have experience of a trauma in which you felt your life was threatened, or have you witnessed someone else's life being threatened?		
7. Feel suicidal?		
8. Think you will make the time to do the exercises in this book (really, honestly and truly)?		
9. Think you will skim the book and feel guilty that you haven't done it properly?		

Table 1.1: Is this book for you?

If you answered 'yes' to any of 1–5 and number 8, then this book may be able to help you.

If you answered 'yes' to number 6, then this book is unlikely to be of help to you, but there is help available: you should speak to your doctor about being referred to someone suitably qualified who can help. If you answered 'yes' to number 7 (you are feeling suicidal), then you should speak to your doctor or visit your Accident and Emergency department immediately.

If you answered 'no' to number 8 or 'yes' to number 9, then this book is probably not right for you just yet. This is because it might not be the right moment for you to be trying to change. Change requires time and commitment. If you are not ready to change, then it won't be helpful to buy a book that stares at you from the bookshelf as a constant reminder that you should do something about your problems. If your problems persist, however, you might consider talking to your doctor about your difficulties instead.

How common are common emotional problems?

Common emotional problems such as depression, anxiety, anger, low self-esteem and stress affect huge numbers of people. It is estimated that around 450 million people worldwide experience a mental health problem at some point in life. Approximately 50 per cent of people with common emotional problems recover after eighteen months, although less affluent people, the long-term sick and the unemployed are more likely to be affected for longer. Women are more likely to be treated for a mental health problem than men (29 per cent compared to 17 per cent).[1] You will find out more about depression, anxiety, anger, stress and low self-esteem in the next chapter.

How to use this book

The book is structured so that you can focus on the areas of most concern to you, learn about the problems, and then begin to make changes. We know that it can be difficult to tackle these kinds of problems for all sorts of reasons. Do try to bear this in mind as you work your way through the exercises in the book, so that you can be forgiving of yourself when times are tough. Remember that the benefits will repay your efforts.

Research shows that self-help books are much more likely to be effective when they are used with someone to support you, rather than alone. This makes sense. We are much more likely to turn up to a fitness class if we have arranged to meet a friend than if we have not, after all. Equally, we are more likely to hand in work if we have committed to a deadline. There are several reasons for this. First, there is social pressure: if you know that someone is going to ask you how you got on with a particular exercise in this book, you are more likely to do the exercise. Second, other people sometimes have good ideas! They can help you if something doesn't make sense, and can also help you to make the exercises personally meaningful and relevant. Third, it's important to have people to support you and cheer you on.

For all of the above reasons, we encourage you to find a 'supporter': someone to help you work through this book and share your journey of recovery. Choose someone whom you trust and see regularly, and with whom you feel you can be completely honest. If you do not have someone in your life that fits this description, or if you decide you are uncomfortable 'burdening' a friend with your problems, then you could find a mental health professional to help you. Your GP surgery may have information available on who could do so and how you can contact them, so talk to your doctor if you think this might be something you would like to pursue.

However, there is also absolutely no reason why you can't use this book on your own, and many people find books such as this helpful without someone else's input. It may be that you want to be able to try out the different techniques and exercises at your own pace, or that you just prefer to tackle your problems alone. It is up to each of us to find what works best, and we are confident that this book will help you however you decide to use it.

How this book works

The book is broken down into three parts. Part 1 focuses on how to identify different emotional problems and introduces a number of questionnaires to measure symptoms, as well as looking at how CBT can start to address problems. We will also introduce you to a number of people in the first part of the book. You will meet Leon, who has depression (Chapter 3), Pearl, who also has depression (Chapter 3), Bea, who has anxiety (Chapter 4), Dez, who has difficulties with anger (Chapter 5), Penny, who has problems with low self-esteem (Chapter 6), Leah, who has difficulties with stress (Chapter 7), and Ash, who has mixed anxiety and depression symptoms (Chapter 8). (These cases are not real people but illustrative examples inspired by our clinical practice.) Part 2 shows you how to use a variety of tried-and-tested CBT strategies to help bring about significant change to your difficulties. Finally, Part 3 focuses on how to make sure these changes last and what to do if you experience a re-emergence of any symptoms.

Throughout this book we will introduce you to a number of questionnaires, scales, measures, tables and charts. These will help illustrate some of the principles and methods used in CBT, but they are also there for *you* to use. A copy of each of these can be found in the Appendix at the back of this book. In the contents list, at the beginning of the book, you'll find a page number to help you locate specific items in the Appendix.

Of course it is important to bear in mind that many people, like Ash for example, experience more than one type of problem. For this reason, many of the measures that we introduce will appear in more than one chapter.

Summary

Every chapter ends with a summary, which you can use in different ways. Use the space below the summary to write down key points from the chapter. Or, if it would be more helpful, use it to make notes of the things that you want to remember from what you have read so far. What was most interesting? Did any one thing resonate in particular for you? What did you find helpful? This can act as a quick guide for you to refer to as you read on.

1. _____

   _____

2. _____

   _____

3. _____

   _____

4. _____

   _____

Part 1

Identifying the problem

2 CBT for emotional problems: An overview

Emotional problems such as depression and anxiety are remarkably common. Many of us will struggle with low mood, anxiety, anger or low self-esteem at one point or another. It is also not uncommon to experience more than one problem at a time. You might, for example, be experiencing quite severe anxiety while suffering from depression.

So how do you know if you have an emotional problem? Symptoms vary across different problems, and some can be common to all. It is not, for instance, unusual to have difficulty sleeping when you are feeling depressed, worried, anxious or pent up with anger. The rest of this chapter offers an overview of different types of problems, and is a good opportunity to find out if this book is for you. We will go into each of these problems in more detail in later chapters.

Depression

Most people will feel low from time to time. Depression, however, is a lowering of mood that is persistent and can make you feel tired, unmotivated, worthless and devoid of hope that things will ever get better. You may find that your sleep, appetite and self-esteem are affected and that you no longer get as much pleasure from doing things that you used to enjoy. Depression can be mild, moderate or severe. Sometimes it will be triggered by a stressful or upsetting event, such as going through childbirth, someone close to you dying, or losing your job. It is common for people with depression to experience anxiety as well. If you are suffering from depression, you may find that your routine is disrupted and that doing ordinary things like opening mail and cooking meals can feel like too much effort.

Anxiety

Most of us feel anxious occasionally. Sometimes it can even be helpful: if you see a large truck hurtling towards you, for example, the adrenaline rush from your anxiety would help you jump to safety. However, anxiety becomes problematic when it seems to happen for no apparent reason, if it lasts too long by continuing after the initial stressor has gone (for example, half an hour after getting out of the way of the truck) or if it is out of proportion to the situation. When anxiety is severe it can interfere with our normal day-to-day activities. Anxiety makes us feel fearful and tense and is often accompanied by unpleasant physical symptoms such as a racing heart, feeling sick, shaking, sweating, a dry mouth, chest pains, over-breathing (breathing too rapidly) and headaches.

Anger

Anger is a natural response to feeling attacked in some way. But it can become a problem when it is too intense, is disproportionate to the situation that causes it, lasts too long and/or leads to violence and aggression. When we are angry we become tense and adrenaline rushes through our body. Because anger can be a normal reaction to certain situations, it is not necessarily the anger itself that is the problem; what matters is how we deal with it. If anger leads to aggressive behaviour such as shouting or violence it can be extremely frightening for others. This, in turn, can lead to the breakdown of relationships with our family and friends. Sometimes people try to suppress their anger, but this can also be unhelpful. Suppressed anger can lead instead to 'passive aggressive' behaviour such as sarcasm or the silent treatment. This book will help you to start to tackle anger in a more constructive and healthy way.

Stress

Stress is extremely common: it's what experts call the experience of being under excessive pressure and feeling unable to cope. This is something most of us will undergo at some stage, because life is demanding and work, relationships and finances can all take their toll. Being stressed affects how we feel physically, our emotions, our thoughts and the way we behave. Common symptoms include having trouble sleeping, experiencing changes in your appetite and suffering from poor concentration. Muscle tension and headaches can also be typical signs of stress. When you are feeling stressed, you might be susceptible to anxiety, find it difficult to get rid of worrying thoughts or feel irritable. Some people drink or smoke more when they are stressed; others find their self-esteem is lower than usual. Of course people react in different ways to stress, so a situation that is stressful to one person may not be to another. Somebody who teaches large groups of students on a day-to-day basis, for example, might find it enjoyable and motivating, while another person might find the prospect of speaking to a large group extremely stressful.

Low self-esteem

Low self-esteem is a feature of numerous emotional problems. When our self-esteem is low we're likely to see ourselves as less valuable than other people. We may dislike ourselves and feel that we're unworthy and unlovable. In this way, depression and low self-esteem can feed off each other. Most of us recognize that the way we see ourselves will have an impact on how we feel and how confident we are with others. When our self-esteem is low it can be difficult to accept compliments, put our needs first or trust our own opinion. In these situations, people sometimes also find it easier to withdraw from others rather than risk doing something that they think may upset those around them.

Of course, depression, anxiety, stress, anger and low self-esteem are all interrelated, and many people have difficulties in more than one area.

This book will both help you to tackle each of these problem areas using CBT, and help you to understand how they are all connected.

Why choose CBT?

People choose CBT for a lot of different reasons. Your reasons might include some of the following:

- You want a treatment that has been proven to work.

- Someone you know has had CBT and recommended it.

- You have read something about CBT and think it might work for you.

- You are taking medication and need something to supplement your treatment.

- Your doctor suggested CBT could be helpful.

- CBT seems to be the only treatment available.

- You have tried other therapies and they have not been helpful.

Whatever your reason for choosing CBT, it is a good place to start to help you improve your mood, anxiety and general stress levels. Of all the therapies available, CBT is the one backed by the most scientific evidence that it works in treating specific emotional problems.

What is CBT?

If you search for 'CBT' on the internet, you may find yourself looking at 'Compulsory Basic Training' for riding motorcycles! Scroll down, however, and you will soon discover that 'CBT' stands for cognitive behavioural therapy. In fact, CBT is not one single therapy but a family of approaches that includes behavioural therapy, behavioural activation, cognitive therapy, exposure therapy and problem-solving. We will look at each of these in this book.

The different forms of CBT all share some important characteristics:

1. CBT therapies are based on the idea that your emotions are not caused by events themselves but by your interpretation of events

Consider the anxiety that you might feel when you hear the buzzing of a bee. The bee buzzes and you think 'there is a bee'. You might also think 'the bee is going to sting me', which is likely to make you feel anxious. But if you find out that the buzzing is coming not from a bee but from a bluebottle fly, you may think 'Great! Now I won't be stung', and your anxiety will pass. The point is that one event – something buzzing – can cause different reactions. In the first situation you felt anxious because you interpreted the buzzing as potentially dangerous, whereas in the second situation you decided that the buzzing was not in fact dangerous, and so your anxiety passed very quickly.

This example can also show how no two people are the same. It may be that you are not frightened of being stung by bees (after all, the pain is temporary and no big deal). If this were the case, then when you first interpreted the buzzing as coming from a bee, you probably wouldn't feel anxious at all. However, you may be very frightened of germs and, believing that bluebottles are germ carriers, end up doing a lot of anxious cleaning if one lands on your kitchen table. In this scenario, it's the buzzing of a bluebottle, and not a bee, that makes you feel worried.

Take a moment now to think of how the way you have interpreted specific events in your own life has affected your mood: for example, made you feel anxious or depressed. The examples in Table 2.1 might help to jog your memory.

Event	Thought	Emotional response
Not being given a promotion.	This is unfair – I work so hard!	Anger.
Note on the door from your boss saying 'Please see me'.	I am in trouble.	Anxiety.
Friend not responding to a text.	She does not like me.	Low mood.
Being too tired to read a bedtime story to the kids.	I am a bad parent.	Guilt.
Trousers too tight.	I have gained weight.	Feeling low/anxious and 'fat'.

Table 2.1: Example interpretations of events

Now use Table 2.2 for your own examples.

Event	Thought	Emotional response

Table 2.2: Your examples of interpretations of events

What should be clear from this exercise is that how we interpret things affects how we react emotionally. For example, when we feel that an injustice has been done, we may feel angry; when we perceive a danger, we may feel anxious; when we experience a sense of loss, we may feel low; when we perceive that we have done something wrong, we may feel guilty; when we perceive a change to our body shape and weight, we may feel fat.

We might presume that it will always be obvious what particular interpretation of events is making us feel a certain way, but this is often not the case. In fact, our emotional response can often be overwhelming, which makes what is going on in our heads that much less clear. One of the goals of this book is to help you to work out what is going on in your head, and how that links to the feelings you are experiencing.

2. CBT therapies are all 'talking therapies' and do not involve medication

You may be taking medication for your emotional problems or you may not. You may have tried medication in the past and found it helpful, or you may have experienced side effects that you weren't comfortable with. Medication can be a wonderful help for many problems. It can make the unbearable just slightly more bearable, no doubt saving countless lives and improving the quality of many others.

If you choose to take medication and it works on its own, then that is great. If you think it is helping you but that there is still room for improvement, then that is fine too. There is no reason why you shouldn't use this book at the same time as taking medication. If this is the case, it might be worth letting your doctor know you are reading this book and doing the exercises it contains so that they can support you.

3. The first step of CBT is to identify what type of problem you are experiencing

In Chapters 3 to 8 we describe in detail the types of problems you may be undergoing in terms of anxiety, depression, anger, stress, self-esteem and so on. Interpreting and identifying the kind of problems you may be experiencing is an important step, and it will help you to devise ways to tackle them. This book will help you to do so.

4. CBT is less concerned with understanding the root of the problem than with understanding why your particular problem is persisting now

It is common in some therapies to discuss your childhood. However, do you *need* to understand what has happened to you in the past in order to change how you feel in the present? The answer is no. Let's take the example of stress. You do not need to know the cause of your stress to know that taking a few minutes out with a cup of tea is likely to help you relax a little bit. Of course, knowing why you felt stressed is helpful in being able to reduce stress, but it is not the priority in the short term. For one thing, there are likely to be lots of causes for your stress, and going back into your childhood may only provide clues as to what happened to cause it in the first place. In fact, sometimes finding a precise cause may be impossible, but this does not have to mean you can't get better. It is more important to know *what is causing your feelings of stress to persist* and what needs to change in order to reduce your stress levels and thereby improve the quality of your life. The same principle applies to all the other areas that we are looking at in this book. Although CBT tends not to focus on the root of the problem, it can still be helpful to put a problem in context. With this in mind, we have included two chapters on how to make sense of your problems (see Chapters 9 and 10).

5. The second step of a CBT approach involves breaking vicious cycles so that your problem improves

Many of us get trapped in vicious cycles. Let's say, for example, that your kids refuse to get dressed in the morning before school, so you shout at them to hurry or else they will be late. They then respond by shouting back at you, by which time you are trapped in a vicious cycle and they are *still* late for school. Shouting doesn't help them get dressed and creates a bad atmosphere in which they are reluctant to do anything they are told – including getting dressed! In CBT we try to identify the vicious cycles that are keeping you trapped, and then find the best way for you to break these cycles, and we do this in Part 2. Usually it is not enough just to be vague and say 'try things a different way'. Specific suggestions are required. Going back to our example of getting your kids dressed on time, practical steps such as putting clothes out the night before, giving stickers to reward your child, or letting them spend any extra time they save by getting dressed quickly on the computer, may help break the pattern of morning shouting matches.

6. The third step involves helping you to stay well

'Old habits die hard' is a familiar expression that indicates that it is tough to change. Sometimes it is even tougher to stick with a new habit you are trying to develop. For example, the vast majority of people who lose weight when they diet go on to regain the weight that they lost. People often find it very hard to stick to their new dietary regimes and give up after a couple of minor setbacks. An important part of CBT involves preparing you for those setbacks, and helping you to deal with them. We cover this in Chapter 21.

7. CBT is time-limited, structured and personal

If you were to see a CBT therapist, you would work with them to identify and help overcome your difficulties. Together you would identify clear personal goals to work towards. CBT is a time-limited therapy in that it rarely lasts for more than twenty sessions (it usually runs to six or twelve sessions). These sessions involve discussing specific problems and learning new ways of dealing with difficulties. They also include agreeing ways of testing out what has been learned in the form of 'homework'.

We've designed this book to work in a similar way. First we will help you to identify your problem, and get an understanding of where it might have come from and what is keeping it going. Then we will help you to identify a set of goals to work towards, teach you some new strategies, and help you devise ways of trying out those strategies.

8. A scientific approach is a very important part of CBT

In the next section, we will briefly mention the research that has been carried out on CBT, including the research that demonstrates that using self-help books can be effective in treating mental health difficulties. You will use a 'scientific approach' as you work through this book: each chapter includes scales and measures for you to use to keep a record of your symptoms as you progress. You will find copies of these scales and measures in the Appendix. We have also included some progress graphs at the end of the book so you can chart how your scores change. The scales, measures and graphs will help you to keep track of your symptoms as you work your way through this book. They will highlight your progress and give you pointers as to what might need additional work.

What are the 'scales and measures'?

There are a number of different scales and measures in this book which are all tools designed to 'measure' your initial symptoms and your progress. These are the same measures that CBT therapists use and unfortunately their names do sound technical – however, they are very easy to use. Relevant additional measures will be introduced in later chapters as appropriate.

- The PHQ-9 (Patient Health Questionnaire) measures low mood.

- The GAD-7 (Generalized Anxiety Disorder scale) measures anxiety levels.

- The Phobia Scales measure very specific anxiety (phobias). This may or may not be relevant to you depending on the nature of your problem.

- The WASAS (Work and Social Adjustment Scale) measures the impact of your difficulties on a number of important areas in your life, and can be helpful to keep track of improvements in each area.

These four measures are generally appropriate for everyone, so you might want to complete them all. It is a good idea to get a 'baseline' for how you are feeling now, so that you can use this to track your progress as you work through this book. To do this, fill in the four short measures, which you will find in the Appendix, pp. 387–92. They won't take long to complete. Once you are finished, you can plot your scores on the graphs provided on pp. 405–8. You can then keep track of your scores each time you repeat the measures; we would recommend filling them in once a week at least. Don't worry about some of the measures asking you to indicate how you have been feeling in the last two weeks if you are filling them in weekly. If this is the case, just think back over the last few days since you completed them. Of course, you might find that you rate so low on a measure that you think it is not worth repeating.

How thinking, emotional responses, bodily sensations and behaviour are linked

Earlier on we described how particular interpretations are linked to certain emotions such as anger, low mood, guilt or anxiety. For example, if you hear a buzzing and interpret the buzzing as coming from a bee, you may feel anxious. If the friend you spot on the other side of the street doesn't acknowledge you, you may interpret it as them being in some way upset with you, and then feel anxious or depressed. But what comes after you experience such emotions? What usually happens is that your body reacts. We all know what it feels like to be anxious in one way or another, whether it's the way our hearts race when we believe we are in danger or the way our stomachs flutter when we go on a first date.

Anxiety is a normal emotion and an important part of life because it acts as a basic survival mechanism, commonly known as the 'fight or flight' response. This is our body's primitive, inborn, automatic response that helps us prepare to confront danger by either facing it head on ('fight') or running away ('flight'). There are many day-to-day situations where it is reasonable to experience some degree of anxiety. For example, if you are about to cross a busy road where there is no pedestrian crossing, then it is realistic that you would feel a little anxious about potentially getting hit by a car. In this scenario, anxiety helps to keep you vigilant and to pay more attention to the cars, thereby keeping you safe. However, for some people anxiety happens too frequently (when they are not faced with real danger), is too intense (for example, it leads to panic attacks) or lasts too long (it goes on longer than the stressful situation lasts). So although anxiety is normal and vital to our survival, in certain circumstances it can be unhelpful and debilitating.

Once your body reacts to a perceived threat, it is likely to cause you to behave in a certain way. Let's return to the example of the buzzing bee to illustrate what we mean. If you are afraid of bees, then when you hear the buzzing your heart may begin to race, you may feel hot and sweaty, and you may even feel sick or panicky. You then have two problems. The first is getting rid of the bee and the second is the unpleasant way you feel.

If you can successfully get rid of the bee by opening the door, you are likely to think 'I am safe'. This feeling of safety will trigger an emotional reaction of relief and your body will *not* react by preparing to fight or flee. Instead your behaviour will be calm and you will be able to stay where you are. On the other hand, it may be that you are so frightened of the bee that you fumble with the door and cannot open it to let the bee out. In this case, you might think 'I'm trapped', and feel highly anxious. Suddenly, there will be a very rapid increase in symptoms in your body. You may find that you are rooted to the spot, paralysed with fear. You may even think 'this stress is going to kill me' and then begin to worry about the damage that such extreme anxiety is causing you.

This example illustrates the close link between our thinking, emotional responses, bodily sensations and behaviour. In CBT we examine the thoughts that lead to emotional arousal, which in turn leads to bodily sensations and affects how we behave, which links back to thoughts. However, it may be that your experience actually begins with bodily sensations (for example, you notice your breathing is a bit faster than usual), or begins with behaviour (for example, walking into a busy supermarket), or it can begin with an emotional response (for example, feeling nervous). Either way, our thoughts, emotions, bodily sensations and behaviour are all interlinked. In addition, other things will be happening at the same time, and these might tip the balance. If you are afraid of bees and are confronted by several on the same day that your washing machine is broken, your partner is being unhelpful and you are experiencing money problems, you may feel completely overwhelmed. Moreover, you may feel that in the absence of all of these you could have responded calmly, rationally and productively to the bee problem.

The diagram in Figure 2.1 illustrates the relationship between thoughts, emotions, physical sensations and behaviour which we will call the 'CBT Model' from hereon. We have chosen to put feelings at the top of the model because the way you are feeling is likely to have motivated you to buy this book. After all, what has led you this far is your feeling that you want to change in order to become happier.

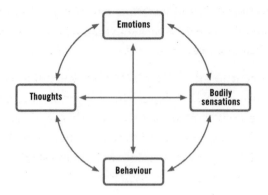

Figure 2.1: CBT model

This book will help you work out how all these elements interact for your own specific problems, and will enable you to make changes to your feelings, thoughts, bodily sensations and behaviour using CBT.

Does CBT work?

There are lots of research studies showing that face-to-face talking therapy with a therapist trained in CBT is helpful. This is true for people with anxiety disorders, eating disorders, depression, personality disorders, substance misuse problems, psychosis, relationship problems and others. Although most people who are referred to a CBT therapist are likely to have between six and twelve sessions with their therapist, it can also be helpful in much lower 'doses'. CBT has been found to be effective across all age groups, including children. In addition, it has also been shown to be effective in self-help book form (especially with a supporter i.e. a mental health practitioner, friend or family member) although many people use such materials successfully by themselves.

CBT is not the only face-to-face talking therapy that has been shown to be effective for these problems. 'Interpersonal psychotherapy' (IPT), for example, is effective for depression and eating disorders. The central idea of IPT is that psychological symptoms, such as low mood, can be understood as a response to current difficulties in relationships and directly affect the quality of those relationships. IPT tends to focus on addressing conflict with another person; life changes that affect how the person feels about themselves and others; grief and loss; and difficulty in starting or keeping relationships going.

Another treatment found to be effective in depression is 'behavioural activation'. When people are depressed, they tend to become less active. They get to the point where they stop seeing friends and family, and give up doing the things they used to enjoy. Behavioural activation aims to get people active again by helping them to re-establish their normal routines, which in turn improves their mood.

While other therapies can be very effective, no other talking therapy has been found to be as consistently effective as CBT in helping people overcome their emotional problems.

To see an improvement in how you are feeling, you will need to commit to carrying out the exercises properly – to setting aside time to read through this book and practise the techniques it contains. If you do this, it is very likely you will start to see positive changes. If, on the other hand, you do not improve as much as you would have hoped, make an appointment with your doctor and explain the work you have done and request some more intensive therapy.

What next?

By now you should have a good understanding of what CBT is, and how using this book might help you. The chapters that follow will help you to:

- Identify what type of problems you are experiencing.

- Understand why your particular problem persists by defining the problem.

- Set 'SMART' goals (i.e. goals that are Specific, Measurable, Achievable, Realistic and Time-orientated).

- Use behavioural activation to start tackling your problem.

- Detect your unhelpful thinking and behaviour.

- Change your unhelpful thinking and behaviour by 1) evaluating your thoughts and 2) using behavioural experiments.

- Reach a new perspective.

- Test out the new perspective in your life.

- Deal with setbacks.

- Make changes last.

First, in Part 1, we will describe in more detail each problem mentioned earlier in this chapter to give you a better understanding of what causes it, how it affects people and what keeps the problem going.

Summary

Use the space below to write down key points or things that you want to remember from this chapter. What did you find out that you didn't know before? Did any one aspect of the common problems that were described ring true for you? Is there anything that caught your attention in this chapter that you want to learn more about? The notes that you make here will be a useful reference guide for you to turn back to as you progress through this book.

1. _____

   _____

2. _____

   _____

3. _____

   _____

4. _____

   _____

3 Depression

Case illustration 1: Leon

Leon is a twenty-eight-year-old single man who lives alone and has a job in a local music shop. He has not been able to work for the last month because of his depression. He became depressed five months ago. The main trigger for this episode of depression was discovering that his life-long best friend and his girlfriend of two years were having a relationship. The discovery occurred when he came home early from work to find them in bed together in the flat he shared with his girlfriend. Leon has felt completely devastated by these recent events and, as a result, has felt unable to cope with his job. His parents separated when he was eight and both live 200 miles away, so he does not get to see them as much as he would like. He has not told either of them what has happened as he does not want them to worry. He has, however, confided in his older brother who has been supportive but also lives far away.

Leon feels betrayed and humiliated by what has happened to him, as well as an overwhelming sense of loss. He has stopped socializing with friends, some of whom he no longer trusts because he believes they must have known about the relationship. He stays in bed most of the day, lacks energy and feels no pleasure or sense of purpose in life. He spends most of his time ruminating over the lost relationships and berates himself for not noticing that the affair was going on. He sometimes thinks that he would be better off dead but does not have any current plans to kill himself.

Many people say they are 'depressed' when they want to convey that their mood is low. Low mood is certainly part of depression, but it is also part of everyday life. It can happen when something goes wrong at work or when you are feeling neglected by your partner. It can even be triggered by something as seemingly small as realizing you can't afford the new shirt you wanted. All sorts of everyday events can leave us feeling low. However, the low mood in depression is persistent. It doesn't get better after a good night's sleep and it affects people in lots of ways. For example, people with depression often have trouble concentrating and sleeping; their appetite for food and sexual intimacy are affected; they think negative thoughts about themselves, their world and their future. Some people find that they have suicidal thoughts, images and urges. Some people cry a lot when they are depressed while others find they cannot cry at all. People who suffer depression feel hopeless, as though things will never change, and often become socially isolated.

Table 3.1: *Key statistics about depression*

- 8–12 per cent of people experience depression in any one year.

- Depression occurs in one in ten adults in the UK at any one time.

- Approximately one in twenty people at any one time experience major (clinical) depression.

- Depression is more common in women than men. One in four women will require treatment for depression at some time, compared to one in ten men. It is not clear why this is, but both social and biological factors may play a part.

- As an older adult, you are more likely to suffer from depression if you are in residential care: one in five older adults living on their own or with family suffer from depression, while two in five living in residential care experience it.

- Depression is expected to be the second biggest global cause of disability (after coronary heart disease) by 2020.[2]

What causes depression?

We know that there are a number of possible causes of depression, including:

- Genetics: If you have a family history of depression, then you may be more likely to develop it than those who do not.

- Chemical imbalance: There is some indication that mood-related chemicals such as serotonin are low in the brain during depressive episodes. This is commonly known as a 'chemical imbalance'. A chemical imbalance may reflect a low mood, but it may also contribute to its persistence or indeed its development in the first place. Mood changes – caused by psychological treatment or medication – can be reflected in changes in brain chemistry.

- Life events: Circumstances such as losing someone important to you, relationship difficulties, divorce and loss of a job can trigger depression.

The signs and symptoms of depression

Not everybody with depression experiences the same symptoms, but we've listed some of the most common signs below. If you experience five or more of the following symptoms for more than two weeks and at least one of the symptoms is either 1.) depressed mood or 2.) loss of interest or pleasure, you should visit your doctor.

- Depressed mood.

- Markedly diminished interest or pleasure in all, or almost all, activities.

- Change in appetite or weight (usually this means a decreased appetite, but sometimes an increased appetite occurs).

- Disturbed sleep such as insomnia or sleeping too much.

- Agitation and restlessness, or being slowed down to a degree that is noticeable to others.

- Fatigue or loss of energy.

- Feelings of worthlessness or excessive or inappropriate guilt.

- Difficulty concentrating or indecisiveness.

- Thoughts of being better off dead or hurting yourself in some way.

Depression is classified into many different levels of severity, which we have listed below. Your level of depression relates to how many of the symptoms listed above you experience, and their impact on your life.

- **Subthreshold depression** is diagnosed when you feel low but experience fewer than five of the symptoms of depression listed above.

- **Mild depression** is diagnosed when you have the five symptoms required to make the diagnosis, and perhaps a few others too. At this level, symptoms result in minor functional impairment (e.g. you don't look after yourself as well as you normally do, for instance by brushing your hair, cleaning your teeth or eating healthily).

- **Moderate depression** is when your symptoms fall between 'mild depression' and 'severe depression'.

- **Severe depression** is when you experience most of the symptoms listed above, and they markedly interfere with your ability to function in day-to-day life (e.g. go to work, look after children). Severe depression can occur with or without psychotic symptoms (e.g.

hallucinations, such as hearing voices, or delusions, which are beliefs that you'd normally recognize are clearly untrue).

The symptoms listed above are common in depression and are required for a diagnosis of depression to be made according to one of the main diagnostical manuals (DSM-5).[3] Other symptoms that are also often experienced by people who are depressed are included in Figure 3.1.

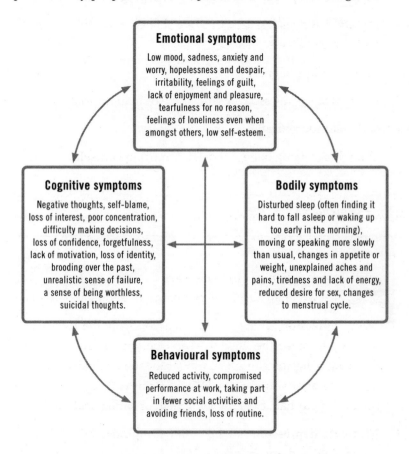

Figure 3.1: Common symptoms of depression

Once you have thought about the symptoms that you might be suffering from, you can start to consider how they may be impacting your life. If you have not already done so, now is a good time to complete the measures introduced in Chapter 2 (PHQ-9, GAD-7, Phobia Scales and the Work and Social Adjustment Scale) in the Appendix, pp. 387–92, so you can begin to chart your progress. It's important to note that you won't need to use all of the measures, just those which relate to the symptoms you are experiencing. However, if you are suffering from depression, you may wish to complete all of them because, for instance, you are quite likely to be experiencing anxiety symptoms as well.

Once you have done this, you can use the measures to assess the extent of your problems now so that, by returning to these measures and using them to reassess your difficulties on a regular basis, you can judge the progress you are making.

Leon, who we described at the beginning of this chapter, completed all four measures (see Table 3.2).

Table 3.2: Leon's completed measures

Leon's completed PHQ-9

Over the last 2 weeks, how often have you been bothered by any of the following problems?	Not at all	Several days	More than half the days	Nearly every day
1 Little interest or pleasure in doing things	0	1	2	**_3_**
2 Feeling down, depressed, or hopeless	0	1	**_2_**	3
3 Trouble falling or staying asleep, or sleeping too much	0	1	2	**_3_**
4 Feeling tired or having little energy	0	1	2	**_3_**

5	Poor appetite or overeating	0	<u>1</u>	2	3
6	Feeling bad about yourself — or that you are a failure or have let yourself or your family down	0	1	2	<u>3</u>
7	Trouble concentrating on things such as reading the newspaper or watching television	0	1	<u>2</u>	3
8	Moving or speaking so slowly that other people could have noticed? Or the opposite – being so fidgety or restless that you have been moving around a lot more than usual	<u>0</u>	1	2	3
9	Thoughts that you would be better off dead or of hurting yourself in some way	0	<u>1</u>	2	3
PHQ-9 total score 18					

Scoring PHQ-9

Add up your scores and see where they fall on this index of severity.

0–4   None

5–9   Mild depression

10–14   Moderate depression

15–19   Moderately severe depression

20–27   Severe depression

If you have a score of 10 or above for more than two weeks and/
or scoring 3 on question 9, you should visit your doctor.

Leon's completed GAD-7

Over the <u>last 2 weeks</u>, how often have you been bothered by any of the following problems?		Not at all	Several days	More than half the days	Nearly every day
1	Feeling nervous, anxious or on edge	0	<u>**1**</u>	2	3
2	Not being able to stop or control worrying	0	1	<u>**2**</u>	3
3	Worrying too much about different things	0	1	2	<u>**3**</u>
4	Trouble relaxing	0	1	<u>**2**</u>	3
5	Being so restless that it is hard to sit still	<u>**0**</u>	1	2	3
6	Becoming easily annoyed or irritable	0	1	<u>**2**</u>	3
7	Feeling afraid, as if something awful might happen	0	1	<u>**2**</u>	3
GAD-7 total score 12					

Scoring GAD-7

Add up your scores and see where they fall on this index of severity.

0–4   None

5–10   Mild anxiety

11–15   Moderate anxiety

16–21   Severe anxiety

If you have a score of 8 or more you may wish to consider visiting your doctor.

Leon's completed Phobia Scales

Choose a number from the scale below to show how much you would avoid each of the situations or objects listed below. Then write the number in the box opposite the situation.

0	1	2	3	4	5	6	7	8
Would not avoid it		Slightly avoid it		Definitely avoid it		Markedly avoid it		Always avoid it

Social situations because of a fear of being embarrassed or making a fool of myself. [0]

Certain situations because of a fear of having a panic attack or other distressing symptoms (such as loss of bladder control, vomiting or dizziness). [0]

Certain situations because of a fear of particular objects or activities (such as animals, heights, seeing blood, being in confined spaces, driving or flying). [0]

Scoring the Phobia Scales

These questions help you track the severity of your phobic anxiety. The higher the score, the more severe the anxiety.

Leon's completed Work and Social Adjustment scale

Using the scale provided below, select the number that you think most accurately describes how you are affected in each section.

1. Work

If you are retired or choose not to have a job for reasons unrelated to your problem, please tick N/A (not applicable).

0	1	2	3	4	5	6	7	**8**	N/A
Not at all		Slightly		Definitely		Markedly		Very severely	☐ I cannot work

2. Home management

Cleaning, tidying, shopping, cooking, looking after home/children, paying bills, etc.

0	1	2	3	4	5	**6**	7	8
Not at all		Slightly		Definitely		Markedly		Very severely

3. Social leisure activities

With other people, e.g. parties, pubs, outings, entertaining, etc.

0	1	2	3	4	5	6	**7**	8
Not at all		Slightly		Definitely		Markedly		Very severely

4. Private leisure activities

Done alone, e.g. reading, gardening, sewing, hobbies, walking, etc.

0	1	2	3	4	5	**6**	7	8
Not at all		Slightly		Definitely		Markedly		Very severely

5. Family and relationships

Forming and maintaining close relationships with others, including the people that I live with.

0	1	2	3	**4**	5	6	7	8
Not at all		Slightly		Definitely		Markedly		Very severely

Total score   31

Scoring the WASAS

This five-item measure can help you track the impact of your problems on your work, home life, social life, private activities and your relationships.

How is depression treated?

There are a number of effective treatments for depression. An important first step to getting the right treatment for you is to visit your doctor. This is important because your doctor will be able to rule out other conditions that have similar symptoms to depression, such as hypothyroidism (an underactive thyroid gland, leading to a variety of symptoms such as feeling low and tired, or putting on weight) or sleep problems. Your doctor will also be able to advise you on whether or not taking antidepressant medication might help.

Since visiting his doctor, Leon has been taking a prescribed antidepressant, and is starting to feel some of the benefits such as an improvement in his sleep and appetite. However, as he has only been taking the medicine for four weeks, it's still early days and further improvements may well follow.

As we explained earlier, the different levels of depression depend on how severe it is. For each of these levels, there are different options for treatment. For anybody who is known or suspected to have depression, there will always be support, psycho-education (education offered to people with a mental health condition), active monitoring (this is sometimes known as 'watchful waiting' when your GP regularly assesses deterioration or improvement in symptoms) and referral for further treatment available. Then, for mild to moderate depression there is also the possibility of low-intensity interventions. These interventions focus on supporting the person to use CBT-informed self-help guides such as this book to tackle their difficulties.

For those who haven't responded well to earlier treatment or who have moderate or severe depression, there are lots of options available, including medication, high-intensity psychological treatment (e.g. one-to-one CBT), combined treatments (such as CBT and antidepressant medication) and collaborative care (the integration of care from a number of health professionals done in a coordinated way rather than all delivered independently).

Finally, for those experiencing severe and complex depression, who pose a risk to life or of severe self-neglect, there is further medication available, high-intensity psychological treatment, crisis service, combined treatments, multiprofessional (involving a number of professionals such as doctors, nurses, psychologists) and inpatient care. Please do seek the help you need as it can really make a difference.

This is all a lot of information about depression. We have thought about the symptoms, the impacts *and* the treatments. Let's now return to Leon's story to see how the interrelation between situations, thoughts, emotions, bodily sensations and behaviours discussed in the last chapter might begin to relate to depression.

Leon's story

As we've seen, Leon is a twenty-eight-year-old single man who has been feeling depressed for the last five months since he broke up with his girlfriend. Since then, his relationships with his friends have become strained and so, as a result, he has become increasingly socially isolated and his work life has also suffered. During a recent incident when his mood was particularly low, Leon decided to monitor his symptoms using the CBT model in Figure 3.2. You can see how his symptoms are interlinked, and how they influence each other.

Figure 3.2: Leon's CBT model

Situation: Woke up on Monday morning and started thinking about the week stretching in front of me.

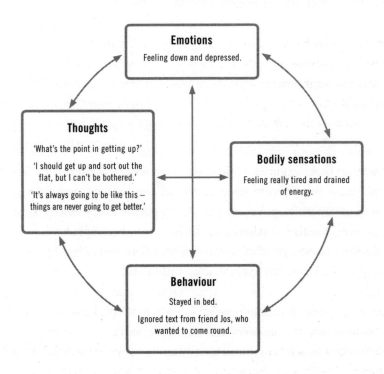

After writing down his symptoms in the CBT model in Figure 3.2, Leon rated his problems with low mood on the mood scale (Figure 3.3). His baseline score, the one he is taking now to assess his starting point, on his overall mood is:

-5	<u>-4</u>	-3	-2	-1	0	+1	+2	+3	+4	+5

Negative   Neutral   Positive
mood   mood

Figure 3.3: Leon's mood scale

To take your own baseline mood scale score, complete the measure in the Appendix, pp. 385–6. That way you can keep track of improvements over time.

For the other measures, Leon's baseline scores are:

PHQ-9: 18.

GAD-7: 12.

Phobia Scale: 0, 0, 0.

WASAS: 31.

Leon's scores indicate that his depressed mood is in the moderately severe range, he is experiencing moderate anxiety, he does not present with any phobic anxiety and that his problems are having a significant impact on his life, particularly home management and both social and individual leisure activities.

Details of where you can find further information about depression can be found in Further Resources, pp. 381–2, and in Part 2 we will be looking at various methods to help you address your difficulties. Before moving on to the next chapter, we want to introduce you to Pearl.

Case illustration 2: Pearl

Pearl is a sixty-nine-year-old married woman who lives with her husband, John. She has been depressed for the past year or so. The onset of her depression coincided with the diagnosis of her husband's Alzheimer's disease. They have one daughter, Tia, who lives and works forty miles away and so is only able to come over at the weekend. John is in the early stages of dementia and Pearl finds she is having to keep a close eye on him to ensure that he does not wander off or try to go somewhere in the car, which he often forgets he is no longer allowed to drive. Pearl has given up doing a lot of the things she used to enjoy, like going to see shows at her local theatre, attending a local supper club and meeting friends for coffee, because she does not feel able to leave John on his own. John's close friend Eddie has offered to come to sit with John while she goes out, but Pearl feels too much like this is an imposition on Eddie.

Apart from two earlier short-lived episodes of depression, Pearl has been a generally happy person and has felt able to cope with all that life has thrown at her. However, she now views herself as a 'waste of space' and fears that, with John's condition, things will only get worse. Pearl has trouble sleeping, mainly waking early, and she feels tired most of the time. She feels tense and anxious a lot as she worries about what the future holds for John. Her mood is low and although she does have occasional suicidal thoughts, she says she would never act on them because she knows her daughter would be devastated.

Pearl was able to think of a recent incident when her mood was particularly low. She used the CBT model diagram in Figure 3.4 to link her symptoms.

Figure 3.4: Pearl's CBT model

Situation: It's raining outside and John is being argumentative.

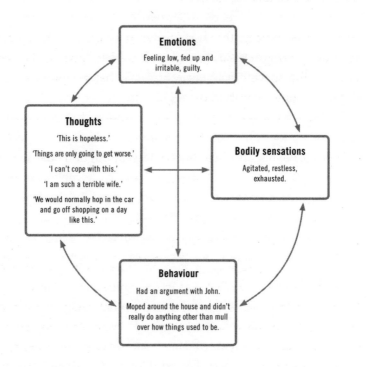

Pearl then rated her mood on the scale (Figure 3.5). Her baseline score on her overall mood is:

-5	-4	**-3**	-2	-1	0	+1	+2	+3	+4	+5

Negative   Neutral   Positive
mood   mood

Figure 3.5: Pearl's mood scale

Pearl then completed the other measures.

Pearl's baseline PHQ-9 score is: 16.

Her baseline GAD-7 score is: 13.

Her baseline Phobia Scale scores are: -1, 1, 0.

Her baseline WASAS score is: 23.

Pearl's scores indicate that her depressed mood is in the moderately severe range, she is experiencing marked anxiety, she does not have any specific phobic anxiety and that her problems are having a significant impact on her life.

We will chart Leon's and Pearl's progress throughout the remaining chapters.

Summary

You can use the space below to make your own summary of the key points from this chapter. What was most important? Did anything you came across in the chapter surprise you? What did you learn about depression that was most helpful to know? Were there any aspects of Leon or Pearl's stories that you will reflect on? Writing a summary here will mean that you have a useful reference to look back on later.

1. _____

_____

2. _____

_____

3. _____

_____

4. _____

_____

4 Anxiety

Case illustration 3: Bea

Bea is a forty-seven-year-old divorced woman. She lives with one of her three grown-up children, Gus, who is twenty-six years old and has a mild learning disability. Her other two sons, who are twenty-eight and thirty, both live close by and visit often. Bea describes herself as always having been a worrier: 'I was born a worrier to a worrier mother.' She has a strong dislike and intolerance of uncertainty (i.e. not being 100 per cent sure that every situation will work out), which is one of the things that put a strain on her marriage. Her husband left her five years ago for what Bea describes as a 'younger model'. Her husband is an owner of a small business and now lives with his secretary, who is twenty-five years his junior. They have just had a baby and he has little interest in his children and grandchildren from his marriage with Bea.

Bea worries about Gus and what will become of him if something happens to her. She worries about her own health and about losing her house, despite being healthy and secure in her job as a bus driver. She also worries about her other sons and their children (they have two each). One of her grandchildren, Lily, was born prematurely and has had ongoing heart problems, which she worries about as well. When visitors come to visit, Bea worries about how clean the house is. She has stopped watching the news as she finds that she takes the worries of the world on her shoulders and struggles to put them out of her mind. She suffers a lot from muscle tension and frequently rubs the back of her neck in an attempt to get rid of the strain. She does not sleep well, and some nights she can struggle to get to sleep because of all of the worries she has taken on board.

Types of anxiety

Anxiety problems take many different forms.

Panic disorder (with or without agoraphobia)

People with panic disorder experience sudden attacks of intense anxiety or fear, during which they feel like they are going to die, lose control in some way or go crazy, and they worry about when another attack might happen. Unpleasant physical symptoms include: increased heart rate, feeling breathless, shaking, light-headedness and chest pain. People with this problem will sometimes avoid situations where they believe they are more likely to have a panic attack, such as going away from home, being in crowded places, etc. – when this is the case, the problem can be considered to be panic disorder with agoraphobia.

Generalized anxiety disorder

Generalized anxiety disorder, or GAD, is a condition in which the person feels in a constant state of anxiety and may be regarded by friends and family as a 'constant worrier'. People who have GAD often describe themselves as suffering from 'free-floating anxiety', which moves from one problem to another as soon as the first issue is resolved. Common symptoms of GAD include a need for certainty; being easily fatigued; loss of concentration and one's mind going blank; feeling irritable; muscle tension; and sleep disturbance.

Specific phobia

This is a term used for unreasonable or irrational fear of a specific object or situation. The person with the phobia will tend to avoid direct contact with their feared stimuli; if particularly severe, even a mention of it can lead to anxiety. The fear or anxiety can be triggered by not only the presence but also the anticipation of being faced with the specific object or situation. Often the person knows logically that their fear is unreasonable, but still feels unable to control it. Specific phobias can be disabling for the person affected. Common phobias include: animals and insects, storms, the dark, injections and going to the dentist or doctor.

Social anxiety disorder (also known as social phobia)

This is a persistent fear of social situations and being around people. It is much more than simply feeling shy; instead social anxiety disorder causes an intense and overwhelming fear of being negatively evaluated by others in what may seem to be routine social interactions such as shopping or speaking on the phone. People with social anxiety disorder frequently worry that they may say or do something that will be perceived negatively by others and that they will feel humiliated. It can be a real problem, disrupting normal life, impairing performance at work and in social situations, and interfering with relationships.

Obsessive compulsive disorder (OCD)

When a person suffers from this condition they experience obsessive thoughts and compulsive behaviours. Obsessions are unwanted, unpleasant thoughts, images or urges that repeatedly pop into a person's mind and cause anxiety. The compulsive behaviour is a repetitive behaviour or mental ritual that someone feels compelled to perform in order to prevent the obsessional thought coming true. For example, someone who is obsessively scared of their property catching fire may feel the need to check that sockets and plugs are switched off when not in use. Generally the person will have an obsessive thought pop into their mind, which will cause anxiety, and the person will react by engaging in the compulsion. This makes the individual feel better temporarily but it does not alleviate the problem in the long-term. OCD can be very disabling for the sufferer and have a severe impact on day-to-day functioning.

Health anxiety (sometimes referred to as hypochondriasis)

This is characterized by obsessive worrying about one's health to the point where it is causing marked distress and affecting the person's ability to function normally. Some people with health anxiety experience unexplained physical symptoms that they assume are a sign of serious illness. The severe anxiety this triggers can persist despite reassurance from a medical professional. Other people with health anxiety might find that they are almost permanently worried about their future state of health (e.g. concerns about developing cancer). People with health anxiety tend to fall into one of the following two categories: those who constantly seek information and reassurance (e.g. by frequent visits to the GP, researching symptoms on the internet, etc.); or those who opt for avoidance (e.g. avoiding seeing the GP, avoiding exertion in case it makes symptoms worse, etc.).

Post-traumatic stress disorder (PTSD)

This disorder is caused by extremely stressful, frightening or distressing events such as serious road traffic accidents, violent personal assaults, witnessing violent deaths, military combat, natural disasters, etc. It is estimated to affect around one in three people who have been involved in a traumatic event. Symptoms of post-traumatic stress disorder include reliving symptoms such as in nightmares and flashbacks; feeling constantly on edge; experiencing difficulty sleeping; and avoidance or numbing symptoms such as avoiding reminders or having difficulty remembering aspects of the event. Symptoms are often severe and persistent, which can have a significant impact on the person's daily life.

The key to understanding anxiety is in recognizing that people with anxiety disorders *overestimate the probability of threat*. In other words, they think that something is more threatening or dangerous than it actually is. One person may overestimate the consequences of a bee sting, for example, while another may overestimate the possibility of catching a disease from a bluebottle fly. To a certain extent, the actual threat is not what is important – it is rather the *perception* of threat. Once someone believes that a threat is real, they feel anxious.

Anxiety is associated with a lot of worries and 'what ifs'. What if the fly lands on my food? What if I need to spend all afternoon clearing up? What if I can't concentrate on what I am doing? What if I lose my job? What if I can't get another job? What if my partner leaves me and takes the kids? What if I drive my partner away with my worrying? *What if I never stop worrying?* If you are a worrier, you will identify with the 'what ifs' and the fact that these worries go round and round in your head until you are ready to scream with the frustration and fruitlessness of it all, and yet it is hard to stop worrying.

You may find that your bodily symptoms of anxiety are affecting you the most. For example, it may be that in anxious situations your heart feels as though it is literally jumping out of your chest, your hands shake so much you can't hold a glass of water, you blush, flush, shake or you can't think what to say. On top of which you are sure others notice these symptoms and think badly of you. Although you want to run away, you feel rooted to the spot. You might have butterflies in your stomach, or feel your throat tightening, while other parts of you might ache with tension. All of these horrible, sometimes frightening, sensations are part of experiencing anxiety.

For some people, anxiety starts quickly, becomes extremely intense, and is over quickly (for example, panic attacks); for others it begins slowly and lasts a long time (for example, generalized anxiety disorder).

Anxiety should, in theory, only last an hour at most before it dies down. But it can be that the anxiety becomes activated again by something else that pops into mind as being threatening before it has the chance to fully subside and in these cases anxiety can feel intense for hours.

For some people the immediate trigger for anxiety is obvious: giving a speech, sitting an exam, going into a crowded place, having to pay bills and so on. For others, however, the trigger may be internal and therefore less obvious. For example, people with obsessive compulsive disorder (OCD) can feel anxious because unwanted thoughts or images seem to 'pop into' their heads. They find these thoughts and images disturbing and interpret them as personally meaningful. As with other anxiety problems though, the *interpretation* is what gives rise to the emotional response of anxiety (i.e. touching something dirty means I am contaminated; not checking the light switches and sockets before going to bed means that I'd be responsible if we have a fire, etc.). This, in turn, provokes behaviour such as hand-washing or compulsive checking.

For other individuals, the trigger for anxiety can be external: people with panic disorder, for example, may become anxious if they visit a crowded supermarket. But the external catalyst soon becomes internal, as people understandably become frightened by the intensity of their emotional and physical reactions until just *the thought of* going to the supermarket ends up provoking the same anxious response as actually *going to* the supermarket. Whether the trigger is internal or external doesn't matter – it may well be a mixture of both – what is important is realizing that both are equally important when it comes to understanding why your problem with anxiety is persisting.

If you are anxious because you have a phobia, OCD or panic disorder it is likely that you will know what the cause is. For example, you may have a phobia of bees or a worry about germs. If you have a more generalized anxiety it may not always be clear what the cause is. This sense of not knowing what is triggering your anxiety has an intensifying effect, which might lead you to worry that there are no solutions to your problems.

Table 4.1: *Key statistics about anxiety*

The Mental Health Foundation gives the following figures for the most common forms of anxiety:

- While 2.6 per cent of the population experience depression, 4.7 per cent have anxiety problems. As many as 9.7 per cent suffer mixed depression and anxiety, making it the most prevalent mental health problem in the population as a whole.

- Women are twice as likely to experience anxiety as men.

- About 1.2 per cent of the UK population experience panic disorders, rising to 1.7 per cent for those experiencing it with or without agoraphobia.

- Around 1.9 per cent of British adults experience a phobia of some description, and women are twice as likely to be affected by this problem as men.

- Agoraphobia affects between 1.5 and 3.5 per cent of the general population in its fully developed form; in a less severe form, up to one in eight people experience this.

- Post-traumatic stress disorder (PTSD) affects 2.6 per cent of men and 3.3 per cent of women.

- Obsessive compulsive disorders (OCD) affect around 2–3 per cent of the population.

- Generalized anxiety disorder affects 2–5 per cent of the population, yet accounts for as much as 30 per cent of the mental health problems seen by GPs. About 55 per cent to 60 per cent of those suffering from generalized anxiety disorder are female.[4]

Symptoms of anxiety

In this book we will focus on generalized anxiety and worry; however, many of the techniques and exercises will still be useful if you suffer from other forms of anxiety.

If you experience excessive anxiety and worry that are difficult to control, alongside three or more of the symptoms listed below, with at least some of the symptoms being present for more days than not for the past six months, you may be suffering from generalized anxiety disorder.[5]

- Restlessness or feeling keyed up or on edge.
- Being easily fatigued.
- Difficulty concentrating or mind going blank.
- Irritability.
- Muscle tension.
- Sleep disturbance (difficulty falling or staying asleep, or restless unsatisfying sleep).

These are the signs a mental health professional would look for in order to make a diagnosis. Figure 4.1 includes some additional symptoms that are commonly experienced by people with all forms of anxiety.

Avoidance and escape

When we are anxious about a given situation or object, we naturally do our utmost to avoid or try to get away from the focus of our fears. Someone with a fear of spiders might avoid entering the garden shed at all costs, or dash from the bathroom screaming if they find one in the bath. They may worry about dying of fright if a spider should ever crawl onto them. Someone else might become anxious at the thought of going

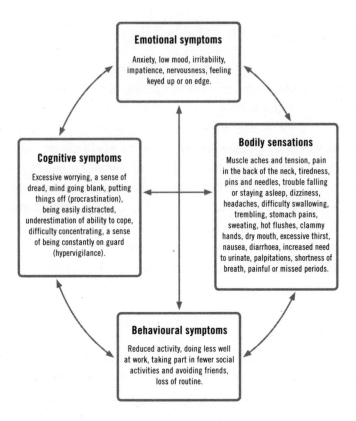

Figure 4.1: Common symptoms of anxiety

into big department stores and so may try to avoid them – or at least leave if they start to feel anxious.

Although it is tempting to avoid or run away from situations that make us feel anxious, avoidance and escape actually help to maintain anxiety problems. The reason for this is that avoiding situations that make you feel anxious means that you deprive yourself of the opportunity to discover that the anxiety you feel does not materialize into the fear you are harbouring. You will not actually die of fright if a spider crawls over you; you will not 'go crazy' if you go into a big department store. Avoiding situations that make you anxious also means that you will not find out that anxiety does not actually maintain its intensity. Rather, it fades over time.

Safety behaviours

Safety behaviours are what people use to prevent their fears from materializing and to help them feel safe. Safety behaviours can be observable behaviours (i.e. the kind of actions other people can see) or they can be internalized (i.e. thoughts). For example, someone who is frightened at the thought of going into a department store might always ensure that a friend is there to accompany them. Someone else might find counting to a certain number in their head helps reduce their anxiety when they find themselves in an anxiety-inducing situation. Although safety behaviours can be helpful in some ways, they can also feed the problem by preventing you from finding out what would actually happen if you did not engage in them. More often than not, the terrible thing that you fear might happen does not.

For example, if you get anxious going into your office canteen because you think people will stare at you, you might only feel able to enter the canteen if you keep your head down, avoiding eye contact and buying something you do not have to wait for and can take away. These safety behaviours might be helpful in enabling you to buy something to eat, but they prevent you from discovering that, if you had managed to look up, you would have seen that everybody was too busy eating and chatting to notice you quietly buying your lunch. Failure to realize this means that your next trip to the canteen is likely to be just as big an ordeal for you.

Safety behaviours are frequently a focus of CBT and we will refer to them throughout this book. In Chapter 18 you will be introduced to people who are experimenting with dropping safety behaviours.

Bea's story

In order to begin tackling her anxiety, Bea completed the PHQ-9, which measures low mood, the GAD-7, which measures anxiety, the Phobia Scales, which measure phobic anxiety, and the Work and Social Adjustment Scale (WASAS), which measures the impact her anxiety is having on her life. She also completed the Penn State Worry Questionnaire, which relates specifically to worry. See Table 4.2 for Bea's completed measures.

Once you have thought about the anxiety symptoms that you are suffering from, you can start to think about how these symptoms impact your life. If you haven't already done so, complete and score the same measures that Bea uses so you can begin to chart your progress. You'll find these measures in the Appendix, pp. 391–410.

Table 4.2: Bea's completed measures

Bea's completed PHQ-9

Over the <u>last 2 weeks</u>, how often have you been bothered by any of the following problems?		Not at all	Several days	More than half the days	Nearly every day
1	Little interest or pleasure in doing things	0	<u>**1**</u>	2	3
2	Feeling down, depressed, or hopeless	<u>**0**</u>	1	2	3
3	Trouble falling or staying asleep, or sleeping too much	0	1	<u>**2**</u>	3

4	Feeling tired or having little energy	**0**	1	2	3
5	Poor appetite or overeating	0	**1**	2	3
6	Feeling bad about yourself — or that you are a failure or have let yourself or your family down	**0**	1	2	3
7	Trouble concentrating on things such as reading the newspaper or watching television	0	1	**2**	3
8	Moving or speaking so slowly that other people could have noticed? Or the opposite – being so fidgety or restless that you have been moving around a lot more than usual	**0**	1	2	3
9	Thoughts that you would be better off dead or of hurting yourself in some way	**0**	1	2	3
PHQ-9 total score 6					

Bea's completed GAD-7

Over the <u>last 2 weeks</u>, how often have you been bothered by any of the following problems?		Not at all	Several days	More than half the days	Nearly every day
1	Feeling nervous, anxious, or on edge	0	1	**2**	3
2	Not being able to stop or control worrying	0	1	2	**3**
3	Worrying too much about different things	0	1	2	**3**
4	Trouble relaxing	0	1	**2**	3
5	Being so restless that it is hard to sit still	0	1	**2**	3
6	Becoming easily annoyed or irritable	0	**1**	2	3
7	Feeling afraid, as if something awful might happen	0	1	**2**	3
GAD-7 total score 15					

Bea's completed Phobia Scale

Choose a number from the scale below to show how much you would avoid each of the situations or objects listed below. Then write the number in the box opposite the situation.

0	1	2	3	4	5	6	7	8
Would not avoid it		Slightly avoid it		Definitely avoid it		Markedly avoid it		Always avoid it

Social situations because of a fear of being embarrassed or making a fool of myself? `2`

Certain situations because of a fear of having a panic attack or other distressing symptoms (such as loss of bladder control, vomiting or dizziness)? `2`

Certain situations because of a fear of particular objects or activities (such as animals, heights, seeing blood, being in confined spaces, driving or flying)? `2`

Bea's completed Work and Social Adjustment Scale

Using the scale provided below, select the number that you think most accurately describes how you are affected in each section.

1. Work

If you are retired or choose not to have a job for reasons unrelated to your problem, please tick N/A (not applicable).

0	1	**2**	3	4	5	6	7	8	N/A
Not at all		Slightly		Definitely		Markedly		Very severely	☐ I cannot work

2. Home management

Cleaning, tidying, shopping, cooking, looking after home/children, paying bills, etc.

0	1	2	**3**	4	5	6	7	8
Not at all		Slightly		Definitely		Markedly		Very severely

3. Social leisure activities

With other people, e.g. parties, pubs, outings, entertaining, etc.

0	1	2	3	4	**5**	6	7	8
Not at all		Slightly		Definitely		Markedly		Very severely

4. Private leisure activities

Done alone, e.g. reading, gardening, sewing, hobbies, walking, etc.

0	1	2	3	**4**	5	6	7	8
Not at all		Slightly		Definitely		Markedly		Very severely

5. Family and relationships

Forming and maintaining close relationships with others including the people that I live with

0	1	2	3	**4**	5	6	7	8
Not at all		Slightly		Definitely		Markedly		Very severely

Total score   18

Bea's completed Penn State Worry Questionnaire

	Statements	Not at all typical	Not very typical	Some-what typical	Fairly typical	Very typical
1	If I don't have enough time to do everything, I don't worry about it.	1	**2**	3	4	5
2	My worries overwhelm me.	1	2	3	**4**	5
3	I don't tend to worry about things.	1	**2**	3	4	5
4	Many situations make me worry.	1	2	3	**4**	5
5	I know I should not worry about things, but I just cannot help it.	1	2	3	**4**	5
6	When I am under pressure I worry a lot.	1	2	3	**4**	5
7	I am always worrying about something.	1	2	**3**	4	5
8	I find it easy to dismiss worrisome thoughts.	**1**	2	3	4	5

9	As soon as I finish one task, I start to worry about everything else I have to do.	1	2	**<u>3</u>**	4	5
10	I never worry about anything.	**<u>1</u>**	2	3	4	5
11	When there is nothing more I can do about a concern, I do not worry about it any more.	1	**<u>2</u>**	3	4	5
12	I have been a worrier all my life.	1	2	3	4	**<u>5</u>**
13	I notice that I have been worrying about things.	1	**<u>2</u>**	3	4	5
14	Once I start worrying, I cannot stop.	1	2	**<u>3</u>**	4	5
15	I worry all the time.	1	2	**<u>3</u>**	4	5
16	I worry about projects until they are all done.	1	**<u>2</u>**	3	4	5
Total 59						

How to score the Penn State Worry Questionnaire

Add up your scores for questions 2, 4, 5, 6, 7, 9, 12, 13, 14, 15 and 16 using a scale of 1–5, where:

1 = not at all typical

5 = very typical.

It is important that you 'reverse score' specific items as follows:

Reverse score questions 1, 3, 8, 10 and 11:

Very typical of me = 1 (circled 5 on the sheet)

Circled 3 on the sheet = 2

Circled 2 on the sheet = 3

Circled 1 on the sheet = 4

Not at all typical of me = 5 (circled 1 on the sheet).

A score of 45 or more would suggest that worrying is a significant problem.

Bea's scores indicate that her mood is mildly depressed, she is experiencing moderately severe anxiety although her phobic anxiety levels are low, and her problems are having a definite impact on her life; her score on the Penn State Worry Questionnaire suggests that worry is a significant problem for her.

How is anxiety treated?

There are a number of effective treatments for generalized anxiety, including self-help books (like this one), psycho-education groups (groups led by mental health professionals with a focus on education around emotional problems and ways of coping), CBT, medication and relaxation (see Chapter 14).

Bea's story

As we have already learned, Bea is a forty-seven-year-old divorced woman who has a long-standing problem with anxiety. Her story can help us to understand the relationship between worry and anxiety and the situations, thoughts, emotions, bodily sensations and behaviours discussed in this chapter. It can also help us to understand how the scales can be used to help measure symptoms.

Bea was able to think of a recent incident when her worry and anxiety were particularly high and made a note of her symptoms on the CBT model diagram (see Figure 4.2). You can see how the components of the diagram are interlinked and how they influenced each other.

Figure 4.2: Bea's CBT model

Situation: Son, Rob, mentioned that he and his wife were taking their daughter Lily to a routine hospital appointment.

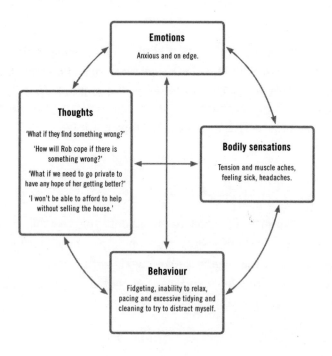

Emotions
Anxious and on edge.

Thoughts
'What if they find something wrong?'
'How will Rob cope if there is something wrong?'
'What if we need to go private to have any hope of her getting better?'
'I won't be able to afford to help without selling the house.'

Bodily sensations
Tension and muscle aches, feeling sick, headaches.

Behaviour
Fidgeting, inability to relax, pacing and excessive tidying and cleaning to try to distract myself.

Bea rated her problems with anxiety on the mood scale (Figure 4.3). Her baseline score on her overall mood is: -3

-5	-4	**<u>-3</u>**	-2	-1	0	+1	+2	+3	+4	+5

Negative   Neutral   Positive
mood   mood

Figure 4.3: Bea's mood scale

As we saw in Table 4.2, Bea's baseline PHQ-9 score is: 6.

Her baseline GAD-7 score is: 15.

Her baseline Phobia Scale scores are: 2, 2, 2.

Her baseline WASAS score is: 18.

Her baseline Penn State Worry Questionnaire score is: 59.

We will chart Bea's progress throughout the remaining chapters.

In Further Resources, pp. 381–2, you will find some guidance as to resources you can use to learn more about anxiety. Part 2 contains more information on various CBT techniques that will help you tackle your problems.

Summary

In the space below, write down any key points that you wish to remember from this chapter and that you might want to refer back to later on. What was most helpful? What did you learn about anxiety that was particularly interesting? Is there anything from this chapter that you are going to bear in mind as you progress on into the next chapters?

1. _____

   _____

2. _____

   _____

3. _____

   _____

4. _____

   _____

5 Anger

Case illustration 4: Dez

Dez is a fifty-two-year-old man who has been living with his partner Corrie for the past fifteen years. Dez has recently moved jobs to become area sales manager for a large food distribution company and, as a result, he now has to travel greater distances on a daily basis. At work he is in charge of a small team of sales people and he has strict sales targets that he has to meet each month. This is a source of great stress for Dez and as a result he can become irritated and impatient with one member of his team in particular whom he feels does not 'carry her weight'. Recently the employee in question accused him of bullying her and threatened to go to his manager. Dez is incensed at the idea of her threatening him and can barely bring himself to talk to her. He feels as though he would do anything to get her off the team.

Because of the greater distance between his new workplace and home, Dez spends a lot more time in the car than he used to. He frequently gets caught up in rush-hour traffic, which he finds extremely irritating. Dez has recently experienced a couple of 'road-rage' incidents, where he drove in an aggressive manner and swore at drivers who cut in front of him. In one incident, he was so angry that he actually got out of his car in stationary traffic and approached another car in order to angrily confront the driver. When he thought back over the incident later that night, Dez realized that he was lucky that the driver had not called the police.

Corrie is finding it increasingly difficult to cope with Dez when he comes home in the evening from work in a rage. Dez frequently takes his anger out on Corrie and can be irritable and shout at her. On occasions he has remained feeling angry for the entire evening, and been uncommunicative and snappy. Although he has never been physically violent towards Corrie, he has punched walls and broken a much-loved photo frame in a rage. Unsurprisingly, Corrie finds this type of behaviour frightening and, although she is used to Dez's temper, she has noticed that he has become much more prone to losing it since he started his new job. Dez doesn't want to give up the new job because it is a significant step up from his old one, but he's worried Corrie may leave him if he doesn't sort himself out.

Anger is a normal emotion and one that we will all have felt at some point, whether as a mild irritation or as an outburst of rage. Sometimes getting angry can be appropriate and is clearly warranted, but when anger is too frequent, too intense or lasts too long, is not proportionate to the situation or leads to violence, it becomes a problem. Sometimes people feel that their level of irritation or anger is justifiable while it is happening, and it is only later, on reflection, that they realize it was excessive. Anger is difficult to live with for the person who is angry, but it is also difficult for those around them. When anger is out of control it can have a negative impact on our work, personal relationships and overall quality of life. At times, we may feel like we are at the mercy of a highly unpredictable and destructive emotion. It is natural for your instinct to be to respond aggressively when you feel angry: anger is a normal response to threat that helps us defend ourselves if we are under attack and can thus be vital to ensuring our survival. However, too much anger is always counterproductive.

Anger is associated with feelings of injustice or unfairness. Knowing this is an important step towards thinking about what is keeping the emotion so intense that you find it difficult to control. Once you are angry, you are likely to experience very similar physical sensations to anxiety – your heart pounds, you feel tension and you may sweat, shake and go red in the face. This is because your body is preparing to fight.

Anger can sometimes, however, quickly turn into uncontrollable rage. You may know that sometimes your emotional response is not proportionate to the situation you are in. In these cases it will help to look at the meanings you attribute to the event that triggered your anger in the first place. For example, it is not the greatest crime in the world to leave an empty packet of cereal in the cupboard rather than throwing it in the dustbin. However, if it makes you uncontrollably angry, it is likely that this event has some sort of significance beyond cereal. For example, the empty packet may make you think, 'My son's so selfish, he only thinks of himself. He eats every last bit of my favourite cereal and then just leaves the packet there. He must either think I'm his servant and will clean up after him, or he's so thoughtless it doesn't even occur to him to throw it away.' If you have these kinds of thoughts about how someone views you, then it is easy to see how a small incident such as their leaving an empty cereal packet in the cupboard might cause you to feel rage.

Like anxiety, anger can be triggered by external or internal events. For instance, you might be angry with someone in particular (for example, your son) or because of an event (the meeting you travelled a long way to attend is cancelled at short notice). These are examples of *external* triggers. If you think back over a past event that made you angry and was not resolved (remembering how irritating it was to find the empty box of cereal), it may cause you to become angry all over again; this is an example of an internal trigger.

Some people do tend to be more irritable than others. If you are one of these people – someone with a 'short fuse' – then you are likely to find it difficult to brush off irritations or let things go.

There are a number of factors that can lower your threshold for anger. These include:

- Being overtired.

- Feeling hungry.

- Sexual frustration.

- Hormonal changes (e.g. premenstrual syndrome, menopause, higher testosterone levels).

- Withdrawal from addictive substances (which leads to cravings for things like nicotine, alcohol, caffeine, illicit drugs).

- Being drunk or under the influence of other substances.

- Feeling unwell.

- Being in pain, whether chronic or acute.

What makes people susceptible to anger?

People who are prone to anger are less able to brush off irritations or manage difficulties well. People who come from families that are poor at dealing with and communicating emotions, and where high levels of anger are expressed, are more likely to develop problems with anger. This may be because such individuals haven't had the opportunity to learn how to resolve problems in a calm, constructive way. Instead, they learn that disagreements escalate and lead to arguments, shouting and intense emotions.

What are the signs and symptoms of an anger problem?

If you answer yes to some of the following questions, then you may have an anger problem:

Do you have a tendency to:

- Shout at people and use violent language?
- Mull over previous episodes of anger and get angry again?
- Be unable to deal with difficult situations without getting irritated?
- Become violent?
- Get angry about situations rather than finding answers to problems or just accepting the situation?
- Experience physical health problems associated with anger (e.g. high blood pressure or problems with indigestion)?
- Be seen by others as an 'angry person' and feared because of this?
- Have a strong dislike for strangers because of something about them (e.g. ethnicity or gender)?
- Avoid situations because of a fear of getting angry?

The above symptoms are common in people with anger problems. There are some other symptoms that are also commonly experienced by people who have issues with anger, and these are included in Figure 5.1.

Table 5.1: *Key statistics about anger*

- Almost a third of people say they have a close friend or family member who has trouble controlling their anger.

- More than one in ten say that they have trouble controlling their own anger.

- More than one in four people say that they worry about how angry they sometimes feel.

- One in five people say that they have ended a relationship or friendship with someone because of how they behaved when they were angry.[6]

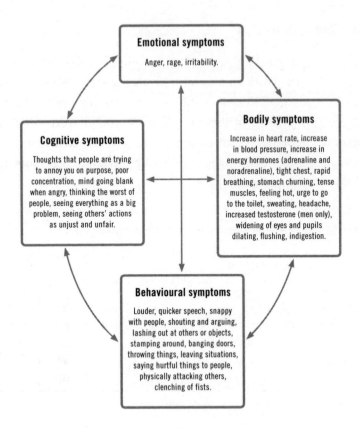

Figure 5.1: Common symptoms of anger

Once you have thought about the anger symptoms that you might be experiencing, it's time to think about how they impact your life. If you haven't already done so, now is a good time to complete and score the measures in the Appendix, pages 391–410, 411–2, so you can begin to chart your progress. We'd suggest completing the PHQ-9, GAD-7, Phobia Scales, the Work and Social Adjustment Scale (WASAS) and the Dimensions of Anger Reactions II in the first instance. If you find that any are not relevant, you might want to stop completing them going forward and just focus on the ones where you have a significant score.

Dez's story

In order to begin tackling his anger, Dez completed the PHQ-9, GAD-7, Phobia Scales, the Work and Social Adjustment Scale (WASAS), and the Dimensions of Anger Reactions II. His responses are reproduced below. You'll remember some of these measures if you've read the previous chapters on depression and anxiety. They are repeated here because depression, anxiety and anger are often interrelated. See Table 5.2 for Dez's completed measures.

Figure 5.2: Dez's completed measures

Dez's completed PHQ-9

Over the <u>last 2 weeks</u>, how often have you been bothered by any of the following problems?		Not at all	Several days	More than half the days	Nearly every day
1	Little interest or pleasure in doing things	0	<u>**1**</u>	2	3
2	Feeling down, depressed, or hopeless	0	<u>**1**</u>	2	3
3	Trouble falling or staying asleep, or sleeping too much	0	1	<u>**2**</u>	3
4	Feeling tired or having little energy	<u>**0**</u>	1	2	3
5	Poor appetite or overeating	<u>**0**</u>	1	2	3

6	Feeling bad about yourself – or that you are a failure or have let yourself or your family down	0	1	2	**<u>3</u>**
7	Trouble concentrating on things such as reading the newspaper or watching television	0	**<u>1</u>**	2	3
8	Moving or speaking so slowly that other people could have noticed? Or the opposite – being so fidgety or restless that you have been moving around a lot more than usual	**<u>0</u>**	1	2	3
9	Thoughts that you would be better off dead or of hurting yourself in some way	**<u>0</u>**	1	2	3
PHQ-9 total score 8					

Dez's completed GAD-7

Over the <u>last 2 weeks</u>, how often have you been bothered by any of the following problems?		Not at all	Several days	More than half the days	Nearly every day
1	Feeling nervous, anxious or on edge	**<u>0</u>**	1	2	3
2	Not being able to stop or control worrying	**<u>0</u>**	1	2	3

3	Worrying too much about different things	**0**	1	2	3
4	Trouble relaxing	0	1	**2**	3
5	Being so restless that it is hard to sit still	0	**1**	2	3
6	Becoming easily annoyed or irritable	0	1	**2**	3
7	Feeling afraid, as if something awful might happen	**0**	1	2	3
GAD-7 total score 5					

Dez's completed Phobia Scales

Choose a number from the scale below to show how much you would avoid each of the situations or objects listed below. Then write the number in the box opposite the situation.

0	1	2	3	4	5	6	7	8
Would not avoid it		Slightly avoid it		Definitely avoid it		Markedly avoid it		Always avoid it

Social situations because of a fear of being embarrassed or making a fool of myself.   `0`

Certain situations because of a fear of having a panic attack or other distressing symptoms (such as loss of bladder control, vomiting or dizziness).   `0`

Certain situations because of a fear of particular objects or activities (such as animals, heights, seeing blood, being in confined spaces, driving or flying).   `0`

Dez's completed Work and Social Adjustment Scale

Using the scale provided below, select the number that you think most accurately describes how you are affected in each section.

1. Work

If you are retired or choose not to have a job for reasons unrelated to your problem, please tick N/A (not applicable).

0	1	2	**3**	4	5	6	7	8	N/A
Not at all		Slightly		Definitely		Markedly		Very severely	☐ I cannot work

2. Home management

Cleaning, tidying, shopping, cooking, looking after home/children, paying bills, etc.

0	1	**2**	3	4	5	6	7	8
Not at all		Slightly		Definitely		Markedly		Very severely

3. Social leisure activities

With other people, e.g. parties, pubs, outings, entertaining, etc.

0	1	2	3	**4**	5	6	7	8
Not at all		Slightly		Definitely		Markedly		Very severely

4. Private leisure activities

Done alone, e.g. reading, gardening, sewing, hobbies, walking, etc.

0	1	2	3	4	5	6	7	8
Not at all	Slightly			Definitely		Markedly		Very severely

5. Family and relationships

Forming and maintaining close relationships with others including the people that I live with

0	1	2	3	4	5	6	7	8
Not at all	Slightly			Definitely		Markedly		Very severely

Total score   16

Dez's completed Dimensions of Anger Reactions II[7]

As accurately as you can, indicate the degree to which the following statements describe your feelings and behaviours. Rate the degree to which each statement applies to you.

1. I often find myself getting angry at people or situations.

0	1	2	3	4
Not at all	A little	Moderately so	Fairly much	Very much

2. When I do get angry, I get really mad.

0	1	2	**3**	4
Not at all	A little	Moderately so	Fairly much	Very much

3. When I get angry, I stay angry.

0	1	2	**3**	4
Not at all	A little	Moderately so	Fairly much	Very much

4. When I get angry at someone, I want to hit or strike the person.

0	1	**2**	3	4
Not at all	A little	Moderately so	Fairly much	Very much

5. My anger interferes with my ability to get my work done.

0	**1**	2	3	4
Not at all	A little	Moderately so	Fairly much	Very much

6. My anger prevents me from getting along with people as well as I would like to.

0	1	**2**	3	4
Not at all	A little	Moderately so	Fairly much	Very much

7. My anger has a bad effect on my health.

0	1	2	3	4
Not at all	A little	Moderately so	Fairly much	Very much

Total score   15

Scoring the Dimensions of Anger Reaction II

This scale measures four areas of anger responses (i.e. frequency, intensity, duration and physical antagonism), and three related to impact on functioning (i.e., adverse effects on social relationships, work and health). Add up your scores across the seven items. A score of 18 or above would be considered to be in the high range and you may wish to talk to your doctor.

Dez's scores indicate that his mood is mildly depressed, he is experiencing mild anxiety and no specific phobic anxiety; his problems appear to be affecting relationships in the main rather than other areas of his life; his score of 15 on the Dimensions of Anger Reactions II measure would suggest that he has moderate anger problems.

How is anger treated?

Studies show that anger responds well to CBT. Many people who experience anger problems see improvements while using appropriate self-help materials or through more formal CBT such as meeting regularly with a trained therapist. We will learn in Part 2 about various CBT techniques that will help you tackle your problems.

Dez's story

Let's return to Dez's story. We can look at it again to help us to understand how the situations, thoughts, emotions, bodily sensations and behaviours that we have covered in this chapter might begin to relate to anger, and how the scales can be used to help measure symptoms. You will remember that Dez is a fifty-two-year-old man who has been having problems controlling his temper.

During a recent incident when his anger was particularly problematic, Dez was able to plot his symptoms in the CBT model diagram (see Figure 5.2). You can see below how his symptoms are interlinked, and how they influence each other.

Figure 5.2: Dez's CBT model

Situation: On way home from work and got stuck in a traffic jam even though left early. It's mine and Corrie's fifteenth anniversary so promised to do something special. Had booked our favourite restaurant for 7.30 p.m.

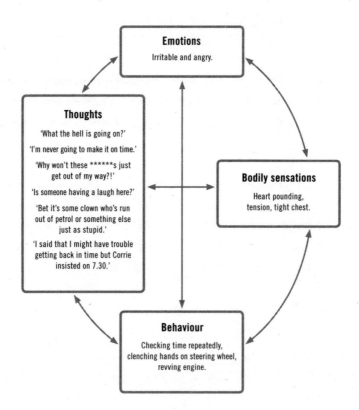

After plotting his diagram, Dez rated his problems with anger on the mood scale (Figure 5.3). His baseline score on his overall mood is:

-5	-4	**-3**	-2	-1	0	+1	+2	+3	+4	+5

Negative mood				Neutral					Positive mood

Figure 5.3: Dez's mood scale

As we saw in Table 5.2, Dez's baseline PHQ-9 score is: 9.

His baseline GAD-7 score is: 5.

His baseline Phobia Scale scores are: 0, 0, 0.

His baseline WASAS score is: 16.

His baseline DAR II score is: 15.

We will chart Dez's progress throughout the remaining chapters. (He will stop filling in measures for which he's scored zero like the phobia scale, and that's something you will probably want to do too.)

Summary

It's time to write down any points that you want to remember from this chapter. Did anything resonate in particular for you? Did any of Dez's reactions surprise you? What was most helpful, and has it made you think about anything differently? As in any previous chapters for which you have written a summary like this, you will be able to use it as a quick point of reference later.

1. _____

_____

2. _____

_____

3. _____

_____

4. _____

_____

6 Self-esteem

Case illustration 5: Penny

Penny is a thirty-two-year-old single woman who lives alone. She has suffered from severe eczema since early childhood. Although it is reasonably well controlled, she still has occasional flare-ups that can last several weeks or more. During a flare-up, the eczema will cover most parts of her body to some degree, including her face, which she finds very embarrassing. Penny was bullied from a young age because of her skin condition. As a result, she grew up with little confidence in herself. Although she has managed to get used to her eczema and is able to control it most of the time, her self-belief and sense of self-worth are poor. She has had a couple of reasonably long relationships in her adult life, but these have not ended well. Penny tends to blame herself for these relationships coming to an end, despite her friends assuring her that they don't believe this to be the case. Because of her lack of self-belief and sense of self-worth, Penny can find herself in relationships where boyfriends take advantage of her vulnerability. She finds her self-belief and self-worth drop even lower as a result of their behaviour and has found herself tolerating behaviour from boyfriends that her friends say they would not put up with. They are keen for her to meet someone 'decent' who will treat her well, and have been encouraging her to try internet dating. However, Penny is not keen as she does not believe that anyone will find her attractive, interesting or lovable. She thinks that internet dating will just end up making her feel worse about herself, so would rather not bother giving it a go at all, even though she has in the past expressed fears that she may spend the rest of her life alone. Instead, she stays at home and watches TV most evenings. When she is not watching TV, she works her way through her Sudoku book. This sedentary lifestyle has meant that Penny has been putting on more weight recently, which is adding to her dissatisfaction with herself and to her low self-esteem.

If you are experiencing an emotional problem, the chances are that you don't feel great about yourself. Some people think badly about themselves because of childhood experiences such as being bullied at school, or being neglected or abused. Others think they are worthless owing to experiences during their adolescence or adulthood such as relationship failures or problems at work. You may be someone who lacks confidence in your own ability or self-worth despite a happy childhood and reasonable relationships. You may say, for example, 'I was born that way' or 'my mother lacks confidence and so do I'. Lacking in confidence is not exactly the same as lacking in self-esteem, but they are closely related. If you don't think well of yourself, it is harder to voice your opinion confidently and to be decisive in every aspect of life. You may be plagued by thoughts that people are only 'pretending' to like you when they don't really, or that they only like you because they don't know the 'real' you underneath.

If you suffer from depression, it is likely you will also have experienced periods of low self-esteem. The same is true for anxiety and other emotional problems. It is not known which comes first: feeling bad about yourself or emotional problems. What *is* likely is that they affect each other. Experiencing an emotional or psychological problem is difficult to live with and many people in this situation become self-critical and lack compassion towards themselves. Feeling bad about yourself, in turn, creates low mood and anxiety. Self-esteem and emotional problems therefore feed from each other in a vicious cycle.

What causes low self-esteem?

Our self-esteem is influenced by a number of different factors, including our physical appearance and weight, our socioeconomic status, peer pressure and bullying.

What are the signs and symptoms?

A person with low self-esteem may display some of the following:[8]

- Heavily self-critical attitude and general dissatisfaction.

- Hypersensitivity to criticism, with feelings of being attacked and resentment towards those who are being critical.

- Chronic indecision, with an intense fear of making mistakes.

- Excessive willingness to please others, and unwillingness to displease anyone.

- Perfectionistic, which can lead to frustration when perfection is unattainable.

- Feelings of extreme guilt, thinking over and magnifying the importance of past mistakes.

- General hostile attitude, general defensiveness and irritability without any obvious trigger.

- Pessimism and a generally negative outlook.

- Envy, general ill will or resentment.

Figure 6.1 shows how the thoughts, feelings, bodily sensations and behaviours associated with low self-esteem are interconnected.

Once you have thought about the low self-esteem symptoms that you might be experiencing, the next thing to do will be to think about how they are impacting your life. If you haven't already done so, now is a good time to complete and score the measures in the Appendix, pp. 389–408, 413–4, so you can begin to chart your progress.

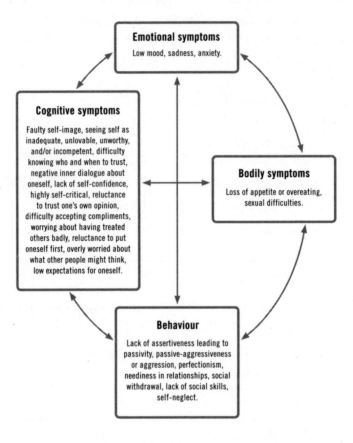

Figure 6.1: Common symptoms of low self-esteem

Penny's story

In order to begin tackling her low self-esteem, Penny completed the PHQ-9, GAD-7, Phobia Scales, the Work and Social Adjustment Scale (WASAS) and the Rosenberg Self-Esteem Scale. You can see her responses in Table 6.1.

Table 6.1: Penny's completed measures

Penny's completed PHQ-9

Over the <u>last 2 weeks</u>, how often have you been bothered by any of the following problems?		Not at all	Several days	More than half the days	Nearly every day
1	Little interest or pleasure in doing things	0	<u>1</u>	2	3
2	Feeling down, depressed, or hopeless	0	<u>1</u>	2	3
3	Trouble falling or staying asleep, or sleeping too much	0	<u>1</u>	2	3
4	Feeling tired or having little energy	0	<u>1</u>	2	3
5	Poor appetite or overeating	0	1	<u>2</u>	3
6	Feeling bad about yourself — or that you are a failure or have let yourself or your family down	0	1	2	<u>3</u>

7	Trouble concentrating on things such as reading the newspaper or watching television	**0**	1	2	3
8	Moving or speaking so slowly that other people could have noticed? Or the opposite – being so fidgety or restless that you have been moving around a lot more than usual	**0**	1	2	3
9	Thoughts that you would be better off dead or of hurting yourself in some way	**0**	1	2	3
PHQ-9 total score 9					

Penny's completed GAD-7

Over the last 2 weeks, how often have you been bothered by any of the following problems?		Not at all	Several days	More than half the days	Nearly every day
1	Feeling nervous, anxious or on edge	0	**1**	2	3
2	Not being able to stop or control worrying	0	**1**	2	3
3	Worrying too much about different things	0	**1**	2	3
4	Trouble relaxing	0	1	**2**	3

5	Being so restless that it is hard to sit still	**0**	1	2	3
6	Becoming easily annoyed or irritable	0	**1**	2	3
7	Feeling afraid, as if something awful might happen	0	**1**	2	3
GAD-7 total score 7					

Penny's completed Phobia Scales

Choose a number from the scale below to show how much you would avoid each of the situations or objects listed below. Then write the number in the box opposite the situation.

| 0 | 1 | 2 | 3 | 4 | 5 | 6 | 7 | 8 |

| Would not avoid it | Slightly avoid it | Definitely avoid it | Markedly avoid it | Always avoid it |

Social situations because of a fear of being embarrassed or making a fool of myself? 5

Certain situations because of a fear of having a panic attack or other distressing symptoms (such as loss of bladder control, vomiting or dizziness)? 0

Certain situations because of a fear of particular objects or activities (such as animals, heights, seeing blood, being in confined spaces, driving or flying)? 0

Penny's completed Work and Social Adjustment Scale

Using the scale provided below, Penny selected the number that she thought most accurately described how you are affected in each section.

1. Work

If you are retired or choose not to have a job for reasons unrelated to your problem, please tick N/A (not applicable).

0	1	2	**3**	4	5	6	7	8	N/A
Not at all		Slightly		Definitely		Markedly		Very severely	☐ I cannot work

2. Home management

Cleaning, tidying, shopping, cooking, looking after home/children, paying bills, etc.

0	**1**	2	3	4	5	6	7	8
Not at all		Slightly		Definitely		Markedly		Very severely

3. Social leisure activities

With other people, e.g. parties, pubs, outings, entertaining, etc.

0	1	2	3	4	**5**	6	7	8
Not at all		Slightly		Definitely		Markedly		Very severely

4. Private leisure activities

Done alone, e.g. reading, gardening, sewing, hobbies, walking, etc.

0	**1**	2	3	4	5	6	7	8

| Not at all | | Slightly | | Definitely | | Markedly | | Very severely |

5. Family and relationships

Forming and maintaining close relationships with others including the people that I live with.

0	1	2	3	4	5	**6**	7	8

| Not at all | | Slightly | | Definitely | | Markedly | | Very severely |

Total score   16

Penny's completed Rosenberg Self-Esteem Scale

	Strongly disagree	Disagree	Agree	Strongly agree
1. I feel that I am a person of worth, at least on an equal plane with others.		✔		
2. I feel that I have a number of good qualities.		✔		
3. All in all, I am inclined to feel that I am a failure.			✔	

	Strongly disagree	Disagree	Agree	Strongly agree
4. I am able to do things as well as most other people.		✔		
5. I feel I do not have much to be proud of.			✔	
6. I take a positive attitude towards myself.	✔			
7. On the whole, I am satisfied with myself.		✔		
8. I wish I could have more respect for myself.			✔	
9. I certainly feel useless at times.			✔	
10. At times I think I am no good at all.			✔	

Scoring the Rosenberg Self-Esteem Scale

Add up the scores, being careful to reverse score some items as indicated below. The scale ranges from 0–30. A score of under 15 suggests low self-esteem.

Scores are calculated as follows:

For items 1, 2, 4, 6 and 7:

Strongly agree   3

Agree   2

Disagree   1

Strongly disagree   0

For items 3, 5, 8, 9 and 10 (which are reversed):

Strongly agree   0

Agree   1

Disagree   2

Strongly disagree   3

Penny's total score: 22

Penny's scores indicate that her mood is mildly depressed, she is experiencing mild anxiety symptoms, has definite symptoms of social anxiety and that her problems are mostly affecting her social leisure activities and relationships; her score of 10 on the Rosenberg Self-Esteem Scale suggests significant self-esteem issues.

How is low self–esteem treated?

Low self-esteem is common and can be a disabling and distressing problem which is often involved in the maintenance of a number of emotional problems such as depression and anxiety. Like many psychological difficulties, we know that low self-esteem responds well to CBT.

Penny's story

Let's return to Penny's story, because it will show us how the situations, thoughts, emotions, bodily sensations and behaviours considered in this chapter might begin to relate to low self-esteem. It will also show us how the scales can be used to help measure symptoms. You will remember that Penny is a thirty-two-year-old woman who has a long-standing skin problem and low self-esteem.

During a recent incident when her self-esteem was particularly low, Penny plotted her symptoms in the CBT model diagram (Figure 6.2). You can see how her symptoms are interlinked, and how they influence each other.

Figure 6.2: Penny's CBT model

Situation: Invitation to friend Schumee's wedding arrived. Started mulling over being alone and not having anyone to take with me.

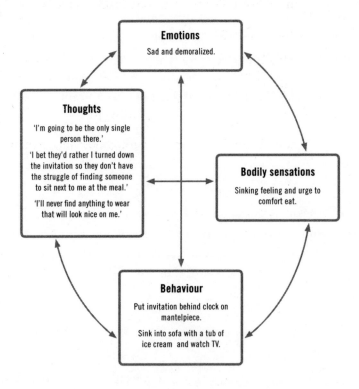

After plotting her diagram, Penny rated her problems with self-esteem on the mood scale (Figure 6.3). Her baseline score on her overall mood is:

-5	**-4**	-3	-2	-1	0	+1	+2	+3	+4	+5

| Negative mood | | | | Neutral | | | | | Positive mood |

Figure 6.3: Penny's mood scale

As we saw in Table 6.1, Penny's baseline PHQ-9 score is: 9.

Her baseline GAD-7 score is: 7.

Her baseline Phobia Scale scores are: 5, 0, 0.

Her baseline WASAS score is: 16.

Her baseline Rosenberg Self-Esteem Score is: 10

We will chart Penny's progress throughout the remaining chapters.

Summary

Use the space below to summarize the key points from this chapter so that you have a useful short reference guide for later on. Did you come across anything that was reassuring? What do you want to remember as being particularly helpful? Were you reminded of anything as you worked through the chapter?

1. _____

_____

2. _____

_____

3. _____

_____

4. _____

_____

7 Stress

Case illustration 6: Leah

Leah is a twenty-five-year-old woman who lives with her partner Jay and works as a reporter for a local newspaper. The newspaper where she works has been losing sales over recent years as more and more people replace their local paper with internet sources and the free newspapers available to commuters. In an attempt to turn around the fortunes of the newspaper, they have brought in an editor from a national paper to 'shake things up a bit'. A number of Leah's colleagues have taken voluntary redundancy and she is aware that more cuts may be made. The advertising department where Jay was employed have reduced their team from ten employees to two. Jay has been unable to find another job, so the couple are starting to struggle financially with just Leah's salary coming in.

Leah works extra-long hours to prove her worth to her company and to her new boss, especially as she wants to ensure she is seen to do things perfectly. She finds that in order to meet tight deadlines on stories and editorials, she regularly has to start work early and finish late. Now that there have been so many redundancies, Leah feels as though her job is under-resourced and that the expectations placed on her are unrealistic. She is too scared to discuss these issues with her boss as she has a substantial mortgage and, with Jay out of work, they would be in real financial difficulty if she lost her job. She finds that she has little time for anything other than work, and not only does this interfere with her weekends but she has also not had a proper holiday for over a year. She is having trouble sleeping, suffers frequently from indigestion and has difficulty getting to sleep at night. She smokes heavily, has a high caffeine intake and snacks on junk food because she gets home so late that she lacks the energy to heat up the meals that Jay has prepared for her.

It is unusual for a day to pass by without us feeling pressured in some way. However, although stress is a feature of life, it can be difficult to define. Richard Lazarus, the American psychologist, suggests that the way to understand it using a cognitive behavioural approach is that it is not *the event* that leads to perceived stress but the person's *perception of that event*.

There are different types of stress. 'Harm' stress refers to psychological damage that has already been done (for example, an irrevocable loss such as a death in the family), and is a type of stress often linked to low mood. 'Threat' stress is the anticipation of harm that has not yet taken place but may be about to take place (for example, being threatened with immediate physical violence). The third type of stress is 'challenge' stress, which results from difficult demands that are placed on us. Challenge stress demands are ones that we feel we can meet and manage, such as working to project deadlines.

Some amount of stress is helpful, and has been shown to be motivating. That being said, too much stress can become counterproductive. The key to knowing whether stress is going to be helpful or unhelpful lies in our ability to cope. Those with emotional problems often underestimate their ability to cope, and if this is true for you, then you are likely to be feeling stressed a great deal of the time.

Table 7.1: *Key statistics*

Work-related stress is defined as a harmful reaction to undue pressures and demands at work.

The latest estimates from the Labour Force Survey (LFS) published by the Health and Safety Executive (http://www.hse.gov.uk/statistics/causdis/stress/index.htm) show:

- The total number of cases of stress in 2011/12 was 428,000 (40%) out of a total of 1,073,000 for all work-related illnesses.

- The estimated cases of work-related stress, both total and new cases, have remained broadly flat over the past decade.

- The industries that reported the highest rates of total cases of work-related stress (three-year average) were human health and social work, education and public administration, and defence.

- The occupations that reported the highest rates of total cases of work-related stress (three-year average) were health professionals (in particular nurses), teaching and educational professionals, and caring personal services (in particular welfare and housing associate professionals).

- The main work activities attributed by respondents as causing their work-related stress, or making it worse, were work pressure, lack of managerial support and work-related violence and bullying.[9]

What causes stress?

The term 'stress' describes the symptoms you experience when you perceive that the demands that are being made of you are greater than your ability to fulfil them. When you feel that you have insufficient time, experience and resources to deal with your current circumstances, you are likely to feel stressed. It is not necessarily that the events are themselves inherently stressful, but that you think that they are. The experience of stress is therefore determined by your appraisal of the demands being made of you and of your resources to meet that demand. Inability to cope with these demands can result in a variety of physiological, emotional, cognitive and behavioural symptoms, as you can see below.

Stress often occurs as a result of major life changes, conflict with others, financial difficulties, issues with children and family, work overload and/or tight deadlines. Loss, such as bereavement, bankruptcy, redundancy, divorce or separation, causes stress, as can long-term illness or disability. In addition, events that are often supposed to make us happy can also cause stress (e.g. getting married, starting a new job, going on holiday and moving house).

What are the signs and symptoms of stress?

Figure 7.1 shows how the thoughts, feelings, bodily sensations and behaviours associated with stress are interconnected.

Think about the stress symptoms you may be experiencing, and then about how they are impacting on your life. If you haven't already done so, now is a good time to complete and score the measures in the Appendix, pp. 389–408, 415–19, so you can begin to chart your progress.

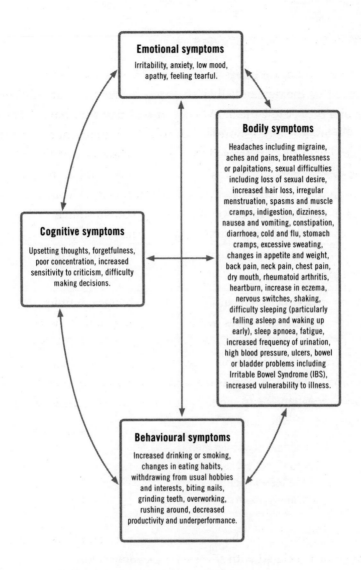

Figure 7.1: Common symptoms of stress

Leah's story

In order to begin tackling her stress, Leah completed the PHQ-9, GAD-7, Phobia Scales, the Work and Social Adjustment Scale (WASAS) and the Perceived Stress Scale: 10 items. Her responses are indicated in Table 7.2.

Table 7.2: Leah's completed measures

Leah's completed PHQ-9

	Over the <u>last 2 weeks</u>, how often have you been bothered by any of the following problems?	Not at all	Several days	More than half the days	Nearly every day
1	Little interest or pleasure in doing things	0	1	<u>**2**</u>	3
2	Feeling down, depressed, or hopeless	0	<u>1</u>	2	3
3	Trouble falling or staying asleep, or sleeping too much	0	1	2	<u>**3**</u>
4	Feeling tired or having little energy	0	<u>1</u>	2	3
5	Poor appetite or overeating	0	1	<u>**2**</u>	3
6	Feeling bad about yourself — or that you are a failure or have let yourself or your family down	0	<u>1</u>	2	3
7	Trouble concentrating on things such as reading the newspaper or watching television	0	1	<u>**2**</u>	3
8	Moving or speaking so slowly that other people could have noticed? Or the opposite – being so fidgety or restless that you have been moving around a lot more than usual	<u>**0**</u>	1	2	3

9	Thoughts that you would be better off dead or of hurting yourself in some way	**0**	1	2	3
PHQ-9 total score 12					

Leah's completed GAD-7

Over the last 2 weeks, how often have you been bothered by any of the following problems?		Not at all	Several days	More than half the days	Nearly every day
1	Feeling nervous, anxious or on edge	0	1	**2**	3
2	Not being able to stop or control worrying	0	**1**	2	3
3	Worrying too much about different things	0	1	**2**	3
4	Trouble relaxing	0	1	**2**	3
5	Being so restless that it is hard to sit still	**0**	1	2	3
6	Becoming easily annoyed or irritable	0	1	**2**	3
7	Feeling afraid, as if something awful might happen	0	**1**	2	3
GAD-7 total score 10					

Leah's completed Phobia Scales

Choose a number from the scale below to show how much you would avoid each of the situations or objects listed below. Then write the number in the box opposite the situation.

0	1	2	3	4	5	6	7	8
Would not avoid it		Slightly avoid it		Definitely avoid it		Markedly avoid it		Always avoid it

Social situations because of a fear of being embarrassed or making a fool of myself?   **2**

Certain situations because of a fear of having a panic attack or other distressing symptoms (such as loss of bladder control, vomiting or dizziness)?   **3**

Certain situations because of a fear of particular objects or activities (such as animals, heights, seeing blood, being in confined spaces, driving or flying)?   **0**

Leah's completed Work and Social Adjustment Scale

Using the scale provided below, select the number that you think most accurately describes how you are affected in each section.

1. Work

If you are retired or choose not to have a job for reasons unrelated to your problem, please tick N/A (not applicable).

0	1	2	3	4	5	**6**	7	8	N/A
Not at all		Slightly		Definitely		Markedly		Very severely	☐ I cannot work

2. Home management

Cleaning, tidying, shopping, cooking, looking after home/children, paying bills, etc.

0	1	2	3	**4**	5	6	7	8
Not at all		Slightly		Definitely		Markedly		Very severely

3. Social leisure activities

With other people, e.g. parties, pubs, outings, entertaining, etc.

0	1	2	3	4	**5**	6	7	8
Not at all		Slightly		Definitely		Markedly		Very severely

4. Private leisure activities

Done alone, e.g. reading, gardening, sewing, hobbies, walking, etc.

0	1	2	3	**4**	5	6	7	8
Not at all		Slightly		Definitely		Markedly		Very severely

5. Family and relationships

Forming and maintaining close relationships with others including the people that I live with.

0	1	2	3	4	**5**	6	7	8
Not at all		Slightly		Definitely		Markedly		Very severely

Total score   24

Leah's completed Perceived Stress Scale: 10 Items[10]

The questions in this scale ask you about your feelings and thoughts during the last month. In each case, please indicate with a check how often you felt or thought a certain way.

1. In the last month, how often have you been upset because of something that happened unexpectedly?

0	1	2	<u>3</u>	4
Never	Almost never	Sometimes	Fairly often	Very often

2. In the last month, how often have you felt that you were unable to control the important things in your life?

0	1	2	<u>3</u>	4
Never	Almost never	Sometimes	Fairly often	Very often

3. In the last month, how often have you felt nervous and 'stressed'?

0	1	2	3	<u>4</u>
Never	Almost never	Sometimes	Fairly often	Very often

4. In the last month, how often have you felt confident about your ability to handle your personal problems?

0	1	<u>2</u>	3	4
Never	Almost never	Sometimes	Fairly often	Very often

5. In the last month, how often have you felt that things were going your way?

0	**1**	2	3	4
Never	Almost never	Sometimes	Fairly often	Very often

6. In the last month, how often have you found that you could not cope with all the things that you had to do?

0	1	2	**3**	4
Never	Almost never	Sometimes	Fairly often	Very often

7. In the last month, how often have you been able to control irritations in your life?

0	1	**2**	3	4
Never	Almost never	Sometimes	Fairly often	Very often

8. In the last month, how often have you felt that you were on top of things?

0	1	**2**	3	4
Never	Almost never	Sometimes	Fairly often	Very often

9. In the last month, how often have you been angered because of things that were outside of your control?

0	1	2	**3**	4
Never	Almost never	Sometimes	Fairly often	Very often

10. In the last month, how often have you felt difficulties were piling up so high that you could not overcome them?

0	1	2	**3**	4
Never	Almost never	Sometimes	Fairly often	Very often

Total score   26

How to score the Perceived Stress Scale: 10 items

Add up all the negatively stated questions – 1, 2, 3, 6, 9 and 10.

Then reverse score the positively stated questions – 4, 5, 7 and 8. For these questions:

$0 = 4$

$1 = 3$

$2 = 2$

$3 = 1$

$4 = 0.$

Add the two scores together.

The higher the score, the more stress you are experiencing at that given time.

Leah's scores indicate that her mood is moderately depressed, she is experiencing anxiety at the top of the mild range, she has some symptoms of social anxiety and panic, and her problems are having an impact on her day-to-day activities, especially the area of work; her score of 26 on the Perceived Stress Scale suggests significant stress levels.

How is stress treated?

Like most common emotional problems, stress responds well to CBT. Many people who are stressed use self-help materials such as this book successfully to learn how to better manage their stress.

This book contains different ways to help you identify your stress and reduce it. These include monitoring your mood (p. 389 and the start of most chapters), problem-solving (Chapter 12), and helping you be realistic about your ability to cope by identifying and evaluating negative thoughts about your coping ability (Chapters 15–17). Reducing stress will also alleviate low mood, anxiety and anger, as well as hopefully improving your self-esteem.

Leah's story

Let's get back to Leah's story, because we can use this to think about how situations, thoughts, emotions, bodily sensations and behaviours relate to stress, and how the scales can be used to measure symptoms. As we said earlier, Leah is a twenty-five-year-old woman who is working long hours and having difficulty coping with the stress of her job and balancing this with her home life.

During a recent incident when her stress levels were high, Leah decided to plot her symptoms in a CBT model diagram, which appears in Figure 7.2. You can see from this diagram how her symptoms are interlinked, and how they influence each other.

Figure 7.2: Leah's CBT model

Situation: Late Thursday evening: arrive home after covering local election. Written up what I can in the office but need to get in early so the overnight results are ready for the following edition. Get home to find Jay hunting for the cat, which hasn't come home in three days.

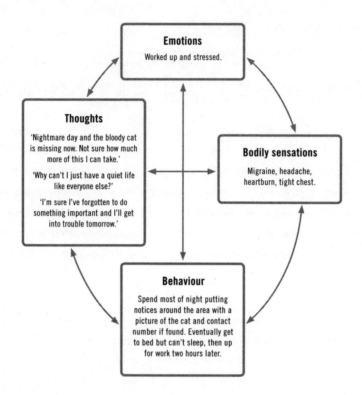

After completing her diagram, Leah rated her problems with stress on the mood scale (Figure 7.3). Her baseline score on her overall mood is:

-5	-4	<u>**-3**</u>	-2	-1	0	+1	+2	+3	+4	+5

Negative   Neutral   Positive
mood   mood

Figure 7.3: Leah's mood scale

As we saw earlier in Table 7.2, Leah's baseline PHQ-9 score is: 12.

Her baseline GAD-7 score is: 10.

Her baseline Phobia Scale scores are: 2, 3, 0.

Her baseline WASAS score is: 24.

Her baseline Perceived Stress Scale is: 26.

We will chart Leah's progress throughout the remaining chapters.

Summary

The space below is for you to use to make your own summary to refer back to as you work through the rest of this book. Write down any important points that you want to remember, either from this chapter or from what you have read so far. Was anything that you read particularly surprising? What was most helpful?

1. _____

_____

2. _____

_____

3. _____

_____

4. _____

_____

8 Symptoms of anxiety, depression and other common problems

Case illustration 7: Ash

Ash is a thirty-nine-year-old married man who lives with his wife and three children in a small country town. Ten months ago Ash was cycling to work through town when a car knocked him off his bike. Ash was terribly shaken by the accident and was taken to hospital where he was treated for two broken ribs. His bike was beyond repair. The driver, who lives in a neighbouring city, had been driving through the small town at speed in order to reach the motorway nearby. The driver was not insured and a court case is now pending. Ash is back to physical fitness but feels 'emotionally scarred' by the accident, although he has not been diagnosed with post-traumatic stress disorder. His wife bought him another bicycle but Ash has felt unable to use it because of the severe anxiety he feels every time he goes near it. He keeps the bike in the garage and avoids even looking at it because seeing it is enough to make him feel anxious.

Ash feels resentful about the position he finds himself in. He now travels to work by bus or car and no longer spends sunny weekends on cycling expeditions with his wife and children. He avoids the news in case he hears anything about cars speeding or cycle accidents. On occasions when he can't avoid the news, he gets anxious. When he thinks about what he is missing out on

Ash gets very angry and low in mood. Often these feelings persist for a long time. The children used to cycle to school but Ash is so worried about how vulnerable they are that he has put a stop to that. His children now take the school bus.

Ash's story reminds us that it is not unusual to experience more than one of the emotional problems described in the earlier chapters. It is common for those who are feeling depressed to also feel anxious or to feel low or angry about their ongoing anxieties. Mixed depression and anxiety is particularly common. It is also common for people with anxiety or depression to have low self-esteem.

Table 8.1: *Key statistics*

- Mixed anxiety and depression is the most common mental health problem in the UK, with almost 9 per cent of the population experiencing enough symptoms to warrant a formal diagnosis.

- Women are more likely to suffer from mixed anxiety and depression than men. In England, 11.8 per cent of women suffer from mixed anxiety and depression compared to 7.6 per cent of men.[11]

What are the signs and symptoms of mixed anxiety and depression?

Symptoms of both anxiety and depression are common. Full details can be found in Chapters 3 and 4.

dy done so, now is a good time to complete and score ne Appendix, on pp. 389–406, so you can begin to chart Ash completed the PHQ-9, GAD-7, Phobia Scale and Work djustment Scale (WASAS), which you can see in Table 8.2.

Ash's story

Table 8.2: Ash's completed measures

Ash's completed PHQ-9

Over the <u>last 2 weeks</u>, how often have you been bothered by any of the following problems?		Not at all	Several days	More than half the days	Nearly every day
1	Little interest or pleasure in doing things	0	<u>1</u>	2	3
2	Feeling down, depressed, or hopeless	0	<u>1</u>	2	3
3	Trouble falling or staying asleep, or sleeping too much	0	1	<u>2</u>	3
4	Feeling tired or having little energy	<u>0</u>	1	2	3
5	Poor appetite or overeating	<u>0</u>	1	2	3
6	Feeling bad about yourself — or that you are a failure or have let yourself or your family down	0	1	2	<u>3</u>
7	Trouble concentrating on things such as reading the newspaper or watching television	0	1	<u>2</u>	3

8	Moving or speaking so slowly that other people could have noticed? Or the opposite – being so fidgety or restless that you have been moving around a lot more than usual	**0**	1	2	3
9	Thoughts that you would be better off dead or of hurting yourself in some way	**0**	1	2	3
	PHQ-9 total score 9				

Ash's completed GAD-7

	Over the last 2 weeks, how often have you been bothered by any of the following problems?	Not at all	Several days	More than half the days	Nearly every day
1	Feeling nervous, anxious or on edge	0	1	**2**	3
2	Not being able to stop or control worrying	0	**1**	2	3
3	Worrying too much about different things	0	1	2	**3**
4	Trouble relaxing	0	**1**	2	3
5	Being so restless that it is hard to sit still	**0**	1	2	3

6	Becoming easily annoyed or irritable	0	1	**2**	3
7	Feeling afraid, as if something awful might happen	0	1	2	**3**
GAD-7 total score 12					

Ash's completed Phobia Scales

Choose a number from the scale below to show how much you would avoid each of the situations or objects listed below. Then write the number in the box opposite the situation.

0	1	2	3	4	5	6	7	8
Would not avoid it		Slightly avoid it		Definitely avoid it		Markedly avoid it		Always avoid it

Social situations because of a fear of being embarrassed or making a fool of myself? ☐ 1

Certain situations because of a fear of having a panic attack or other distressing symptoms (such as loss of bladder control, vomiting or dizziness)? ☐ 2

Certain situations because of a fear of particular objects or activities (such as animals, heights, seeing blood, being in confined spaces, driving or flying)? ☐ 8

Ash's completed Work and Social Adjustment Scale

Using the scale provided below, select the number that you think most accurately describes how you are affected in each section.

1. Work

If you are retired or choose not to have a job for reasons unrelated to your problem, please tick N/A (not applicable).

0	1	**2**	3	4	5	6	7	8	N/A
Not at all		Slightly		Definitely		Markedly		Very severely	☐

I cannot work

2. Home management

Cleaning, tidying, shopping, cooking, looking after home/children, paying bills, etc.

0	1	2	**3**	4	5	6	7	8
Not at all		Slightly		Definitely		Markedly		Very severely

3. Social leisure activities

With other people, e.g. parties, pubs, outings, entertaining, etc.

0	1	2	3	4	5	**6**	7	8
Not at all		Slightly		Definitely		Markedly		Very severely

4. Private leisure activities

Done alone, e.g. reading, gardening, sewing, hobbies, walking, etc.

0	1	**2**	3	4	5	6	7	8
Not at all		Slightly		Definitely		Markedly		Very severely

5. Family and relationships

Forming and maintaining close relationships with others including the people that I live with.

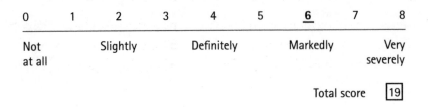

0	1	2	3	4	5	**6**	7	8
Not at all		Slightly		Definitely		Markedly		Very severely

Total score   19

Ash's scores indicate that his mood is moderately depressed, he is experiencing anxiety at the top of the mild range, he has some symptoms of social anxiety and panic, and his problems are having an impact across functioning and most markedly affecting the area of work.

How is mixed anxiety and depression treated?

Depression and anxiety often exist together and it is estimated that more than two-thirds of people with major depression also suffer from a degree of anxiety. As with depression and the anxiety disorders, there is good evidence to indicate that CBT is an effective treatment for *mixed* anxiety and depression. We will look at various techniques for this in Part 2.

Ash's story

Ash's story can help us to understand how situations, thoughts, emotions, bodily sensations and behaviours can interact to trigger and sustain mixed anxiety and depression. It should also become clearer how the measures can be used to help evaluate the severity of symptoms.

During a recent incident when his symptoms were particularly intense, Ash made a note of his symptoms in the CBT model diagram in Figure 8.1. You can see how the symptoms are interlinked and how they influence each other.

Figure 8.1: Ash's CBT model

Situation: Monday evening: walked into the living room and accidentally caught a news item about a drunk-driving hit-and-run incident that left a four-year-old boy critically ill in hospital.

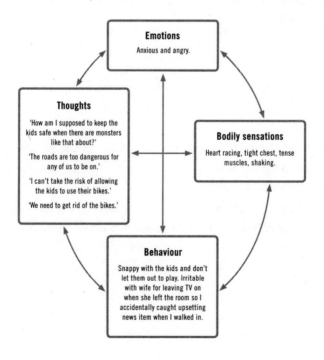

After filling in his diagram, Ash rated his problems with anxiety and anger on the mood scale (Figure 8.2). His baseline score on his overall mood is:

-5	**-4**	-3	-2	-1	0	+1	+2	+3	+4	+5

Negative mood	Neutral	Positive mood

Figure 8.2: Ash's mood scale

As we've seen in Table 8.2, Ash's baseline PHQ-9 score is: 9.

His baseline GAD-7 score is: 12.

His baseline Phobia Scale scores are: 1, 2, 8.

His baseline WASAS score is: 19.

We will chart Ash's progress throughout the remaining chapters.

Summary

Use the space below to write down some of your thoughts about this chapter. You might like to note things that you found particularly interesting or important, or that you found especially relevant to your own experiences. What do you want to remember from this chapter? Is there anything that you'd like to think about and come back to later on?

1. _____

   _____

2. _____

   _____

3. _____

   _____

4. _____

   _____

9 Making sense of your problem

We hope that having read the descriptions of the characteristics of depression, anxiety, anger, low self-esteem and stress, and filled in the measures in the Appendix, you will have a better idea of the type of problem you are experiencing.

We saw in the previous chapters how Leon, Pearl, Bea, Dez, Leah, Penny and Ash each created a diagram based on a specific incidence of their particular problem during a time when it felt acute. Doing this helped them to start making sense of their problem. Now it's your turn.

My symptoms diagram

1. Begin by thinking of a recent incident when your problem caused you particular difficulties, and make a note of that situation in the diagram in Figure 9.1.

2. Plot your emotional, physical, behavioural and cognitive symptoms (i.e. your thoughts) under the relevant headings.

3. Check to see if you are able to identify how each one is interlinked with the other and how they influence each other (e.g. seeing a link between not getting out of bed and how you feel about yourself, or identifying a link between feeling your heart race and thinking you might be having a heart attack, etc.). If you get stuck, you can always look back over the examples from the previous chapters.

4. Once your diagram is complete, sit back and look at it. Does the situation you've plotted and your response seem typical for you?

5. Why not try making another diagram of another recent event when your problem caused you particular difficulty? See pp. 437–9 for more blank diagrams. Are there any similarities between the diagrams? Is there anything you think you could learn from this comparison?

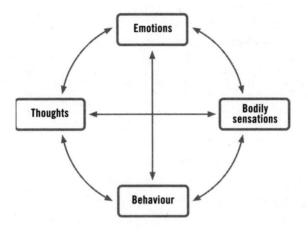

Figure 9.1: My CBT model

Now rate your current mood on the mood scale in Figure 9.2.

-5	-4	-3	-2	-1	0	+1	+2	+3	+4	+5

Negative mood	Neutral	Positive mood

Figure 9.2: My mood scale

If you haven't already, now turn to pp. 389–408 in the Appendix and complete the PHQ-9, GAD-7, Phobia Scale, and WASAS in order to generate your 'baseline' scores. After you record your scores below, plot them on the graphs on pp. 405–8.

My baseline PHQ-9 score is:

My baseline GAD-7 score is:

My baseline Phobia Scale scores are:

My baseline WASAS score is:

Are you ready to change?

You might be reading this book last thing at night because that is the only opportunity you have to sit down and read. If you have ten or fifteen minutes a night that you can dedicate to making changes, then that is terrific. If you only have ten or fifteen minutes once a month, then you will need to try to free up some more time that you can use to focus on the exercises in the book. Even when you have a lot of time to dedicate to making changes, it is still hard. However, it is almost *impossible* to see and do things differently if you have almost no time in which to do so. If you are unable to prioritize changing at the moment, then it may be that this is not the right time to start. Maybe wait until a holiday, or a bank holiday, or even take a day's annual leave to read through this book and begin some of the exercises. It would be demoralizing if you started the book, made a few changes, and then felt it was too difficult to continue because you do not have sufficient time to stick at it.

Even if you do have time you can dedicate to this book, you also need to *want* to change. The benefits of changing have to be clear to you, as do the disadvantages of staying the same. Change can sometimes seem unachievable at first, but when you start reaping the benefits of your hard work, change can feel fantastic! It is a bit like starting a healthy eating and exercise plan after a holiday; at first it can be difficult to get started but once you start noticing how much better you feel, it is self-motivating.

Remember Leon, who suffers from depression, triggered by discovering that his girlfriend had been having a relationship with his best friend?

He wrote down the benefits of changing and disadvantages of staying the same in Table 9.1.

Table 9.1: Leon's table of advantages of changing and disadvantages of staying the same

Advantages of changing	Disadvantages of staying the same
I'll get back to work.	I'll go down to half pay in five months' time and will find it hard to survive financially.
I'll hopefully feel less miserable.	
I might meet someone else although that feels unlikely right now.	My boss might decide to get rid of me.
I can work towards coming off my medication.	I will probably lose the few good friends I have as they will get fed up of contacting me and being ignored.
I can get my life back and feel normal again.	
Leon's conclusion: Although everything feels overwhelming right now, I know I definitely don't want to stay this way. If I make changes little by little, then I should start noticing improvements – and particularly if I can get back to work sooner rather than later.	

Using Leon's table as an example, fill in the table of advantages and disadvantages in Table 9.2. This will help you to work out the benefits you will experience if you are able to make improvements to your mental health, as well as the disadvantages of things staying the same. It might be worth tearing out this page or making a copy of it and sticking it on the fridge to remind you about what there is to gain by trying to see your situation from a different perspective.

Table 9.2: My advantages of changing and disadvantages of staying the same

Advantages of changing	Disadvantages of staying the same
My conclusion:	

Another blank table is given in the Appendix, p. 443.

The combination of your view of how life is for you at the moment, the descriptions above and your scores on the measures might lead you to decide that your difficulties do not need addressing at this point in time. If, however, you consider that you are experiencing some emotional problems that need to be addressed right now, and you are ready to address them using CBT, the next chapters will provide you with helpful ways of making improvements.

Summary

As you come to the end of Part 1 of this book, take some time to reflect on what you have found most important or useful so far. What do you want to remember about Part 1 as you continue to progress through the book? Is there any one thing in particular that you want to take away from this chapter in particular? Making some notes now will mean that you have a valuable summary to turn back to later on.

1. _____

   _____

2. _____

   _____

3. _____

   _____

4. _____

   _____

Part 2

Methods of breaking vicious cycles

10 Problem statements and SMART goals

In Chapters 1 and 2 we described the aims of this book and explained how CBT works. In the following chapters we looked at the sort of problems you may be experiencing, to help you try to make sense of them.

Now it is time to start making changes.

Measuring your symptoms

Before starting to make changes, it is important to measure your symptoms. There are three reasons for this:

1. By filling in a measure of your mood and anxiety, etc. at the start of each chapter you read, and plotting it on a graph, you will be able to see how things are improving.

2. More specifically, you will be able to see the areas that are improving and the areas that require more work and need more of your attention.

3. Research has shown that recording your mood and anxiety this way can improve outcomes by helping you to stay on track.

Rate your current mood on the mood scale in Figure 10.1.

-5	-4	-3	-2	-1	0	+1	+2	+3	+4	+5

Negative   Neutral   Positive
mood   mood

Figure 10.1: Mood scale

- The PHQ-9 provides a measure of low mood. You can find this in the Appendix on pp. 391–6. You may have already filled it in as part of the previous chapter. If not, you should fill it in now. Plot your score on the graph on pp. 423–5.

- The GAD-7 is a measure of anxiety. You can find a copy of this in the Appendix on pp. 397–9. If you have not already done so, please complete it now and plot your score on the graph on p. 426.

- The Phobia Scale is self-explanatory. Like the other measures, it can also be found in the Appendix, on pp. 400–2. Go ahead and complete this scale, and then plot your score on the graph on pages 429–34.

- The Work and Social Adjustment Scale (WASAS) provides a measure of the impact of a problem on various aspects of life, including work and home life. This scale is in the Appendix on pp. 403–8. If you have not already completed this scale, then please do so now and plot your score on page 435.

- As its title suggests, the Penn State Worry Questionnaire is used to measure worry. Like the others, you will find this in the Appendix, on pp. 409–10. If this measure seems relevant to your problems and you have not yet completed it, please do so now. Once you have finished the questionnaire, plot your score on page 436.

- The Dimensions of Anger Reactions II is a measure of anger, which is provided in the Appendix, on pp. 411–12. If anger is relevant to your problems and you have not already done so, complete this measure now and plot your score on page 437.

- The Rosenberg Self-Esteem Scale provides a measure of self-esteem. This scale is in the Appendix, on pp. 413–14. If this measure seems relevant to your problems and you have not already completed it, please do so now and plot your score on page 438.

- If stress is a relevant feature of your problem, then please complete the Perceived Stress Scale (10- and 4-item versions), which are given on pp. 415–19.

You should rate your mood on the mood scale at the beginning of this chapter, as well as complete the PHQ-9 and GAD-7 and any other relevant measures, at the start of every chapter. This is a good habit to get into because you will be able to measure your progress, which is self-reinforcing if things are going well, and a good signal that it might be worth trying a different tactic if things are not going so well. We will include the mood scale at the beginning of the following chapters as a reminder.

Using problem statements to help identify your problems

As we mentioned in Chapter 2, the first step in addressing your difficulties using CBT is to identify the types of problems you are experiencing. This is easier said than done, although reading the earlier descriptions about the various types of emotional problems and completing the measures will have helped you to achieve this.

Breaking down the problems you have been experiencing into what are known as 'problem statements' will help you further identify the types of problem you are experiencing, as well as giving you some ideas as to why they persist.

What is a problem statement?

A problem statement should summarize your difficulties in a nutshell. There are three key elements to a problem statement and they are: the *trigger* (in *italics*), the **symptoms** (in **bold**) (emotional, physical, cognitive and behavioural), and the consequences or impact (underlined). Problem statements tend to contain words such as 'leading to', 'as a result' or 'consequently'.

Let's look at a few examples of problem statements in Table 10.1.

Table 10.1: Examples of problem statements

Leon's problem statement

As we've seen, Leon is a twenty-eight-year-old single man who has been feeling depressed for the last five months since he broke up with his girlfriend.

'My main problem is **feeling tired all the time** and **low in mood** particularly *on waking*, leading me to **stay in bed**; as a result I am finding it <u>difficult to work and see friends</u> and worrying that **I can't stop mulling over the break-up** and that **things will never get any better**.'

Pearl's problem statement

Pearl is a sixty-nine-year-old married woman who has been depressed for the past year or so. The onset of her depression coincided with the diagnosis of her husband's Alzheimer's disease.

'*Every morning* I get up having **not slept well** and feel **generally miserable in myself; I worry about John and what the future holds** and have **given up pretty much all the things I used to enjoy doing**. Consequently <u>my days are empty apart from looking after John</u> and <u>I feel like a useless non-coper</u>.'

Bea's problem statement

Bea is a forty-seven-year-old divorced woman who has a long-standing problem with anxiety.

'Difficulty dealing with *problems that arise* leading to lots of **worrying** and **feeling keyed up** and **tension all over my body, particularly my shoulders,** and **difficulty sleeping**; I seem to spend all my time **fretting** which is <u>wearing me down</u>.'

Dez's problem statement

Dez is a fifty-two-year-old man who has been having problems controlling his temper since starting his new job.

'Whenever I am *stuck in traffic* or *dealing with staff whose sales figures are lower than I would like* I start **thinking people are doing things on purpose to get at me**, my **muscles get tense**, I get **angry** and I sometimes **shout and lash out verbally at people**; as a result I have <u>lost friends</u> and it is <u>putting a strain on my relationship with my partner</u>.'

Leah's problem statement

Leah is a twenty-five-year-old woman who is working long hours and having difficulty coping with the stress of her job.

'*Pressure at work* and *threat of redundancies* are leading me to work **very long hours** as I feel like **I need to prove my worth** to my boss, feeling s**tressed, difficulty sleeping** and proneness to **headaches**; consequently I am <u>left with no energy or time to spend with Jay or to see friends</u>.'

Penny's problem statement

Penny is a thirty-two-year-old woman who has a long-standing skin problem and low self-esteem.

'**Lack of confidence and self-belief** that *seems to be there all the time* and which **gets me down**; I cope by **staying in alone** and **over-eating,** which is leading me to feel even more <u>dissatisfied with myself</u>.'

Ash's problem statement

Ash is a thirty-nine-year-old married man who was knocked off his bike on his way to work. Ash was terribly shaken by the accident and still feels 'emotionally scarred'.

'My main problem is my **avoidance** of *travelling anywhere by bike* due to physical symptoms such as **racing heart** and **shaking** and a **fear** that **I'll be knocked off again,** leading me to become increasingly <u>restricted about how I get to and from work</u>.'

My problem statement

Use Table 10.2 to identify the different ways your problem affects you, from its triggers through to its impact. Once you have written down the different aspects of the problem, pull it together into a sentence like the ones in Table 10.1. If you are experiencing more than one problem then just use the blank table in the Appendix, p. 444, as many times as you need to.

Table 10.2: How my problems affect me

Symptoms

Trigger	Emotions	Behaviours	Physical	Thoughts	Impact

Now transfer the various aspects of your problem into Table 10.3 to come up with your own problem statement.

Table 10.3: Problem statement

_____

_____

_____

_____

_____

Next, rate each problem on a scale of 0–100, to indicate how severe it is for you currently (Figure 10.2).

Problem severity scale (0–100)

0	50	100
Not a problem	Moderate problem	Very severe

Figure 10.2: My problem severity scale

Now it is time to decide which problem you would like to tackle first. Often, this is the one that causes the most disruption to your life and it is usually the most severe.

Try to return to your original statement about each problem every now and again (perhaps every couple of weeks or so) to track any improvement as you work your way through your problem.

Now that you have written your problem statement, do you have a better idea of why your problem persists? By looking at triggers, symptoms and consequences, you will have formulated some ideas not only about what your problem is but what is keeping it going. This understanding of what is keeping your problem going is important to achieve, because it is necessary in order to make changes.

SMART goals

Setting goals is a great way to identify exactly what you want to achieve by putting into practice the strategies you are going to learn over the following chapters. The best goals are:

- Specific

- Measurable

- Achievable

- Realistic, and

- Time-limited (or 'SMART').

Goals should be directly related to your problem statement. Setting goals this way can really help when it comes to maintaining a focus on where you want to be, which in turn will enable you to assess your progress.

Let's go back to the people we met earlier. Leon told us that he wants to 'feel normal again'. This is a very understandable and reasonable goal. It is also a realistic goal. However, it isn't particularly 'SMART'.

Making your goals SMART will help ensure that you achieve them. Being *specific* about *what* you are setting out to achieve means that you will know *where* to begin to try to achieve it. If you have a goal that is not *measurable*, then you won't know if you have met it or not. If your goal is not *achievable* and *realistic*, then it may end up feeling like another thing you've failed at. If it is not *time-limited*, then you risk losing interest and focus.

Leon's goal of 'wanting to feel normal again' could be made 'SMART' by thinking through what he would be doing differently if this was the case. For him, this would be working, socializing with friends and keeping his apartment in good shape – three goals that would make Leon feel like his normal self again.

Let's have a look at a few examples of SMART goals in Table 10.4.

Table 10.4: Examples of SMART goals

Leon's SMART goals

1. To work at the music shop five days a week from 10 a.m. to 6 p.m.

2. To socialize with friends 2–3 times a week for a minimum of two hours each time.

3. To spend half an hour each day cleaning and tidying the apartment.

Pearl's SMART goals

1. To organize regular respite care for John from professional carers and friends for a minimum of three hours twice a week.

2. To go out with friends at least once a week for a minimum of two hours.

Bea's SMART goal

1. To learn and use new ways of tackling everyday real-life and hypothetical problems to help reduce worry time to no more than twenty minutes a day.

Dez's SMART goals

1. To travel to and from work on a daily basis without getting so irritable.

2. To meet with colleagues to discuss sales targets without appearing irritable.

Leah's SMART goals

1. To leave work by 6 p.m. at least twice a week.

---

2. To go to the gym for one hour, three times a week.

3. To go out with Jay for a minimum of three hours, once a week.

4. To meet with friends for a minimum of half an hour, once a week.

Penny's SMART goals

1. To meet with friends for a minimum of one hour, three times a week.

2. To 'treat myself' at least once a week, even if it's something small like buying myself a nice coffee.

3. To join a dating agency and communicate with and go out for dates with suitable men.

Ash's SMART goals

1. To cycle to and from work five days a week.

2. To go cycling with wife Kay and kids most weekends (weather permitting).

3. To allow kids to cycle to and from school five days a week.

4. To watch the news at least once a day without becoming distressed.

You may have more than one SMART goal that you would like to achieve by the end of this book. Be sure to make your goal(s) as SMART as possible. Your supporter, if you have one (a close friend or professional, who is helping you work through this book), could help you come up with some if you're having difficulty with this. Once you have thought of a few, write them down in Table 10.5.

Table 10.5: My SMART goals

Goal 1

_____

_____

_____

_____

Goal 2

_____

_____

_____

_____

Goal 3

_____

_____

_____

_____

Goal 4

_____

_____

_____

_____

Summary

Use the space below to write down key points or things that you want to remember from this chapter. What was most helpful? What did you learn from making your problem statement and SMART goals? Is there anything in particular that you want to bear in mind as you go on to the next chapter?

1. _____

_____

2. _____

_____

3. _____

_____

4. _____

_____

11 Examining activity

Before we begin ...

Before starting this chapter, rate your current mood on the mood scale in Figure 11.1.

-5	-4	-3	-2	-1	0	+1	+2	+3	+4	+5

Negative mood				Neutral					Positive mood

Figure 11.1: Mood scale

Next, take a moment to record your mood or anxiety again using the PHQ-9 and GAD-7 and anxiety, stress or self-esteem. Plot your scores on your graphs whatever else you are recording such as on pp. 423–8.

Hopefully the work we did in the previous chapter identifying your problems and giving some thought as to why they persist will have made you feel more optimistic that change is possible. Such optimism may be reflected in your scores, but don't be too concerned if they have not yet changed or have even become a bit worse. Remember that you have only just started to think about your problems and how you want to change them! Whatever is going on in your life right now is an important factor in influencing your emotions, bodily sensations, behaviour and thoughts, and may be affecting the way you are feeling at the moment.

In this chapter we will look at how *what you actually do* affects your mental health, and how changing your behaviour can help to break vicious cycles.

Activity

Think back to your problem statement. Did you use the words 'isolation', 'staying in bed' or 'being too busy' at all? One of the most common and powerful reasons that emotional problems persist is because they cause us to become isolated and unmotivated. This is particularly true for depression. It can also be true for anxiety, low self-esteem, stress and anger, when people avoid situations because of fear, guilt, feeling under pressure, and irritation.

Let's go back to Leon, Penny and Ash. Leon avoids seeing friends and talking to his parents because he feels humiliated following the break-up of his relationship. Penny avoids socializing as she fears people will find her boring. Ash avoids going out for cycle rides with the family in case harm comes to his children. This kind of avoidance can lead to isolation. The opposite is also true, as it can also be the case that you are doing too much. Being busy all the time is sometimes necessary, but it is not healthy to be constantly busy on a long-term basis. In fact, living your life as though it is a sprint rather than a marathon is one factor that leads to stress – being able to pace yourself is important. Whether you are doing too much or too little can be very important to improving your mental health.

The *types* of activity you are doing are also very important. Are your days full of pleasurable activities like talking to your friends, reading and arranging fun things to do? Or are they full of activities such as making breakfast for the family, commuting, going to work, answering emails, cleaning, paying bills and sorting out the mess that other people seem to have left for you? If the latter is more typical, then you might be able to see why your mood could be low and your stress levels high.

In addition to doing less, people who experience ongoing feelings of sadness often suffer from a loss of routine. Leon, for example, writes in his activity diary (below) that he stays in bed because he feels so depressed and unable to face the day. Because of this he ends up staying away from the people and activities that may actually help to bring about an improvement in his mood. This is not unusual for someone who is experiencing depression, but it disrupts a normal routine and is likely to worsen an already low mood. By isolating himself, Leon is less likely to experience things that might bring a sense of pleasure or accomplishment.

Rather than *waiting* to feel better and for routine to re-establish itself, an effective way of treating depression is to take an 'outside-in' approach (i.e. doing things rather than waiting to feel better on the inside first) and re-establish routine and increase activity, particularly activities that bring about a sense of achievement and pleasure.

Your activity

The best way to find out if you are doing too much or too little, and whether there are enough (or indeed any) pleasurable activities in your life, is to monitor your daily activities over the course of a week. Becoming aware of your daily activities will also help you to identify a pattern in your behaviour and mood, and may motivate you to change some aspects of your daily routine for a healthier and more enjoyable lifestyle.

Leon rated the activity of watching TV as 4/10 for enjoyment and 3/10 for importance (Table 11.1). This implies that he doesn't find watching TV very enjoyable or important in his life.

Use the Daily Activities Worksheet (Table 11.2), to keep a diary of your hourly activities, rate how much you enjoyed each activity, and make a note of its importance to you. Rate the activities as enjoyable or important on a scale of 0–10. A score of 0 would imply that the activity is not enjoyable at all or not important in your life, while a score of 10 suggests that the activity is very enjoyable or the activity is of highest importance in your life.

At the bottom of the Daily Activities Worksheet, there is space for you to provide a rating for your overall mood that day, between 0 (negative mood) and 10 (positive mood).

Table 11.1: Leon's completed Daily Activities Worksheet

Time	Activity	Enjoyment (0–10)	Importance (0–10)
5–6 a.m.	Sleeping	4	4
6–7 a.m.	Sleeping	4	4
7–8 a.m.	Sleeping	4	4
8–9 a.m.	Sleeping	4	4
9–10 a.m.	Sleeping	4	4
10–11 a.m.	Sleeping	4	4
11–12 a.m.	Sleeping	4	4
1–2 p.m.	Sleeping	4	4
2–3 p.m.	Lay in bed	3	2
3–4 p.m.	Watched TV	4	3
4–5 p.m.	Watched TV	4	3
5–6 p.m.	Watched TV	4	3

6–7 p.m.	Had a snack	5	4
7–8 p.m.	Watched TV	4	3
8–9 p.m.	Lay on settee	4	2
9–10 p.m.	Used Facebook	4	2
10–11 p.m.	Used Facebook	4	2
11–12 p.m.	Used Facebook	4	2
12–1 a.m.	Played video games	5	2
1–2 a.m.	Played video games	5	2
2–5 a.m.	Slept	4	3
Overall mood for the day (0–10) **4**			

The best way to complete the Daily Activities Worksheet is to fill it in hour by hour for every single thing you do, even when it might seem like you are not really doing anything (e.g. sitting looking out the window, lying in bed thinking about work, sleeping). Keeping a diary like this for a week can seem a bit tedious. However, the more accurate it is, the better. It will certainly be worth the effort in the long run.

Table 11.2: My Daily Activities Worksheet

Time	Activity	Enjoyment (0–10)	Importance (0–10)
5–6 a.m.			
6–7 a.m.			
7–8 a.m.			
8–9 a.m.			
9–10 a.m.			
10–11 a.m.			
11–12 a.m.			
1–2 p.m.			
2–3 p.m.			
3–4 p.m.			
4–5 p.m.			
5–6 p.m.			

6–7 p.m.			
7–8 p.m.			
8–9 p.m.			
9–10 p.m.			
10–11 p.m.			
11–12 p.m.			
12–1 a.m.			
1–2 a.m.			
2–5 a.m.			
Overall mood for the day (0–10) ____			

What now? Introducing Behavioural Activation

If you are returning to this book after a week of monitoring your daily activities, take a moment to rate your mood and anxiety (and anything else you are recording) and plot it on the graphs on pp. 420–39. If you see any changes, take a moment to reflect on what may have caused them; if not, have a think about why there may not have been any change.

Now is the time to try things differently. It is encouraging if you have noticed some change, but this may not be the case. Regardless, this is a good time to either build on what is already going well or to try to do things differently. It would be very easy simply to suggest that you increase routine and pleasurable activities in your life, and this can help enormously, but for many people it would only solve part of the problem. Your thoughts and feelings are also a key part of the problem and need to be attended to. Research shows that if we change the daily activities that are contributing to the persistence of an emotional problem such as depression, this will often have a positive impact on how we feel. It is actually very difficult to feel depressed if you are doing lots of things that are enjoyable or bring a sense of accomplishment!

When we are feeling depressed, anxious, under stress or angry it is natural to want to do less and withdraw from the activities we used to pursue. This can seem like the best way to cope when life feels overwhelming. The problem is that this approach does not really help in the long term, and actually feeds the problem (e.g. doing less, like not going to the gym, leads to even lower mood). The best way to stop this negative downward spiral is to force ourselves to become more active, which will then impact our thoughts and feelings. This approach is called Behavioural Activation and it is a tried-and-tested approach for treating depression.

To become more active, we first need to identify the important aspects of our life and our values, because this will guide us in our choice of activities. It is no good just finding any old activities to fill up our time. We need to choose activities that are truly important to us and are worthwhile and enjoyable.

Though this approach to becoming more active can feel uncomfortable and difficult at first, there is a lot of research evidence to show that it really works. However, that is not to say that this approach works for *everyone*. Some people will prefer to focus more on their thoughts, feelings, physical symptoms or relationships. So for you, this approach might simply be a first step or it might complement another method you are trying.

The first step in Behavioural Activation is to monitor your daily activity for a week, which you may have already done in your Daily Activities Worksheet above. This provides an accurate snapshot of your current level of activity.

It is interesting how we can think we have a good sense of how we are spending our time but can still be surprised at what it looks like when written down. Sometimes people find that they are less active than they thought they were, and this new information can spur them on. Conversely, some people find that they are doing more than they expected – and that can be a big boost to morale.

Monitoring your activities for a week is a very good starting point as you can compare future weeks with this first one to see whether this approach is helping you to become more active. It may also help you to think about when during the day you have free time to add an activity to your schedule that you enjoy doing.

Activity assessment

Now that you know exactly what you are and are not doing and the way each activity is affecting your mood, the next step is to think about how you would like to change your daily activities.

To do this, we will focus on the most important areas of your life. In particular, we will develop new activities based on your personal values in each area. Take some time to think through the areas of your life in Table 11.3, and note any difficulties that you are currently experiencing across these areas.

Table 11.3: My activity assessment

1. Relationships (forming and maintaining close relationships with others including family, friends and/or romantic partner)
2. Education/career (this could be formal education or self-learning, paid or voluntary employment)
3. Recreation/interests (leisure time, having fun or relaxing, volunteering)
4. Mind/body/spirituality (physical and mental health, religion and/or spirituality)
5. Daily responsibilities (obligations and responsibilities to others and to your belongings. This could include things like cleaning, tidying, shopping, cooking, looking after home/children, paying bills)

Now write down what you would like to achieve in each of these five areas. In case you need help with ideas, we've included Pearl's list in Table 11.4:

Table 11.4: *Pearl's completed Activity Assessment*

1. Relationships

I'd like to see my friends more often as I've stopped doing this over recent months. I'd also like to spend more time with Tia.

2. Education/career

Having previously been a piano teacher, I'd like to go back to giving weekly piano lessons to local children.

3. Recreation/interests

I'd like to spend half an hour or so every week reading the local newspaper and getting the garden back into shape, as I used to enjoy it so much.

4. Mind/body/spirituality

I'd like to start back doing meditation once or twice a week as it used to help me relax.

5. Daily responsibilities

I'd like to get back into checking my bank accounts at least once a week. It would also be good if I could get back to spending more time on keeping the house tidier. I might even be able to get John to help if I am close by to keep an eye on things. It would be a way of doing things together. I'd also like to get back to baking once or twice a week.

An important step in selecting enjoyable and important activities to include in your schedule involves identifying your values in each of these important areas of your life. A value is a strong belief in a certain way of living.

In order to get a sense of your values, ask yourself the following two questions:

1. What is important to me about each of these areas of my life?

2. What do I want out of each?

Table 11.5: *Pearl's values*

1. What is important to me about each of these areas of my life?

They really define who I am. I am a sociable person and need the company of others but I also like some 'me-time' so that I can recharge my batteries.

2. What do I want out of each?

I want to regain some control over these areas so that I can feel like my old self again and for life to be more fulfilling.

The Life Areas, Values and Activities Inventory

Now that you have identified the areas of your life that you want to tackle and the values that you want to apply to them, you are ready to start thinking through the activities you might want to pursue. Use the Life Areas, Values and Activities Inventory below as your guide towards change. Using the inventory is easy: simply write down your important value and corresponding activities in support of it. Pearl, for example, may state in the 'Relationships' section the value of wanting to be a good wife to her husband. A related activity to this might be to prepare a home-cooked meal for him.

It is very important that the activities you identify are observable (the sort of thing you can actually see) and measurable. Also, if an activity seems to present too big a step at the moment, remember that you can break it down into smaller steps. For example, Pearl found it difficult to get out of the house and go shopping for groceries, so she avoided it by shopping online. Grocery shopping can be quite a tiring task for somebody who has intense feelings of sadness and disinterest, and one way of dealing with this could be to break it down into smaller steps, like making a grocery list, getting ready, getting the car out of the garage, driving to the supermarket and parking, and then shopping and going home.

Fill out the Life Areas, Values and Activities Inventory in Table 11.6. If there isn't enough space to record all of the activities you would like to pursue, simply use extra sheets of paper.

Table 11.6: My Life Areas, Values and Activities Inventory

Life area: Relationships

Value:	Enjoyment (0–10)	Importance (0–10)
Activity 1:		
Activity 2:		
Activity 3:		
Activity 4:		
Activity 5:		

Life area: Education/career

Value:	Enjoyment (0–10)	Importance (0–10)
Activity 1:		
Activity 2:		
Activity 3:		
Activity 4:		
Activity 5:		

Life area: Recreation/interests

Value:	Enjoyment (0–10)	Importance (0–10)
Activity 1:		
Activity 2:		
Activity 3:		
Activity 4:		
Activity 5:		

Life area: Mind/body/spirituality

Value:	Enjoyment (0–10)	Importance (0–10)
Activity 1:		
Activity 2:		
Activity 3:		
Activity 4:		
Activity 5:		

Life area: Daily responsibilities

Value:	Enjoyment (0–10)	Importance (0–10)
Activity 1:		
Activity 2:		
Activity 3:		
Activity 4:		
Activity 5:		

Troubleshooting

If you get stuck you might want to look at the Activity checklist in Table 11.7. Some of the activities on the list may not appeal to you, but there may be others that you want to put a tick beside as something that could possibly interest you and that corresponds to one of your values. It tends to be a good idea to opt for a variety of activities, ranging from fun things through to necessary or routine obligations. If you think an activity is likely to make you feel happier or give you a sense of accomplishment, then you are probably right, so it is worth noting it down.

The aim is to increase your activity levels, re-establish a routine and maximize your feelings of accomplishment and pleasure. Planning activities in advance can help alleviate any difficulties making decisions and putting things off (procrastination). Some people get stuck at this point because they have trouble motivating themselves to follow through with the activities they are already committed to, let alone take on more. If you feel like you might be getting stuck, then it is important to remind yourself that we are using the 'outside-in' approach, in which we re-establish routine to make ourselves feel better, rather than waiting to feel better before we re-establish our routine.

Try to ensure that the activities you are choosing are behaviours rather than new ways of thinking or feeling (e.g. 'schedule date nights with John' as opposed to 'think more positively about my relationship with John'). Activities designed around thinking or feeling in new ways are not ideal because it is so difficult to measure our success in achieving them. It is also a good idea to vary the level of difficulty in the activities you set for yourself, because if they are all really tough to do, then it will be hard to get started. One idea is to include one or two activities from your Daily Activities Worksheet that you are already doing. For example, Leon included watching his favourite TV programme and reading his weekly music magazine, even though he is doing them already. You could try including only a couple of really difficult activities, as too many can be demotivating.

Table 11.7: Activity checklist[12]

Excursions/community	✔
1. Taking a trip or holiday.	
2. Going to a fair, carnival, circus, zoo or amusement park.	
3. Going to the beach.	
4. Going on a picnic.	
5. Going out to dinner.	
6. Taking a road trip.	
7. Riding on an aeroplane, hot-air balloon, helicopter.	
8. Staying at a hotel or bed and breakfast.	
9. Camping.	
10. Going to a museum or exhibition.	
11. Shopping, car boot sales, flea markets.	
12. Going to the library or a bookshop.	
13. Going out to the countryside.	
14. Other:	
Interactions with others or social activities	✔
1. Going to or hosting a party.	
2. Giving and receiving physical affection.	
3. Reminiscing, talking about old times.	
4. Group activities.	
5. Having a frank and open conversation.	
6. Getting together with friends.	

7. Discussing a topic of interest (sports, fashion, politics, news).	
8. Having family to visit or visiting family.	
9. Meeting someone new.	
10. Eating out with friends or associates.	
11. Visiting friends or having friends to visit.	
Other:	
Education	✔
1. Learning something new (a language, how to play a musical instrument, etc.).	
2. Learning something artistic (painting, pottery, knitting, etc.).	
3. Reading.	
4. Taking a course on something of interest.	
5. Writing stories, novels, plays, poetry, essays, reports, etc.	
6. Reading a 'How To Do It' book or article.	
7. Going to a lecture or to listen to a speaker of interest.	
8. Going back to school/college/university.	
9. Taking a course in computers.	
10. Other:	
Domestic activities	✔
1. Cleaning the house.	
2. Baking.	
3. Cooking.	
4. Working in the yard, gardening, landscaping.	

5. Washing the car.	
6. Sewing.	
7. Being exempt from a domestic activity.	
8. Buying flowers and plants.	
9. Rearranging or redecorating a room or house.	
10. Freshening up the house with potpourri or flowers.	
11. Fixing things around the house or working on the car.	
12: Other:	
Pampering self and other leisure activities	✔
1. Having free time.	
2. Playing with or having a pet.	
3. Meditating or doing yoga.	
4. Taking a bubble bath or soothing bath.	
5. Being alone.	
6. Writing in a journal or diary or keeping a scrapbook or photo album.	
7. Sleeping late.	
8. Subscribing to a magazine.	
9. Breathing fresh air.	
10. Listening to music.	
11. Sunbathing.	
12. Listening to the sounds of nature.	
13. Telling and listening to jokes.	
14. Going to a spa.	

15. Daydreaming.	
16. Reading the newspaper or magazine.	
17. Walking barefoot in sand.	
18. Sitting around a fire.	
19. Staying up late.	
20. Other:	
Entertainment	✔
1. Watching TV or listening to the radio.	
2. Playing the lottery or bingo.	
3. Going to the cinema.	
4. Going to concerts.	
5. Going to the races (horse, car, boat, etc.).	
6. Going to a play, musical, comedy show.	
7. Going to a sporting event.	
8. Other:	
Sports and games	✔
1. Swimming, snorkelling or scuba diving.	
2. Biking, skating or roller-blading.	
3. Hunting or shooting.	
4. Playing lawn sports (croquet, bowls).	
5. Jogging, hiking or walking.	
6. Tennis, table tennis, squash, badminton.	
7. Golf.	

8. Fishing.	
9. Bird-watching.	
10. Playing board games.	
11. Playing card games.	
12. Puzzles, crosswords, Sudoku, brain-teasers.	
13. Rock climbing or mountaineering.	
14. Football or netball.	
15. Boating (canoeing, kayaking, sailing, river cruising).	
16. Pool, billiards or snooker.	
17. Computer games.	
18. Other:	
Hobbies, arts & crafts, and the arts	✔
1. Playing a musical instrument.	
2. Singing.	
3. Dancing.	
4. Craft and art work (drawing, painting, sculpting, pottery, model-making).	
5. Needlework (knitting, crocheting, embroidery).	
6. Restoring antiques or refurbishing furniture.	
7. Photography.	
8. Woodworking or carpentry.	
9. Collecting things.	
10. Other:	

Health and appearance	✔
1. Having photograph taken.	
2. Buying new clothes, shoes or jewellery.	
3. Putting on make-up or purchasing it.	
4. Getting a haircut.	
5. Getting a manicure or pedicure.	
6. Getting a massage or body rub.	
7. Putting on perfume or aftershave.	
8. Preparing self to go out.	
9. Improving one's health (having teeth fixed, new glasses or contact lenses, eating more healthily, starting an exercise programme).	
10. Getting a makeover or facial.	
11. Getting a workout.	
12. Other:	
Treats	✔
1. Chocolate.	
2. Favourite sweets.	
3. Ice cream.	
4. Dessert.	
5. Beverage.	
6. Favourite dish.	
7. Other:	
Altruistic acts	✔
1. Volunteering for a special cause.	

2. Charity work.	
3. Doing favours for others.	
4. Making contributions to religious, charitable or other groups.	
5. Giving gifts.	
6. Helping or counselling someone.	
7. Defending or protecting someone.	
8. Other	
Religious and charitable activities	✔
1. Going to a place of worship.	
2. Attending a wedding, baptism, bar mitzvah, religious ceremony or function.	
3. Other:	
4.	
5.	
6.	
Miscellaneous pleasant activities	✔
1.	
2.	
3.	

Once you have come up with fifteen activities, write them down in Table 11.8. It doesn't matter what order you put them in, but once you have written them in, try to rank them from 1–15 according to how difficult you think you will find them (with 1 being the easiest and 15 the hardest). To give you an idea of what you're aiming for, we have also included Pearl's table (see Table 11.9).

Table 11.8: My activity list

Activity	Indicate level of difficulty (1–15)

Table 11.9: Pearl's activity list

Activity	Indicate level of difficulty (1–15)
Make a Skype call to a friend.	8
Baking.	6
Play a board game with John (and maybe Tia).	9
Go for a walk alone.	10
Have a lie-in.	15
Skype/email niece in Australia.	7
Sort the garden.	11
Sudoku.	4
Line dancing.	13
Read a magazine.	3
Listen to music.	1
Go to café with friends.	12
Cook a meal.	2
Go to theatre and supper club.	14
Do the Sunday newspaper crossword.	5

Getting started

Now you have compiled your activity list, the next step is to plan how to get started on the actual activities, and how you are going to keep an eye on your progress. You can use the Daily Activities Worksheet (on pp. 446–51) to timetable in your new activities.

Start by scheduling in the activities and chores you can't skip (taking the kids to school, perhaps, or shopping for dinner): that way you'll be able to see how much time you have left over for other things.

Then choose 1 to 3 of your easiest activities and add them to your blank Daily Activities Worksheet for next week. So, for instance, Pearl put listening to music, cooking a meal and reading a magazine into her diary. Make sure to specify the day and time for the chosen activity, and think about the likely feasibility of carrying out this activity then. Pearl may decide, for example, that she will read a magazine on Saturday afternoon at 4 p.m. and on Tuesday afternoon at 5 p.m., and she will write this down on her Daily Activities Worksheet beforehand.

Sometimes activities can seem too big, and this can be discouraging. For example, Pearl and John's garden has been neglected for several months now, and although Pearl is generally a keen gardener, it is hard to know where to start as the garden is so overgrown. It is also unlikely that she will be able to get it back into shape in one session. In situations such as these, it can be a good idea to break big activities down into smaller, more manageable steps (e.g. 'sort the garden' could be broken down into mowing the lawn, weeding, etc.). You can do this by qualifying the activity according to specific time limits. For example, you can decide to 'spend 10 minutes sorting through mail' as opposed to 'sort out mail'. Once Pearl broke down the gardening into half-hour chunks, she felt she could achieve her goal of getting the garden into shape. She could survey the progress she made after each half-hour chunk until the garden was back to how she liked it. This proved to be an enormous boost, and meant that she and John could enjoy sitting outside on sunny days.

You might think that activities like sorting the mail or weeding the garden are not particularly pleasurable; instead they may seem like daunting chores, and as such perfect candidates for breaking down into more manageable activities. It can, however, be just as helpful to break down pleasurable activities too. For example, Leah was a keen runner but due to her work commitments she has not exercised for months, so it's a good idea to make time for a twenty-minute jog and to build on this prior to joining her friends at the local running club for half-marathon training.

As well as making goals more manageable, it is equally important to schedule each activity at a time that makes sense each day. If you are in work between 9 a.m. and 5.30 p.m. Monday to Friday, then you'll need to schedule your activities around your working hours: in other words, evenings and weekends, and perhaps your lunch hour if time allows.

Difficulties in getting started

Getting started can be tough and there may be several reasons why it is difficult for you to introduce more activities into your life, whether they be pleasurable or routine and necessary. Reintroducing pleasurable activities, for some, can be particularly difficult. For example, you may feel too unmotivated, or unable to think of anything that you can be bothered to do. It might be that you have so many demands on your time that you do not have time for anything for yourself, or you may have – or feel as though you have – nobody to do anything with. You may be fixated on the fact that you have no money and that pleasurable activities are costly, or you may feel that pleasurable activities are point- less, self-indulgent things that you do not deserve and feel guilty about. Let's look at each of these reasons in turn.

Are you feeling unmotivated?

If you are unmotivated to try any pleasurable activities, then it is likely you are caught in a vicious cycle of feeling low. Breaking the cycle has to start somewhere, so take a moment to identify something that may be pleasurable for you, such as browsing your favourite newspaper/ magazine/websites. Take another moment to predict how pleasurable it will be on a scale of 0–10 and make a note of it. Now browse the newspaper. How pleasurable was it? Many people who feel low predict that pleasurable activities won't be particularly enjoyable, and they also easily forget the level of enjoyment they experienced from doing that activity in the past.

Are you finding it hard to think of activities to do?

Remember that we all have different ideas about what constitutes a good time. Roz likes country music, for example, while Pam does not. Pam likes dressing up and going out, while Roz prefers relaxing in comfy clothes and eating pizza in front of the TV at home. Everyone is different. The list of possible and mostly reasonably cheap activities in the activities checklist, above, can be used to help stimulate your ideas about pleasurable activities, but it is a good idea to think back to what you used to do before you became depressed, anxious or stressed. Did you go out with your friends? Did you go for bike rides or play sport? If so, there is a good chance that if you found those activities enjoyable in the past, then reintroducing one or two of them will be a good place to start right now.

What if you feel that you don't have time for new activities?

You may have many important demands on your time. For example, you may be the carer for a child or elderly relative; you may be working and taking care of the home; or you may be juggling several jobs. The reality is that in order to be a good care-giver, home-maker, or worker, you need to take care of yourself. If you neglect your diet, sleeping and basic need for a bit of time for yourself, then it is likely your mood and wellbeing will suffer. So take a moment to think about where you can squeeze in ten minutes in the day just for you. It may be that you use this time to read the newspaper, or paint your nails, or do some exercises. It doesn't really matter what exactly you do. What's important is that the time is for *you*, so that you have the benefit of that break in the day. Moreover, by making time for yourself, you are also giving yourself the important message that your needs are as important as those of the people around you (which they are).

What if you feel you don't have anyone to do things with?

It can be difficult if, for example, you want to join an exercise class but don't want to go on your own and can't think of anyone to go with. It may be that there is nobody who would be interested or able to go with you, but at other times it may be shyness or a fear of rejection that means you never ask. If it is the latter, then you could carry out a 'behavioural experiment' and ask someone to go with you to a particular event or class. (We'll learn more about behavioural experiments in Chapter 18, and discover how testing out new ways of behaving can have a positive impact on how we think and feel.) If there really is nobody interested in doing a particular activity with you, then you need to decide whether you are able to go on your own. If you don't feel able to, you could instead find an activity that someone else is likely to want to do with you, or you could find a group such as a book club at the local library, which encourages and expects new people to come along on their own.

What if you don't have much money?

There are many pleasurable activities that are expensive and unaffordable for most of us. However, there are also many that are free or inexpensive, and there are lots of good sources of information about these. It would be worth spending some time searching the internet for 'free' and 'activities' for your local area and then trying some of the suggestions that come up.

What if it all feels pointless?

This is similar to feeling unmotivated and so being aware of what happens when you do try to break the cycle of inactivity is important. It is also helpful to examine your thoughts about the activity to see if they are getting in the way – you might think, for example, that the activity is too much of a hassle to arrange, or that it won't be as much fun as it used to be.

Viewing activities as pointless is likely to be connected to being low in mood. Although it is hard to make the first step and try something different, it is well worth a go, because there's lots of evidence to indicate that getting more active can have a positive impact on mood.

Do you feel as though you're being self-indulgent?

Sometimes people feel guilty and self-indulgent for spending time doing activities they used to enjoy. There are many reasons for this reaction. They might think that if they are going to do anything at all, it should be something they have been neglecting, like opening mail or tackling an unruly garden. Of course it is important that these 'necessary' activities are tackled but it is equally important to ensure that you have time for yourself. Becoming more active is generally easier if you plan something that is likely to make you feel good rather than something that feels like a chore and that you have otherwise been avoiding. Try to achieve a balance between routine, necessary and pleasurable activities.

Review

Once the day or week is up, it's time to revisit your Daily Activities Worksheets to record how you've fared. Before you begin, take a moment to record your mood and anxiety (and whatever else you are recording such as worry, stress levels, anger and irritability, or self-esteem) and plot them on the graphs on pp. 420–39 to see if there have been any changes. If there have been changes, what may have caused these? If there has not yet been any change, can you think of any reasons why?

Now, looking at your Daily Activity Worksheets, circle each of the planned activities if you completed them. If you did not manage to complete a given activity, put a line through it and write down the activity you did instead, then reschedule any missed activity for another time within the same day or week. Ask yourself, what was the reason for not completing the activity at that time? What was the barrier? Can this barrier be overcome the next time you schedule the activity, and if so how?

Table 11.10: Leon's completed planning on his Daily Activities Worksheet

Time	Activity	Enjoyment (0–10)	Importance (0–10)
5–6 a.m.			
6–7 a.m.			
7–8 a.m.			
8–9 a.m.			
9–10 a.m.			
10–11 a.m.	Call a friend.		
11–12 a.m.	Go to coffee shop to read.		
1–2 p.m.			
2–3 p.m.			

3–4 p.m.			
4–5 p.m.	Go for a 10-min walk.		
5–6 p.m.			
6–7 p.m.			
7–8 p.m.			
8–9 p.m.			
9–10 p.m.			
10–11 p.m.	Write a note to Mum.		
11–12 p.m.			
12–1 a.m.			
1–2 a.m.			
2–5 a.m.			
Overall mood for the day (0–10) ___			

Table 11.11: Leon's completed monitoring Daily Activities Worksheet

Time	Activity	Enjoyment (0–10)	Importance (0–10)
5–6 a.m.	Sleep	6	6
6 – 7 a.m.	Sleep	6	6
7–8 a.m.	Sleep	6	6
8–9 a.m.	Sleep	6	6
9–10 a.m.	Sleep	6	6
10–11 a.m.	**Call a friend**	8	4
11–12 a.m.	**Go to coffee shop to read**	8	7
1–2 p.m.	Watch TV	4	2
2–3 p.m.	Lie down for a nap	5	1
3–4 p.m.	Watch TV	4	1
4–5 p.m.	~~Go for a 10-min walk~~ Watch TV	5	2
5–6 p.m.	**Watch TV**	4	4
6–7 p.m.	Go for a 10-min walk	6	6
7–8 p.m.	Lie on settee	4	2
8–9 p.m.	Play video game	5	2

9–10 p.m.	Play video game	6	2
10–11 p.m.	Write a note to Mum	6	6
11–12 p.m.	Watch TV	4	3
12–1 a.m.	Watch TV	4	2
1–2 a.m.	Sleep	6	6
2–5 a.m.	Sleep	6	6
Overall mood for the day (0–10) **5**			

Leon successfully completed all the activities he planned to. He chose to stay in to watch a favourite television programme instead of the walk at 5 p.m. but he rescheduled it to a little later. He also found all the scheduled activities reasonably pleasurable, especially calling his friend and going to the coffee shop and he noticed a general improvement to his overall mood, which he scored as 5.

Keep adding activities over the coming weeks until you are able to regularly complete your fifteen activities. You can even add other activities as you progress if you feel you have time in your week for them. Keep hold of your completed Daily Activity Worksheets so that you can chart your progress over the coming weeks. Comparing worksheets from week to week can be very encouraging as you can see how much more active you are becoming. Remember also to keep checking to see what effect this is having on your measures – are you seeing any changes or improvements to your scores? Use Table 11.12 to make a note of the impact of focusing on your activity levels.

Table 11.12: Impact of working on activity

Were you able to make changes to your activity? If so, what were the changes you made? List them all here:

_____

_____

_____

_____

What was the impact of each of them?

_____

_____

_____

_____

Were there any surprises? If so, what were they?

_____

_____

_____

_____

What conclusions can you draw from increasing the activities you engage in? What will you continue to do from now on?

_____

_____

_____

_____

Summary

You can use the space below to write your own summary of important points from this chapter. What was most interesting? Was there any one thing that was particularly helpful? Making some notes here will mean that you have a useful reference guide to turn back to later on as you progress through the book.

1. _____

   _____

2. _____

   _____

3. _____

   _____

4. _____

   _____

12 Problem-solving

Before we begin ...

Start off by rating your current mood on the scale in Figure 12.1. Regular monitoring of your mood will help you notice any improvements as you go along.

-5	-4	-3	-2	-1	0	+1	+2	+3	+4	+5

Negative mood   Neutral   Positive mood

Figure 12.1: Mood scale

If you are returning to this book after a break of a few days or more, also take a moment to measure your mood and anxiety (and whatever else you are recording). Next, plot them on the graphs on pp. 420–39 to see if there have been any changes. If so, take a moment to reflect on what may have caused the changes; if not, take a moment to think why there has not yet been any change.

It may also be helpful to review your problem statements (see p. 135) and re-rate those. And, finally, review your SMART goals and any progress you are already making towards reaching them (see p. 139).

An introduction to problem-solving

Problem-solving is a very effective way of improving mood and relieving distress. Some people are natural 'problem-solvers' and others are not. For all of us, however, going through the steps of problem-solving one by one, slowly and methodically, can be really helpful.

Problem-solving can be a particular challenge for people with anxiety and depression. The techniques described below are based on the work of Art and Christine Nezu, who have written about Problem-Solving Therapy.[13]

The therapy starts from the insight that problem-solving is a useful skill that can benefit everyone. It aims to help us to:

- Begin to see problems as an opportunity for learning and growth rather than a threat.

- Spend more time and energy tackling stressful problems head on as opposed to avoiding them.

- Develop confidence in our ability to tackle stressful situations.

- Learn to respond to difficult problems in a thoughtful way, rather than trying to avoid them, opting for a 'quick fix' or being overwhelmed by upsetting emotions.

Problem-solving style

The Nezus identified two important aspects of problem-solving: how we think about problems and our problem-solving style.

1. How we think about problems

How do you currently view stressful problems and your ability to cope with them? Do you tend to take the attitude 'I can sort this out although it may take a bit of time and effort'? Or are you more likely to take a stance of 'I can't deal with this'? If you have a positive attitude towards stressful life problems and your ability to cope with them, then you are more likely actively to try and cope with a problem rather than avoid it. If, on the other hand, you tend to view life problems as a major threat, see yourself as being unable to cope with them, and get overwhelmed by negative emotions, then you are likely to do your best to avoid problems.

2. Our 'problem-solving style'

'Problem-solving style' refers to what we do when we are trying to cope with a life problem. There are three main types of coping style:

1. The **quick fix** style, which might mean that the problem is not dealt with completely.

2. The **avoidant** style, in which you put off dealing with the problem and might even pretend it doesn't exist or let other people deal with it instead.

3. The **rational** style, which means that you identify the problem, look for possible solutions, decide the best way to deal with it, put that into action and review how it has gone.

No prizes for guessing which one is the most helpful way of dealing with problems! See Table 12.1 for a list of the steps to successful problem-solving.

Table 12.1: Steps to successful problem-solving

1. Identify your problem precisely.
2. Write down as many possible solutions as you can.
3. Think through the pros and cons of each solution.
4. Select the best possible solution.
5. Plan how to carry out the solution.
6. Put the plan into action.
7. Review what happens.

Let's look at each of these steps in more detail.

1. Identify your problem precisely

The good news is that you have already done something similar to this. In Chapter 10 you wrote down a problem statement (or perhaps more than one). In order to begin problem-solving, you could start with that problem statement or you may wish to focus on a specific problem in a bit more detail, such as 'I'm exhausted every night'.

The remainder of the problem statement is less relevant to this section (i.e. '… leading me to feel tired throughout the day and unable to do as much as I would like to do and being bad-tempered with my partner.').

Another example of a specific problem is: 'They are cutting jobs at work and I might be on the "at risk" list.'

2. Write down as many possible solutions as you can

Try to be as creative as possible when you come to writing down possible solutions. The idea is not to come up with purely practical, sensible solutions but to just think of all the possibilities, no matter how outlandish. You can pass judgement on them later. For now, thinking 'outside the box' is going to help you to start to think differently about situations that have been troubling you for a long time.

3. Think through the pros and cons of each solution

This is where you need to go through the possible solutions you have just brainstormed, and think about the pros and cons of each one. To help you begin, rule out any that are immoral, illegal or impractical! You should be left with a few practical possibilities, which, if implemented, will improve your life.

4. Select the best possible solution

Now that you have thought through the pros and cons and come up with some different options, it's time to decide which of these solutions you feel able to try. To do this, consider how each option will help you solve your problem. Think about the short- and long-term benefits of each, the time and effort each solution will require and the consequences for you and those around you of choosing that solution.

5. Plan how to carry out the solution

By now you have come up with a potential solution. It is worth thinking about how you will carry out your solution in some detail. Are there any resources you will need? What needs to happen to enable you to try the solution? What particular steps will need to be undertaken?

6. Put the plan into action

Go for it!

7. Review what happens

Once you have carried out your solution, take the time to record your mood and anxiety (and whatever else you are recording), and plot them on the graphs on pp. 420–39 to see if there have been any changes. If there have been changes, what do you think may have caused them? If there haven't, take a moment to reflect on this too.

It is now time to evaluate your solution. What happened? Did it go better or worse than expected? What have you learned from your attempt to problem-solve? What will you take from the experience for the future?

Many people say that they problem-solve in their head (i.e. they work through the problem and possible solutions in their mind rather than writing them down or talking about them). The trouble with this approach is that very often the minds of people who are experiencing problems such as depression, anxiety, stress, anger and low self-esteem are full of negative thoughts and images, and worries and anxieties. Writing things down can help you to see things from a different point of view and more clearly, so it is worth making a note of your thoughts and ideas as you go through the steps above. You can use the form in Table 12.3 to do this, but first let's see how Bea went about this (Table 12.2).

Table 12.2: *Bea's completed problem-solving steps*

Bea, who is suffering from generalized anxiety, worked through the problem-solving process set out above to address an ongoing worry she has about what will happen to her youngest son Gus, who has mild learning disabilities, if she dies or stops being able to look after him.

1. Specify your problem precisely

I feel concerned that Gus will be on his own if something happens to me.

2. Write down as many possible solutions as you can

1. Carry on as usual.

2. Leave the house to Gus in my will so that he can continue living here alone.

3. Leave the house to Gus in my will and organize a carer to live with him.

4. Leave the house to all three of my sons and leave them to sort out the issue.

5. Ask one of my other sons to take him into his home.

6. Ask one of my other sons to move in to the house to live with Gus here.

7. Arrange for Gus to move into supported independent accommodation where there are carers employed to keep an eye on him.

8. Arrange for Gus to move into residential care.

9. Arrange for Gus to move in with his father.

10. Provide in my will for Gus to stay in the house but divide my assets equally between all three boys.

3. Think through the pros and cons of each solution

Solution 1: Carry on as usual.

Pros	Cons
It means I don't need to do anything.	It will continue to worry me.
	It is unfair on Gus to leave him vulnerable in the event of something happening to me.
	It will be extra work for the boys to sort everything out.

Solution 2: Leave the house to Gus in my will so that he can continue living here alone.

Pros	Cons
It means that I know he will be able to carry on living in the family home.	I don't think he would be able to cope with looking after himself and the house.
He will continue to have the security of being at home.	My other sons would need to visit often which puts a lot of responsibility onto them.
	Seems unfair not to leave part of this asset to the other boys.

Solution 3: Leave the house to Gus in my will and organize a carer to live with him.

Pros	Cons
It means that I know he will be able to carry on living in the family home.	He might not like the carer.
	It would be difficult for him to live with someone else.
He will continue to have the security of being at home.	The carer might be impersonal.
If there are any problems the carer is there on hand.	Unfair not to leave the other boys a share in this asset.

Solution 4: Leave the house to all three of my sons and leave them to sort out the issue.

Pros	Cons
It means that the boys will come to some arrangement together as to how it will work best for them.	It places a lot of responsibility on the boys.
	They may not be able to agree what to do.

Solution 5: Ask one of my other sons to take Gus into his home.

Pros	Cons
He will be with someone who loves him.	The other boys have their own lives and families so it would be hard for them to manage this.
	Both Rob and Will live in smallish houses so Gus wouldn't have his own room.

Solution 6: Ask one of my other sons to move in to the house to live with Gus here.

Pros	Cons
Gus will be able to continue living at home.	The boys have their own families so not really in a position to look after Gus too.
He will have another family member with him.	It is unlikely that either of them would want to move their families in here.

Solution 7: Arrange for Gus to move into accommodation where he can live independently but with carers around to keep an eye on him.

Pros	Cons
He will be safe.	He is likely to miss his home.
The accommodation might be shared so he will get to know some new friends.	The upheaval may be unsettling for him.
There will be somebody on hand if he is having any problems.	

Solution 8: Arrange for Gus to move into residential care.

Pros	Cons
He will be safe.	He is likely to find a residential care home a scary place.
There will be somebody there to help if he is experiencing any difficulties.	He has only a mild learning disability and some of the other residents may have much more severe difficulties so it might be hard for him to fit in.
	I don't want him to live in a home.
	I want him to live independently but supported.

Solution 9: For Gus to move in with his father.

Pros	Cons
He would be with his father.	His father has shown no interest in any of the family since he moved out.
He would be safe and looked after.	He has a new wife and children so unlikely to want Gus living there too.
	Not sure he has the room.

Solution 10: Provide in my will for Gus to stay in the house but divide my assets equally between all three boys.

Pros	Cons
It would mean that his future is secure.	Same as no 3 in that he might find it difficult to get used to living with a carer.
It would mean he could continue living at home.	
This could be supported by a carer as in solution 3.	
All boys are receiving a share of the assets.	

4. Select the best possible solution

Solution: Provide in my will for Gus to stay in the house but divide my assets equally between all three boys (solution 10).

5. Plan how to carry out the solution

Find a solicitor who knows about this kind of thing.

Look on the internet for a suitable law firm.

Contact them to arrange an appointment.

Dig out all the documents in relation to the house, insurance, etc

6. Put the plan into action

Found a law firm in town that I have heard good things about. Phoned them up and made an appointment. Took all my papers and met with one of the solicitors there. Set up things so that Gus will be able to stay in the house, with Rob and Will getting equal shares of my other assets.

7. Review what happens

This has been a source of worry for me for years and I have always just tried to put it to the back of my mind as something to address another day. I feel a huge sense of relief now that it is sorted and I know that Gus is going to be secure in his own home. The next thing that I need to do is to start looking at different care agencies and the support they provide so we can consider what options are available should anything happen to me. I shall plan that next.

Table 12.3: Your problem-solving steps

1. Identify your problem precisely

....

....

....

....

....

2. Write down as many possible solutions as you can

1. ....

2. ....

3. ....

4. ....

5. ....

6. ....

7. ....

8. ....

9. ....

10. ....

3. Think through the pros and cons of each solution

Solution 1: ....

Pros	Cons
....	....
....	....
....	....
....	....
....	....
....	....

Solution 2: ....

Pros   **Cons**

....

...:...   ....

....

....

....

....

Solution 3: ....

Pros   **Cons**

....

....

....

....

....

....

Solution 4: ....

Pros   **Cons**

....

....

....

....

....

....

Solution 5: ....

Pros	Cons
....	....
....	....
....	....
....	....
....	....
....	....

Solution 6: ....

Pros	Cons
....	....
....	....
....	....
....	....
....	....
....	....

Solution 7: ....

Pros	Cons
....	....
....	....
....	....
....	....
....	....
....	....

Solution 8: ....

Pros   **Cons**

....

....

....

....

....

....

Solution 9: ....

Pros   **Cons**

....

....

....

....

....

....

Solution10:..

Pros   **Cons**

....

....

....

....

....

....

4. Select the best possible solution

Solution: ....

5. Plan how to carry out the solution

....

....

....

....

....

6. Put the plan into action

7. Review what happens

....

....

....

....

....

....

....

....

....

....

....

....

....

If the solution that you opted for doesn't turn out to be as successful as you had hoped, then review what you have learned and think about whether it could be modified in any way to make it more successful or if you need to try a different solution.

Summary

Use the space below to reflect on what you have read and done in this chapter and to write down any points that you especially want to remember. What was most helpful? What did you learn that you wouldn't necessarily have thought of before? Is there anything that was striking and that you will try to bear in mind as you continue working through this book?

1. _____

   _____

2. _____

   _____

3. _____

   _____

4. _____

   _____

13 Using graded exposure to face your fears

Before we begin ...

Rate your current mood on the mood scale in Figure 13.1.

-5	-4	-3	-2	-1	0	+1	+2	+3	+4	+5

Negative   Neutral   Positive
mood   mood

Figure 13.1: Mood scale

If you are returning to this book after a break of a few days or more, take a moment to record your mood and anxiety (and whatever else you are recording, such as worry, anger, stress and self-esteem) and plot them on the graphs on pp. 420–39. Keeping track of your mood can help you review progress. Have there been any changes? If so, why do you think that might be? If not, can you think of any reasons?

It may also be helpful to review your problem statements (see Chapter 10, p. 135) and, re-rate those using the 0–100 problem-severity scale. Have there been any changes? Finally, review your SMART goals (see Chapter 10, p. 139) and make a note of any progress that you have made towards reaching them.

This chapter is relevant for many types of problems where avoidance is a feature. As we said earlier, avoidance is very common in depression and anxiety, and when we are under stress. It is also a common way to react to situations in which we feel angry or when we feel self-conscious because of a lack of self-esteem.

In this chapter we will introduce you to 'graded exposure', which is a proven way of helping people to face their fears in a controlled way.

What is graded exposure?

Exposure therapy has been around for a long time and it is based on research showing that a response (an emotional reaction, for example) becomes less intense when you are repeatedly exposed to its stimulus (i.e., whatever is causing the response).

Repeated exposure to the fear reduces anxiety but it must be graded with a hierarchy of exposure to increasingly difficult situations. You can think of it as a kind of stepladder of feared situations: from the least anxiety-provoking to the most feared of all. A person using this approach is encouraged to start with the least anxiety-provoking task in the hierarchy, focusing on the task in hand and not trying to distract themselves, and sticking with it for at least an hour or until the anxiety has waned. When they feel ready, they move on to the next step in the hierarchy. The person is encouraged to practise as frequently as possible (most often on a daily basis), until their fear is conquered.

If you think exposure could be helpful for you, there are a couple of things to think about when coming up with your hierarchy. First, it can be useful to include the factors that affect the amount of anxiety you experience. For example, it may be that the time of day, number of people around or being alone are all significant contributors to how anxious you feel. Secondly, to help determine the steps on your hierarchy it is worth asking yourself the questions in Table 13.1.

Table 13.1: Exposure questions

What would make this feared situation easier for you?

_____

_____

_____

_____

What would make this feared situation more difficult for you?

_____

_____

_____

_____

Following his bike accident, Ash has developed a number of anxieties around cycling. He is keen to start cycling regularly again and is also concerned that because of his fears his children have not got as much freedom as they used to have to use their bikes. He came up with the following hierarchy of feared situations for graded exposure in Table 13.2.

Table 13.2: *Ash's graded exposure hierarchy*

1. Spend time in the garage touching my bike and sitting on it.
2. Cycle round the garden.
3. Go round the local cycle track to the park and back.
4. Cycle round the local industrial estate in the evening.
5. Cycle round the local streets at a quiet time of day.
6. Cycle round the local streets at a busy time of day.

---

7. Do my cycle route to work and back at a quiet time of day.

8. Do my cycle route to work and back at rush hour.

9. Cycle to the park with my wife and kids.

10. Cycle with wife and kids on longer cycle routes we used to go on.

Ash managed to work through steps 1 and 2 very quickly and on the same day tackled step 3. Later he was also able to tackle steps 5 and 6. Over time he successfully tackled the remainder of his hierarchy so that he was able to enjoy spending time with his wife and children on routes they had previously enjoyed together.

Troubleshooting common difficulties with graded exposure

Not all problems lend themselves easily to graded exposure. For example, some fears are impossible to put on a hierarchy (signing one's name, for instance: some people fear that their hands will shake and that others will think badly of them for it) or impractical to do very often (e.g. an aeroplane journey). For this reason, it is sometimes helpful to use exposure in your imagination so that you can help grade the exposure practice before doing it in real life. You will see that this 'imaginal exposure' is what Bea has done below.

Another difficulty that sometimes arises when planning graded exposure is if you have what appears to be a number of unrelated fears (for example, standing in queues, using lifts, sitting at the back of a bus and so on). If this is the case, you may need to make more than one hierarchy. However, if you can spot a recurring theme within the various avoided situations (for example, a fear of being trapped) then you could just use one hierarchy.

Finally, if the feared situation is one that is over very quickly (for example, passing a cat on a garden wall, asking someone for directions, signing one's name), the best thing to do would be to repeat the activity regularly, as grading would not be possible.

Case illustration 3: Bea

As is common for most people with generalized anxiety, Bea has difficulty in tolerating uncertainty. This means that she finds uncertainty extremely stressful, dislikes anything unexpected happening, and finds that living with uncertainty affects her ability to function normally. Her worries are generally more hypothetical than real (i.e. 'I *may* get ill'; 'I *might* lose my job'), and so they do not lend themselves well to a problem-solving approach, which requires a concrete basis (i.e. a definite situation that you can begin to deal with). However, they do lend themselves well to alleviation through exposure, and in particular, imaginal exposure.

Bea learned how to visualize the feared situation of losing her job. She trained herself to 'sit with' the worry and tolerate it until the feelings of anxiety it created gradually subsided. At first this was daunting for Bea, who used avoidance as one of her main coping strategies as a worrier: that is, she did her best not to think what it might be like to lose her job. Over time, however, she became more and more adept at tolerating the anxiety of losing her job in her imagination. With her new ability to cope with the uncertainty, Bea found herself spending less time worrying over other anxiety-provoking situations as well. She combined this approach with working on her thoughts (see Chapters 15–17).

You can use an Exposure Diary to try out your own graded exposure. In case you want to have a look at a couple of examples, we've included Ash's and Bea's Exposure Diaries in Tables 13.3 and 13.4 respectively. The last one is blank one for you to use (Table 13.5). As you'll see, the diary isn't just designed to record what you do, but also how you feel when you do it. Aim to complete it as soon as possible after the event so you don't forget any details; if you can do so while you're actually engaged in the activity, that's even better.

Table 13.3: *Ash's Exposure Diary*

Anxiety scale

0	25	50	75	100
No anxiety	Mild anxiety	Moderate anxiety		Severe anxiety/panic

Date/Time	Activity	Anxiety level (using scale above: 0 = no anxiety, 100 = severe panic anxiety)
Sun 5th 6.30–9 p.m.	Went into the garage and stood near my bike (a little easier to start than I thought it would be and soon came down to 0).	50–0 [i.e. started at 50 and declined to 0]
	Stood beside bike and held it by handlebars (a bit more anxious doing this but surprised at how quickly my anxiety eased).	70–10
	Sat on bike in garage (this started about the same but got down to 0).	70–0
Mon 6th 8–9.30 p.m.	Took bike into garden and cycled round (I think the last step helped prepare me for this as I didn't peak so highly).	60–10
	Went on local cycle track from bottom of garden to local park. (This was hard!)	80–50
	Went on local cycle track to park again (easier this time).	60–20

Table 13.4: *Bea's Exposure Diary*

Anxiety scale

0	25	50	75	100
No anxiety	Mild anxiety	Moderate anxiety		Severe anxiety/panic

Date/Time	Activity	Anxiety level (using scale above: 0 = no anxiety, 100 = severe panic anxiety)
Sun 27th 4.30–5.15p.m.	Repeatedly went through a scenario in my head about losing my job and all the implications that would have for me, Gus and the rest of the family.	75–20
Mon 28th 3.15–3.45 p.m.	Went through same scenario again about losing my job and all the implications it would have for us all.	60–10

Table 13.5: My Exposure Diary

Anxiety scale

0	25	50	75	100
No anxiety	Mild anxiety	Moderate anxiety		Severe anxiety/panic

Date/Time	Activity	Anxiety level (using scale above: 0 = no anxiety, 100 = severe panic anxiety)

Using graded exposure for different problems

Hierarchies and graded exposure can be useful techniques for many problems, not just anxiety. Leon used graded exposure to help him return to work, Leah used it to get back into running and thereby tackle her stress, Penny used graded exposure to tackle her concerns about what others will think of her if they see her eczema scars and Dez used graded and imaginal exposure to learn to manage his anger more effectively.

Dez came up with a hierarchy of situations (Table 13.6) that made him angry.

Table 13.6: *Dez's graded exposure hierarchy*

He used the hierarchy to try out coping strategies such as controlled breathing (which combats the shallow and rapid breathing that anxiety provokes) and relaxation techniques while facing progressively difficult situations (see Chapter 14).

Dez's hierarchy

1. Trying to concentrate when someone keeps making a noise.

2. Someone starts to talk to me while I'm trying to watch TV.

3. Someone looking over my shoulder while I'm working.

4. Corrie starts having a go at me the minute I wake up in the morning.

5. Carrying something (e.g. a drink) and someone bumps into me.

6. Someone cancels on me at the last minute.

7. Being stuck in a traffic jam.

8. Driving and someone cuts me up.

9. Being constantly contradicted.

10. Being accused of something I didn't do.

Like Ash, Dez used his hierarchy to gradually work his way up to increasingly challenging situations. However, many of the situations on Dez's hierarchy could not be planned (for example, someone cancelling an engagement) so he used imaginal exposure to practise a number of the scenarios. That way he could try out relaxation techniques and healthy breathing when in increasingly difficult imaginary situations, in order to prepare him for when they happened in real life.

Leon used a graded exposure approach to prepare himself to return to work (Table 13.7).

Table 13.7: *Leon's graded exposure hierarchy*

1. Getting in touch with boss to arrange meeting to discuss return to work.

2. Meet with boss.

3. Go in to see colleagues over a break time.

4. Go back to work two afternoons in first week.

5. Work five afternoons the second week.

6. Work three afternoons and two full days the next week.

7. Work a full week

Leah used a hierarchy to get herself back into running (Table 13.8). She had convinced herself that she didn't have time to spend on exercise and was anxious that she wouldn't enjoy it and that it would interfere with her work too much.

Table 13.8: *Leah's graded exposure hierarchy*

1. Go for a 15-minute walk every day (not working up a sweat so time out is literally 15-minutes).

2. Go for a 15-minute run three times a week (time for shower on return).

3.   Go for a 30-minute run three times a week.

4.   Go for a 30-minute run twice a week and once for an hour.

5.   Go for two 40-minute runs and one 30-minute run a week.

6.   Go for three 50-minute runs plus an hour at the gym in the week.

7.   Exercise for a minimum of one hour for four days in the week.

Penny feels self-conscious about her skin condition and the scars she has gained over the years. She worries about how people will view her and so tends to keep her body covered up. This makes going swimming and visiting a beautician difficult. Penny decided to create a hierarchy so that she could address some of her anxieties about her skin (Table 13.9).

Table 13.9: *Penny's graded exposure hierarchy*

1.   Get a manicure from a beautician.

2.   Get a pedicure from a beautician.

3.   Get a facial from a beautician.

4.   Get a neck massage from a beautician.

5.   Get a back massage from a beautician.

6.   Get a full body massage from a beautician.

7.   Go swimming at a quiet time for a minimum of an hour twice a week.

8.   Go swimming at a moderately busy time for a minimum of an hour twice a week.

9.   Go swimming at a busy time for a minimum of an hour twice a week

A blank hierarchy is provided in Table 13.10 allowing you to design your own hierarchy.

Table 13.10: My graded exposure hierarchy

1. _____

   _____

2. _____

   _____

3. _____

   _____

4. _____

   _____

5. _____

   _____

6. _____

   _____

7. _____

   _____

8. _____

   _____

9. _____

   _____

10. _____

   _____

Summary

Now that you are at the end of this chapter, it's time to make a quick summary so that you can reflect back on it later on. What was most important or most memorable? Was anything reassuring, or particularly striking? Is there anything that you want to find out more about in the Further Resources section?

1. _____

   _____

2. _____

   _____

3. _____

   _____

4. _____

   _____

14 Managing your anger

Before we begin ...

Start by rating your current mood on the mood scale in Figure 14.1.

-5	-4	-3	-2	-1	0	+1	+2	+3	+4	+5

Negative mood				Neutral					Positive mood

Figure 14.1: Mood scale

If you are returning to this book after a break of a few days or more, take a moment to record your mood and anxiety (and whatever else you are recording, such as worry, anger, stress and self-esteem) and plot them on the graphs on pp. 420–39. Keeping track of your mood can help you review progress. Have there been any changes? If so, why do you think that might be? If not, can you think of any reasons?

It may also be helpful to review your problem statements (see Chapter 10, p. 135) and, re-rate those using the 0–100 problem-severity scale. Have there been any changes? Finally, review your SMART goals (see Chapter 10, p. 139) and make a note of any progress that you have made towards reaching them.

When we are angry, we often experience physical symptoms, such as increased heart rate, flushing, sweating, muscle tension and breathing quickly. Learning to control such physical sensations can help reduce the level of anger you experience, and in this chapter we will look at how to do so by regulating your breathing and relaxing your muscles. Managing your anger requires practice and should be used alongside other strategies like working on your thoughts (see Chapters 15–17).

Regular breathing

When we become angry we tend to breathe more quickly (this is known as over-breathing), which increases the amount of oxygen going through our bodies. This in turn provides us with the energy we need to deal with the danger we perceive that we are in (see 'fight or flight', p. 22) by preparing our bodies for physical aggression or flight from a dangerous situation. In this state the heart beats faster to carry blood to the main muscle groups and the brain, and sweating helps prevent the body from overheating. The effects of these responses, and of over-breathing in particular, can result in a person taking in too much oxygen and consequently breathing out too much carbon dioxide. This over-breathing can increase some of the other physical sensations of anger, including a tight chest and muscle tension. Over-breathing like this is not dangerous, but it is uncomfortable.

Learning how to breathe in a more controlled way and to relax are life skills that are especially useful when we are feeling irritable or angry. However, they are less helpful for people with panic symptoms or phobias, because they can become safety behaviours. Safety behaviours are behaviours that people put into place in the belief that that they will prevent a particular feared outcome (see p. 53).

If you can learn to control your breathing when you are feeling irritable or angry, you are likely to find that other bodily symptoms will subside. One of the aims of this chapter is to teach you how to breathe calmly and slowly, which might not be as easy as it sounds. Over-breathing makes us feel like we need more air, and so breathing more slowly can seem extremely difficult because it feels as though we are getting even less air. The best way to get the hang of regular breathing is to practise when you are feeling calm, and to do it for a few minutes until you get used to it. For best results when trying to manage your anger, try to get back to regular breathing as soon as you start to feel angry, rather than waiting until you are in the midst of a full-blown rage.

Follow the steps in Table 14.1 to help regulate your breathing:

Table 14.1: Eight steps to regular breathing

1.	Take a deep breath and fill your lungs with air. Imagine you are filling a flask from the bottom up. Your stomach should expand as your lungs fill up.
2.	Exhale slowly.
3.	Repeat steps 1 and 2 a couple of times. Try to make sure that you are not breathing in a shallow way, from the chest, or too deeply (filling your lungs all the way).
4.	Keep your breathing slow and calm.
5.	Breathe in through your mouth and out through your nose.
6.	Try breathing in slowly, saying to yourself 'one elephant, two elephant, three elephant, four ...' This might sound strange, but adding 'elephant' to the number takes about a second to say, and therefore helps regulate the speed of your breathing.
7.	Let the breath out slowly to a count of six 'elephants': 'one elephant, two elephant ...' Sometimes looking at the second hand of a watch can help to slow down breathing too, rather than counting 'elephants'.
8.	Repeat steps 5, 6 and 7 until you feel calm and your breathing is regular.

If you are using this strategy when you feel angry, it is a good idea to follow it up with some work on the thoughts you are experiencing. Are you aware of what thoughts are going through your mind? Are there any unhelpful thoughts you can identify? Chapter 17 provides you with more information on some of the techniques you can use to try to evaluate the thoughts you are having.

Learning to relax

Being able to relax is a useful skill for us all, and learning how to relax can be particularly helpful if you are experiencing anger problems or suffering from stress. If you are looking to tackle your anxiety you might find other techniques such as graded exposure (see Chapter 13) more helpful.

Relaxation techniques can be easily learned. One of the first steps is to try to identify the early signs of physical tension. Once you can do this, you can put the relaxation techniques into practice, thereby alleviating the physical tension that you feel. Some people find it easier to relax using less formal strategies such as reading a book, listening to a favourite piece of music, soaking in a bath, exercising, watching television or doing yoga. These informal strategies can be just as good as the relaxation techniques. However, being able to use formal relaxation techniques can be a handy skill for us all to have.

Most forms of formal relaxation are based on variations of *progressive muscle relaxation*. Over the following pages is a typical relaxation routine based on a sequence of exercises described by Lars-Göran Öst from Stockholm University in 1987. You don't need to do all six in the same session; practise exercise 1 and when you're ready move on in your next session to exercise 2, and so on to exercise 6. (Some people don't like this formal type of relaxation and actually find that it makes them feel even more tension; if you're one of them, don't be discouraged and focus instead on informal techniques.)

Exercise 1

This first exercise involves tensing and then relaxing various muscle groups. Work your way through your body, tensing each of the muscle groups below and holding for ten seconds each time.

1.   Lower arms: tighten your fists and pull them up towards your body.

2.   Upper arms: tense your arms by the side of your body.

3. Lower legs: extend your legs and point your feet up.

4. Upper legs: push your legs together.

5. Stomach: pull your stomach in towards your spine.

6. Upper chest and back: inhale and hold for a count of ten seconds.

7. Shoulders: pull your shoulders up towards your ears.

8. Back of the neck: tilt your head back.

9. Lips: purse your lips but without clenching your teeth.

10. Eyes: tightly close your eyes.

11. Eyebrows: frown, and push your eyebrows together.

12. Upper forehead: raise your eyebrows.

Remember to release each part of the body after ten seconds. You can do this exercise while sitting or lying down. It is a good idea to practise this exercise a few times.

One of the drawbacks of the first exercise is that it is not easily transferable to stressful situations. If you become agitated or anxious while in a busy queue at the post office, for example, there may not be a chair nearby in which you can sit down to progressively relax your muscles. Besides, you may feel rather conspicuous doing a relaxation exercise such as this in public!

Nonetheless, this first exercise is still very important, partly because it can be a great way to relax in itself, and also because it'll help you with the other exercises.

Exercise 2

Once you have mastered the relaxation exercise above, you are ready to move on to the next exercise. This time you will tense and relax larger groups of muscles, which shortens the time tensing muscles and helps with moving towards even larger muscle groups in exercise 3, so there are only eight points instead of twelve. Again, work your way through your body, tensing each of the muscle groups below and holding for ten seconds each time.

1.   Whole arms: slightly extend your arms with your elbows bent and fists tightened.

2.   Whole legs: extend your legs with your toes pointing upwards.

3.   Stomach: pull your stomach in towards your spine.

4.   Upper chest and back: inhale and hold for a count of ten.

5.   Shoulders: pull your shoulders up towards your ears.

6.   Back of the neck: tilt your head back.

7.   Face: scrunch up your eyes and lips.

8.   Forehead and scalp: raise your eyebrows.

Try to practise this exercise a couple of times a day until you feel that you've mastered it.

Exercise 3

Once you have practised the exercise above and are able to relax with relative ease, you will be ready to progress to the next exercise. This time you will tense and relax just four muscle groups. Again, work your way through your body, tensing each of the muscle groups below and holding for ten seconds each time.

1.   Whole arms: slightly extend your arms with your elbows bent and fists tightened.

2.   Upper chest and back: inhale and hold for a count of ten.

3.   Shoulders and neck: lift your shoulders and tilt your head back.

4.   Face: scrunch up your eyes and lips.

These manoeuvres are much more adaptable, so you can practise them in a number of different situations such as when standing or walking around.

Exercise 4

In this exercise, you do not tense any muscles. Instead, you will focus on the various muscle groups and try to notice if there is tension in any of them. If you do notice tension, focus on relaxing the muscles, without tensing first. This is called *release-only relaxation*. Like the previous exercise, practise this in a number of different scenarios such as those above, including standing, walking around, driving, sitting at a desk, etc.

Exercise 5

When you are confident that you can fully relax using exercise 4, you can move on to exercise 5. Once you are relaxed having used the techniques in exercise 4, take between one and three deep breaths and think of the word 'relax' with each exhalation. While you are exhaling, scan your body for any tension. If you locate any tension, try to release it.

Once you are able to do this, try to practise without doing the release-only relaxation beforehand (exercise 4). By limiting yourself to the word 'relax', the word alone can in time become a signal to your body to do just that. Try to practise this exercise several times throughout the day in various settings. As you may not be used to relaxing this frequently, it can be easy to forget to repeat the exercise. You might therefore find it useful to put in place some reminders to relax (for example, whenever the phone rings, when sending a text, looking at your watch or the clock, sitting at traffic lights, making a drink and so on).

Exercise 6

In this final exercise, you can apply what you have learned in the previous exercises to situations where you need relaxation most of all. If, for example, you need it in anger-provoking situations, then by now you will hopefully be well aware of the early signs of anxiety, tension or anger, and therefore be in a good position to apply the relaxation techniques before your symptoms become intense.

What now?

You may need to persevere with the exercises for a while until you get the hang of them. But once you have mastered them you're likely to find them really helpful – as indeed did Dez. Dez often experiences outbursts of anger, and he decided to try this exercise because he isn't particularly good at relaxing in general. He struggled at first, particularly with the first two exercises, but after a while got the hang of it. Within a few weeks he was at exercise 6. He didn't do the exercises successfully every time, because sometimes he let his anger build too much before applying the techniques, but over time he found them more and more effective. He found them most helpful during his car journeys, particularly because he was able to revert to earlier exercises easily, such as exercise 2 and 3, and nobody could see him.

Guided imagery

Guided imagery is a strategy which involves recreating in your imagination a pleasant environment of relaxation, for example lying on a beach, having a warm bubble bath or lounging on the settee. This strategy can be a powerful stress-reduction technique, especially if it is combined with the relaxation exercises and regular breathing we described above. The key to guided imagery is being able to imagine your chosen situation vividly, because this is likely to make it more relaxing. You might try to imagine a scene that you remember as being safe, warm, peaceful and happy. You should try to include your other senses while you are imagining this place. Imagine what you are smelling (perhaps a salty sea breeze or freshly mown grass), what you can feel (perhaps the touch of silk or the warmth of the sun), what you can taste (perhaps champagne on your tongue or a juicy strawberry) and what you can hear (perhaps birds singing or waves lapping) while you are picturing your scene.

Another way to use guided imagery is to visualize any stress and tension leaving your body as the causes of the stress are packed up in boxes and put into a locked cupboard.

As with progressive muscle relaxation, it is important to practise guided imagery until you become good at it (i.e. able to conjure up pleasant images without difficulty). Try to set some time aside each day to practise. You should allow yourself around ten to fifteen minutes each time. Do be careful of timings and set an alarm if you need to be somewhere afterwards, as sometimes people find it so relaxing they fall asleep!

Table 14.2 provides the five steps for successful guided imagery.

Table 14.2: Steps for guided imagery.

1.	Either lie down somewhere comfortable or sit in a comfortable chair.
2.	Use the regular breathing and progressive muscle relaxation techniques described earlier in the chapter to relax your body, and close your eyes.
3.	When you are feeling relaxed, begin to imagine yourself in the pleasant surroundings of your safe, calm and peaceful environment.
4.	Bring in all of your senses to include smells, sounds, tastes and touch.
5.	Stay in that pleasant environment for as long as you like. When you are ready to come back to the real world, count back from ten and tell yourself that when you arrive at one you will feel calm and peaceful.

Once you have tried regular breathing, relaxation techniques and guided imagery, you might decide that it makes sense to use a combination of all these approaches in your life rather than just favouring one. Being able to apply different techniques in different situations can help you feel better equipped to manage your anger more of the time.

Case illustration 4: Dez

Dez found guided imagery worked well for him, especially when he was at home and his anger was lasting longer than it should. He also found that there were times when he was unable to use the technique, such as when he was driving. At these times he would use the regular breathing techniques and the relaxation techniques he had learned.

Summary

You can use the space below to write down key points or things that you want to remember from this chapter or from what you have read so far. Did any one thing resonate in particular for you? What was especially useful? Making some brief notes here will mean that you have a helpful reference guide to turn back to later on.

1. _____

_____

2. _____

_____

3. _____

_____

4. _____

_____

15 Unhelpful thinking patterns

Before we begin ...

Start the chapter by rating your current overall mood on the mood scale in Figure 15.1.

-5	-4	-3	-2	-1	0	+1	+2	+3	+4	+5

Negative mood   Neutral   Positive mood

Figure 15.1: Mood scale

If you are returning to this book after a break of a few days or more, take a moment to record your mood and anxiety (and whatever else you are recording, such as worry, anger, stress and self-esteem) and plot them on the graphs on pp. 420–39. Keeping track of your mood can help you review progress. Have there been any changes? If so, why do you think that might be? If not, can you think of any reasons?

It may also be helpful to review your problem statements (see Chapter 10, p. 135) and, re-rate those using the 0–100 problem-severity scale. Have there been any changes? Finally, review your SMART goals (see Chapter 10, p. 139) and make a note of any progress that you have made towards reaching them.

How thoughts link to feelings and behaviours

In Chapter 2 we used the CBT model diagram in Figure 15.2 to look at how symptoms interlink.

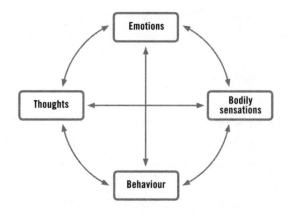

Figure 15.2: CBT model

We then showed you diagrams for a number of situations that had arisen for Leon, Pearl, Bea, Dez, Penny, Leah and Ash. We hope that you had a go at filling in one of the blank diagrams provided on pp. 440–42.

The four symptom areas (thoughts, emotions, bodily sensations and behaviour) all interact with each other within every one of us, as they do in the diagram. Sometimes it is not always obvious which symptoms should go under a particular heading. For example, would you put 'tearfulness' under bodily sensations, emotions or behaviour? Would you put 'feeling slowed down' under behaviour or bodily sensations? Where would 'feeling on edge' go – under emotions or bodily sensations? The answer is that they should go wherever makes most sense to you.

What is important is *being able to tell the difference between thoughts and emotions*. This can be confusing because we often talk about thoughts as though they are emotions. For example, 'I feel like he is really angry with me' is not an emotion despite the words 'I feel'. This is a thought because there is no 'he is really angry with me' emotion. A more accurate representation of what the person might be trying to say would be something like: 'I think he is really angry with me and it is making me feel anxious.' In this sentence, anxiety is an emotion that is being expressed in a thought. It is very common for us to talk about our feelings when we are talking about our thoughts (e.g. 'I feel he doesn't like me', 'I feel like

I'll get into big trouble for this'). Emotions tend to be expressed in just one word, like angry, anxious, sad, jealous, embarrassed, guilty, frightened, worried, upset and so on. This is important to remember when we come on to Thought Diaries later on in this chapter.

CBT is based on the idea that the way we make sense of events affects how we feel and what we do. It is not the event itself that makes us feel a certain way, otherwise everyone would react in exactly the same way to a given situation – and we know that is not the case. You will be able to think of lots of examples of when one of your family or friends has viewed something completely differently to you. Even dreadful situations like being diagnosed with a life-threatening illness will not result in the same response from everyone. So why is this? In CBT, we believe the range of different reactions triggered in people by a particular situation is a result of the range of different thoughts or interpretations (meanings) that the given situation triggers in those people.

In Table 15.1 is an example of how one situation can be interpreted in a number of ways. The one thing that stays constant is the situation. It is the thought or interpretation that is different. The meaning of the situation to the person will therefore determine how the person feels (we'll come on to this later).

As you can see from this example, the situation remains the same, but there are a variety of different thoughts that Lucy has while waiting for Paul in the café. You may be able to think of some other thoughts that a person might have in this situation and, importantly, how you might react if *you* were waiting for Paul. What we've also shown in the chart below is how one thought can lead to another (e.g. 'Paul is never late' leading to 'something awful must have happened' to 'he must have been involved in a car crash').

Any event can result in a number of thoughts and sometimes they will be negative in nature. With so many possible interpretations of any one situation, it is impossible for us all to be right all of the time; naturally we can all make errors in our interpretations of events. However, this can be particularly troublesome if we are experiencing a mental health problem, because we're likely to be prone to more frequent negative thoughts, which are also more strongly held and therefore more difficult to discount. People experiencing depression, for example, are more likely to interpret events in a negative way, looking at the world through a pair of blue-tinted glasses. Someone experiencing anxiety meanwhile is likely to make more anxiety-related interpretations.

Table 15.1: Interpretations of a situation

Situation	Thought
Lucy is meeting a friend for lunch at a café at 12.30; it is now 1.15 and he has not arrived. Lucy knows that he dropped his mobile phone and broke it last week so she is unable to contact him by phone.	Paul is never late ... something awful must have happened ... he must have been involved in a car crash.
	He obviously finds me so dull that he has forgotten about meeting me ... why would anyone want to meet up with me? I can't blame him ... I am so forgettable ... I am such a loser.
	Well this just shows exactly how selfish that Paul is ... imagine not even turning up ... how dare he ... who the hell does he think he is!
	How awful, everyone is looking at me... they think I've been stood up ... I bet I've gone bright red.
	Yikes, did we agree this café? I know we talked about Café Bella too, which is on the other side of town ... I bet I'm in the wrong place and Paul is waiting for me there.
	I noticed that the traffic was getting pretty heavy when I arrived, I was lucky to have missed it ... Paul is probably caught up in it.

The problem with this is that most of us have a tendency to just accept our thoughts as true and leave them unchecked. If we were right all of the time then that would be fine, but as we can see from the example above, this is unlikely to be the case. Many of us treat our thoughts like they are facts (for example, 'I know that she hates me'). However, just because we *believe* a given thought, it does not make it a fact. If Roz thinks her favourite singer is the best singer in the world, it does not mean that this singer is actually the best, and Pam would be sure to disagree! In just the same way, if you think you are a bad person, it does not mean that *you are* a bad person.

Lucy's thoughts in the example above are what we call *automatic thoughts*: they just pop into her mind (unlike purposeful thoughts when we consciously turn our minds to something). Automatic thoughts can be positive, negative or neutral. A positive automatic thought might be 'I love my new hair', triggered by passing a mirror. A neutral automatic thought might be 'Ah, I need toothpaste too', triggered by walking past the toothpaste aisle in a supermarket. Negative automatic thoughts tend to be rapid and brief, and the content harsh and usually highly convincing (for example, 'I am such a loser for mislaying those concert tickets'). Negative automatic thoughts generally lead to equally negative emotions.

Going back to Figure 15.1 at the beginning of this chapter, the reason we placed 'emotion' at the top is because we are often most aware of the feelings that a thought produces. Let's return to the example of Lucy waiting for Paul in a café, and look at which emotions might link with her thoughts (Table 15.2).

Now you can see how the emotion is determined by the thought, rather than the situation. Moreover, how strongly Lucy feels the emotion will be determined by how strongly she believes the thought. If she strongly believes that Paul has been in an accident, her level of anxiety is likely to be very high. If she thinks that it is pretty unlikely, even though the thought did pop into her head, then any anxiety is likely to be a lot less intense. Of course if Paul suddenly appears having been held up for a genuine, unavoidable reason, these upsetting emotions will disappear.

Table 15.2: Linking emotions and thoughts

Situation	Thought	Emotion
Lucy is meeting a friend for lunch at a café at 12.30; it is now 1.15 and he has not arrived. Lucy knows that he dropped his mobile phone and broke it last week so she is unable to contact him by phone.	Paul is never late ... something awful must have happened ... he must have been involved in a car crash.	Worry and Anxiety
	He obviously finds me so dull that he has forgotten about meeting me ... why would anyone want to meet up with me? I can't blame him ... I am so forgettable ... I am such a loser.	Sadness
	Well this just shows exactly how selfish that Paul is ... imagine not even turning up ... how dare he ... who the hell does he think he is!	Anger
	How awful, everyone is looking at me ... they think I've been stood up ... I bet I've gone bright red.	Humiliation and embarrassment
	Yikes, did we agree this café? I know we talked about Café Bella too, which is on the other side of town ... I bet I'm in the wrong place and Paul is waiting for me there.	Anxiety
	I noticed that the traffic was getting pretty heavy when I arrived, I was lucky to have missed it ... Paul is probably caught up in it.	Unconcerned

Not only do our automatic thoughts determine how we feel in response to a given situation, they also influence the bodily sensations we experience. In table 15.3 you will see a slightly amended continuation of the café example. Put yourself in the position of truly believing each of the thoughts and strongly feeling the accompanying emotions in this situation. Now ask yourself, what might you experience in your body?

Table 15.3: Linking bodily sensations to thoughts and emotions

Situation	Thought	Emotion	Bodily Sensations
You are meeting a friend at a restaurant at 6 p.m. It is now 6.30 and your friend is nowhere to be seen.	My friend is never late... something awful must have happened... he must have been involved in a car crash.	Worry and Anxiety	Racing heart, shaking
	He obviously finds me so dull that he has forgotten about meeting me ... why would anyone want to meet up with me? I can't blame him ... I am so forgettable ... I am such a loser.	Sadness	Sinking feeling in the pit of stomach
	Well this just shows exactly how selfish he is ... imagine not even turning up ... how dare he ... who the hell does he think he is!	Anger	Tense muscles, becoming red in the face
	How awful, everyone is looking at me ... they think I've been stood up ... I bet I've gone bright red.	Humiliation and embarrassment	Feeling hot, sweaty, blushing
	Yikes, did we agree this restaurant? I know we talked about another restaurant, which is on the other side of town ... I bet I'm in the wrong place and he is waiting for me there.	Anxiety	Racing heart, feeling hot
	I noticed that the traffic was getting pretty heavy when I arrived, I was lucky to have missed it ... he is probably caught up in it.	Unconcerned	No change

Our automatic thoughts don't just determine how we feel emotionally and in our body in response to a given situation, they also influence what we do (our behaviour).

Here is the café example again. As before, imagine truly believing each of the thoughts and strongly feeling the accompanying emotions. This time, also ask yourself what you might do in this situation.

You will see from the situation in Table 15.4 how our behaviours are also determined by our thoughts. The symptoms don't necessarily occur in the order in which they appear in the table (i.e. thoughts, then emotions, then bodily sensations and finally behaviours), but the thought generally precedes the emotion. However, it is more often than not the emotion that we notice first. Depending on how much you believe it, the thought will determine how strongly you feel the related emotion and how likely you are to change what you are doing.

The important thing to bear in mind here is that our automatic thoughts do not only affect our emotions but also our behaviours, which can then work against us by helping to maintain our negative thoughts and emotions. For instance, by going home and retreating to bed, Lucy might never find out that Paul was unavoidably delayed, and if she angrily decides to have no more contact with him she may also never discover that her interpretation of the situation was mistaken.

In summary, our reactions following an event are more likely to be:

Event → Thought/interpretation → Reactions (emotions, bodily

sensations and

behaviours)

Instead of:

Event → Reactions

Table 15.4: Linking behaviours to thoughts, emotions and bodily sensations

Situation	Thought	Emotion	Bodily Sensations	Behaviour
You are meeting a friend at a restaurant at 6 p.m. It is now 6.30 and your friend is nowhere to be seen.	My friend is never late ... something awful must have happened ... he must have been involved in a car crash.	Worry and Anxiety	Racing heart, shaking	Call his home, work, partner and maybe even the police.
	He obviously finds me so dull that he has forgotten about meeting me ... why would anyone want to meet up with me? I can't blame him ... I am so forgettable ... I am such a loser.	Sadness	Sinking feeling in the pit of stomach, tearful	Go home and retreat to bed.
	Well this just shows exactly how selfish he is ... imagine not even turning up ... how dare he ... who the hell does he think he is!	Anger	Tense muscles, flushing	Phone him at home and leave an angry message and block any of his calls.
	How awful, everyone is looking at me ... they think I've been stood up ... I bet I've gone bright red.	Humiliation and embar–rassment	Feeling hot, sweaty, blushing	Look down, try to avoid eye contact, fidget.
	Yikes, did we agree this restaurant? I know we talked about another restaurant, which is on the other side of town ... I bet I'm in the wrong place and he is waiting for me there.	Anxiety	Racing heart, feeling hot	Try to find phone number for other restaurant and call to see if he is there.
	I noticed that the traffic was getting pretty heavy when I arrived, I was lucky to have missed it ... he is probably caught up in it.	Uncon–cerned	No change	Perhaps browse through the menu to decide what to order when he shows up.

Thinking errors

When we realize that the problems we're experiencing are not caused directly by events but rather by our *interpretation* of those events, then it makes sense to try to tackle some of those interpretations. To help you, it's worth being aware of some patterns of thinking that are common and can be particularly troublesome for people experiencing emotional problems. These are usually referred to as 'thinking errors'. We have listed some of the key thinking errors in Table 15.5, along with examples of how they work in the lives of the people we have already met (Leon, Pearl, Bea, Dez, Leah, Penny and Ash).

Table 15.5: Examples of thinking errors

Thinking error	Description	Example
'All or nothing' thinking, 'dichotomous', or 'black and white', thinking	You do not do things by halves – there is no middle ground or shades of grey. People are either successful or a failure; they either like you or hate you; you are either right or wrong.	Dez is irritated with the woman on his sales team whose sales returns for the last two months have been lower than average, although she had previously been a top seller. This causes him to think that 'Trudie is completely useless'.
Overgeneralizing	You take one specific event and apply it to lots of others in your life; this includes a negative evaluation of yourself. If, for example, someone doesn't let you out of a side-street while you are driving, your thought may be: 'nobody ever does anything nice for me'.	Ash: 'Getting knocked off my bike has made me realize how vulnerable cyclists are. No one is ever totally safe'.

Minimizing and maximizing	You blow things out of proportion, making mountains out of molehills; you underplay and undervalue your strengths but emphasize your weaknesses. For example, you maximize how difficult you find it to be on time, but you minimize how kind you are to other people.	Leah has her annual individual personal review coming up at work and is worried about it. She thinks that 'getting a bad or mediocre review proves just how inadequate I am' although 'getting a good one doesn't really mean anything'.
Fortune-telling	You predict that things will turn out badly, no matter what you say or do. For example, you predict that nobody will speak to you at the party or be interested in what you have to say.	Penny concludes that 'there is no point in joining a dating agency because I won't meet anyone that will like me anyway'.
Emotional reasoning	You base your judgement of the situation on how you are feeling. You feel anxious so you think there must be danger.	Pearl sits down and has a cry after a long day looking after John, whose memory has been particularly bad today. Feeling upset, she concludes that she is a 'waste of space' rather than seeing herself as others would – as someone who is doing incredibly well in very difficult circumstances.

Selective abstracting	You focus on one, negative, aspect of an event rather than taking all aspects into account. For example, you call out the name of the wrong child during a football match and evaluate that entire afternoon as a disaster.	Leah had two minor errors in a long editorial piece, which were picked up by the newspaper's sub-editor. Rather than congratulating herself on completing such a substantial piece of work she became preoccupied by the two small errors, which made her feel anxious and upset.
Discounting the positive	You discount positive things about yourself. For example, you don't think it is important that you are reliable and trustworthy.	Leon was forwarded a letter by his boss from a grateful customer whom Leon had helped to find a rare record to add to his collection. Leon dismissed the letter because 'anyone could have done that'.
Personalizing	When something goes wrong, you blame yourself. For example, if you host a dinner party and someone is rude, you blame yourself for inviting them. However, the same is not true if it goes right. For example, if you host a dinner party and everyone has a great time you would put it down to luck or some reason other than your hosting skills.	Leon decides that 'the relationship break-up is all my fault'.

| Mind reading | You think you know what others are thinking. This is very common and usually involves thinking they are thinking something bad about you. For example, if a friend does not text back for a couple of days, you assume they do not want to be friends with you any more. | Penny at her friend's wedding: 'Everyone thinks I'm a sad old lonely spinster because I'm here by myself.' |

Why are these thinking patterns important?

How we think affects how we feel and behave, as well as what happens in our body. Our thoughts, emotions, bodily sensations and behaviours are all interconnected.

Can you take a compliment? No? Imagine that someone says: 'You're looking well today.' If you think 'they are only saying that, they don't really mean it' (thinking error: 'discounting the positive'/'mind reading'), then you are likely to continue to feel low. If, on the other hand, you can say 'thank you', and believe that you are truly looking well, then such a compliment is likely to improve your mood.

In general, if you are prone to catastrophizing, then changing this aspect of your thinking is going to be important in helping you to reduce your heightened emotion. If you tend to discount the positive aspects of yourself, changing that thinking error should improve how you feel about yourself.

Think back to some recent events that triggered feelings of anxiety, low mood, anger, or stress in general. Can you identify your thinking errors?

Table 15.6: Identifying my thinking errors

Events	Feelings	Thoughts	Possible thinking errors

Now, we would like you to complete the form in Table 15.6 *as and when* your feelings of anxiety, low mood, anger or stress occur. There are two reasons for this:

1. Writing things down at the time they happen (or as close to the time as possible) will provide more accurate information about your thoughts and possible thinking errors because the event will be fresh in your mind.

2. Writing things down helps you distance yourself from your thoughts. This will help you to think more objectively about your thoughts and the situation, which will be very helpful in breaking the thinking habits contributing to your feelings of distress.

Identifying my thinking errors

Complete the form in Table 15.7 for events that are upsetting/stressful in the next week.

In filling out these charts, you have started the process of *thinking about your thinking*! This is a crucial step in helping you to change any negative thought patterns. In the next chapter, we describe further methods to help you work out what you are thinking, how your thoughts relate to your feelings and how you can think differently.

Table 15.7: Identifying my thinking errors

Events	Feelings	Thoughts	Possible thinking errors

Summary

Now it is time for you to make a quick summary of the points that you found most helpful and interesting in this chapter. What was most relevant? What will you try and bear in mind from this chapter as you go on to the next chapters? Is there any one thing in particular that you would like to learn more about?

1. _____

_____

2. _____

_____

3. _____

_____

4. _____

_____

16 Identifying unhelpful thinking

Before we begin ...

Start the chapter by rating your current overall mood on the mood scale in Figure 16.1.

-5	-4	-3	-2	-1	0	+1	+2	+3	+4	+5

Negative   Neutral   Positive
mood   mood

Figure 16.1: Mood scale

If you are returning to this book after a break of a few days or more, take a moment to record your mood and anxiety (and whatever else you are recording, such as worry, anger, stress and self-esteem) and plot them on the graphs on pp. 420–39. Keeping track of your mood can help you review progress. Have there been any changes? If so, why do you think that might be? If not, can you think of any reasons?

It may also be helpful to review your problem statements (see Chapter 10, p. 135) and, re-rate those using the 0–100 problem-severity scale. Have there been any changes? Finally, review your SMART goals (see Chapter 10, p. 139) and make a note of any progress that you have made towards reaching them.

Identifying interpretations

In the previous chapters we demonstrated how our feelings, thoughts and behaviours are closely related. In this chapter we are going to think in more depth about the kinds of thoughts that occur automatically in various situations. In particular, we will discuss the negative interpretations of events that arise automatically and that lead us to feel anxious, depressed, angry or stressed, and that lower our self-esteem.

Let's look at examples of automatic thinking by reviewing Leon, Pearl, Bea, Dez, Leah, Penny and Ash's four-column thought diaries in Table 16.1.

Table 16.1: Example of four-column thought diaries

Leon's Thought Diary (depression)

Date	Situation	Emotion Rate intensity 0–100 per cent	Thought Rate belief 0–100 per cent and circle the most upsetting thought
Fri 6th	Sitting watching TV but unable to concentrate. I keep on thinking about the break-up.	Sad 100 per cent	I should have realized that something wasn't right. (80 per cent) She was the one. (100 per cent) **I'll never feel like that again about anyone. (100 per cent)**

Pearl's Thought Diary (depression)

Date	Situation	Emotion Rate intensity 0–100 per cent	Thought Rate belief 0–100 per cent and circle the most upsetting thought
Tues 14th	Appointment card arrives in post to John for memory clinic.	Miserable 80 per cent	What's the point in attending? They'll just confirm that John is deteriorating. (80 per cent) I should be stronger than this. (100 per cent) John needs me to be there for him at his time of need and I'm struggling. (100 per cent) **I am a waste of space.** **(100 per cent)**

You will have noticed that Pearl included a question in her thought column, but that it remained unrated. That is because it is very difficult to rate your belief in a question. If you do have a question in mind, it's best to turn it into a statement. Your rating will then indicate how much of a question mark there is over that statement. For example, 'what's the point?' could be changed to 'there is no point' and Pearl could rate how much she believed this statement. The higher she rates it, the less she questions its validity.

Bea's Thought Diary (generalized anxiety)

Date	Situation	Emotion Rate intensity 0–100 per cent	Thought Rate belief 0–100 per cent and circle the most upsetting thought
Mon 5th	Sitting waiting for a lift from Rob who is now 30 minutes late.	Worried 100 per cent	Rob is never late. (70 per cent) Something bad must have happened. (90 per cent) **He is not answering his phone because he has been in a crash. (100 per cent)**

Dez's Thought Diary (anger)

Date	Situation	Emotion Rate intensity 0–100 per cent	Thought Rate belief 0–100 per cent and circle the most upsetting thought
Fri 2nd	Driving home from work. Driver cuts in front of me, causing me to brake sharply.	Angry 100 per cent Raging 100 per cent	He did that on purpose. (90 per cent) What an idiot. (100 per cent) I could have crashed. (80 per cent) I must have 'mug' written on my forehead! (80 per cent) **He thinks I'm a soft touch. (100 per cent)**

Leah's Thought Diary (stress)

Date	Situation	Emotion Rate intensity 0–100 per cent	Thought Rate belief 0–100 per cent and circle the most upsetting thought
Fri 30th	At work and struggling to get an editorial piece finished that I've been working on for weeks and that is due on Monday. Boss came over to ask me how I was getting on with it.	Anxious 90 per cent Stressed 100 per cent	I'm way behind on this. (100 per cent) I'll never get it finished on time. (90 per cent) My boss thinks I can't cope. (100 per cent) **I'll lose my job. (100 per cent)**

Penny's Thought Diary (low self-esteem)

Date	Situation	Emotion Rate intensity 0–100 per cent	Thought Rate belief 0–100 per cent and circle the most upsetting thought
Sat 16th	Rena said she would call and didn't.	Upset 100 per cent Sad 100 per cent	She's forgotten about me. (80 per cent) She doesn't even like me. (90 per cent) She just said she'd call because she felt obliged but didn't want to. (80 per cent) **Nobody likes me. (90 per cent)**

Ash's Thought Diary (mixed anxiety and depression)

Date	Situation	Emotion Rate intensity 0–100 per cent	Thought Rate belief 0–100 per cent and circle the most upsetting thought
Sun 10th	Lovely sunny day. Kay and the kids want to go for a bike ride to the park.	Anxious 90 per cent	Someone will hit one of us on the road. (80 per cent) It's not worth the risk. (100 per cent) **It will be all my fault if one of the kids gets hurt. (100 per cent)**

Note that all the emotions are described in one word (i.e. sad, depressed, miserable, worried, anxious, angry, raging, stressed, upset) and that it is possible to experience more than one emotion at a time.

When you make your own Thought Diary, remember that the emotion should make sense in relation to the thought you are recording. For example, let's say you found yourself in a large department store and rated your anxiety at 70 per cent. Your emotion isn't linked to your thought that 'this place is enormous', but instead to the thought that 'I'm going to panic and not be able to find my way out of here'. Look back over the examples above and think whether you would feel the same as Leon, Pearl, Bea, Dez, Leah, Penny and Ash if you believed their thought as much as they did. Would you feel differently, and if so in what way? Why do you think you feel differently?

My Thought Diary

Now it is time to try this exercise for yourself using the four-column thought diary in Table 16.2.

1. First, think back to a recent upsetting event and then write down the answers to the following questions:

    *   Write the date in the first column.

    *   What was the event or situation? Where were you? What were you doing? Who were you with? Write this down in the second column below.

    *   What was the emotion you experienced (e.g. anger, sadness, anxiety)? Remember, this is likely to be just one word. Write this in the third column.

    *   What went through your mind at the time (e.g. 'nobody wants to talk to me')? Remember that it is best to turn any questions into statements. Add this to the fourth column.

2. Now take a moment to rate the intensity of the emotion you felt at the time using a percentage scale where 0 per cent is 'not at all', 100 per cent is extremely high intensity and 50 per cent is moderate. Feel free to be as specific as you want with the number you select.

3. Once you've done that, take another moment to rate how much you believed the thought that went through your mind at the time. If there were lots of thoughts (and very often many negative thoughts come rushing into our minds at times like this), then circle the one that is most upsetting.

Table 16.2: Four-column thought diary

Date	Situation	Emotion	Thought
	Where were you? What were you doing? Who were you with?	**Rate intensity 0–100 per cent**	What was going through your head just as you started to feel the emotion? List all thoughts and images. **Rate belief 0–100 per cent and circle the most upsetting thought**

Analysing your thinking in this way is not easy. When you've completed the exercise, you deserve to feel good about yourself and can legitimately pat yourself on the back. In the next chapter, we will be looking at how to change your thinking patterns.

The next task builds on the previous exercise by asking you to use the blank form in Table 16.3 over the next week. This time, complete the form *as and when* the feelings of anxiety, depression, sadness, anger or stress occur. As we mentioned in the previous chapter, there are two good reasons for this. First, if you write things down when the events are fresh in your mind, the information you record about your thoughts and possible thinking errors is more likely to be accurate. Secondly, writing things down is a way of distancing yourself from your thoughts. It will help you to think more objectively about your thoughts and the situation and thus make it easier to break any negative thinking habits.

Table 16.3: Four-column thought diary to complete during the next week

Date	Situation	Emotion	Thought
Include day of week and time of day where relevant	Where were you? What were you doing? Who were you with?	**Rate intensity 0–100 per cent**	What was going through your head just as you started to feel the emotion? List all thoughts and images. **Rate belief 0–100 per cent and circle the most upsetting thought**

Summary

Here is some space for you to summarize the most important points from this chapter. You can use it to flag up things that you found most helpful and that you want to be able to refer back to later on. What was most interesting? Was any one thing especially striking?

1. _____

   _____

2. _____

   _____

3. _____

   _____

4. _____

   _____

17 Thinking differently

Before we begin ...

Start the chapter by rating your current mood on the scale in Figure 17.1.

-5	-4	-3	-2	-1	0	+1	+2	+3	+4	+5

Negative   Neutral   Positive
mood   mood

Figure 17.1: Mood scale

If you are returning to this book after a break of a few days or more, take a moment to record your mood and anxiety (and whatever else you are recording, such as worry, anger, stress and self-esteem) and plot them on the graphs on pp. 420–39. Keeping track of your mood can help you review progress. Have there been any changes? If so, why do you think that might be? If not, can you think of any reasons?

It may also be helpful to review your problem statements (see Chapter 10, p. 135) and, re-rate those using the 0–100 problem-severity scale. Have there been any changes? Finally, review your SMART goals (see Chapter 10, p. 139) and make a note of any progress that you have made towards reaching them.

Evaluating interpretations

By now you will have identified and recorded your thinking in various situations that you find upsetting. You will have also spent some time recording your thinking errors. Now it is time to put these two pieces of work together. Evaluating thoughts can be a powerful strategy in dealing with difficult emotions.

In this chapter we'll look in depth at how to change your thinking by identifying your thinking errors. In addition, you will learn to check whether there is any information you can use to challenge the interpretation of events that causes you distress, and to help you arrive at an alternative perspective. We call this 'evaluating interpretations' because weighing up the evidence for and against a given thought helps you judge whether it's valid or not. We will go through this process slowly and start by using Bea as an example.

Case illustration 3: Bea

Bea's son was thirty minutes late to meet her one day. She had many thoughts, including 'Rob is never late' and 'something bad must have happened'. Her most upsetting thought was: 'He is not answering his phone because he has been in a crash.' Her reason for thinking this (i.e., her 'evidence' that Rob had been in a crash) was that Rob had not called to explain why he was late, as he usually did. On this occasion, when Bea phoned Rob, the phone went straight to voicemail.

In this scenario, Bea is definitely catastrophizing. Taking a step back and realizing this, would allow Bea to come up with evidence against this most upsetting thought. Such evidence includes the traffic being heavy because of the local football match, the possibility that his phone battery is dead or he has no reception, as has happened in the past, or that Rob's work meeting might have overrun which has also happened previously.

Having weighed up the evidence for and against the thought that Rob has been in a car crash, Bea's next task is to come up with an alternative, more balanced thought. Her alternative thought is that Rob is late because he has probably been delayed by traffic or a meeting. This more balanced thought is believable to Bea which means that her belief in the original catastrophizing thought subsides, as does her emotion. She can then think about what to do next. Bea's example is given in Table 17.1.

Table 17.1: Bea's Nine-Column Thought Diary

Date	Situation	Emotion Rate intensity 0–100%	Thought Rate belief 0–100% and circle the most upsetting thought (100 per cent)	Evidence for the most upsetting thought	Evidence against the most upsetting thought	Alternative thought and rate belief in it	Re-rate belief in upsetting thought and intensity of emotion	What to do next
Mon 5th	Sitting waiting for a lift from Rob who is now 30 minutes late.	Worry 100%	Rob is never late. Something bad must have happened. (90%) **He is not answering his phone because he has been in a crash. (100 per cent)**	On the one occasion that Rob was late before, he rang me to say he was held up. The phone is just ringing and ringing without being picked up.	The traffic is heavy because of the local football derby match being on tonight. Rob has not picked up calls from me in the past having lost signal or battery power. Rob was in a work meeting just before planning to come over so this is possible. I have a habit of catastroph-izing. Maybe I'm doing it again here.	Considering the amount of traffic and the fact that Rob had an important meeting towards the end of the working day, it is most likely that he has been delayed and that his phone is out of charge.	He is not answering his phone because he has been in a car crash. (40%) Worry (60%)	Call Mum for a catch-up while I wait. If he doesn't turn up in the next 30 minutes, I'll call his work to see what time he left.

Evaluating your own interpretations

Think about the past couple of weeks, and try to select examples of when you became distressed, whether that be angry, fearful, depressed, stressed or you felt low about yourself. Can you identify any of your own thinking errors?

Step 1

Choose an example of something that happened and caused you some distress. Try not to choose the most distressing event or situation, as it could be overwhelming, and difficult to use the strategy right away. Identify the main emotion caused by the situation and rate its intensity. Similarly, identify the thoughts you had, rate the extent to which you believed them, and circle the most upsetting thought. Can you spot a thinking error? Use the nine-column thought diary in Table 17.2 to help you.

Step 2

Now consider the evidence that exists for the most upsetting thought being true. If you find this tricky, ask yourself the following questions:

- What is the evidence you have for the upsetting thought?

- What makes you come to that conclusion?

- You believe the thought ___ %. What is it that makes you believe it so strongly?

Write the answers to these questions in the 'Evidence for the most upsetting thought' column. Be careful only to use factual evidence rather than another negative thought. For instance, 'Everybody can see I'm anxious' is likely to be another negative thought unless you have been told by every single person where you are that you appear anxious. Similarly, 'Something always goes wrong' is also likely to be another negative thought (an overgeneralization), because it is most unlikely that something goes wrong absolutely every time you do something. 'I've never achieved anything' is also definitely not true and another overgeneraliza-tion. Facts, on the other hand, are things that are indisputable. 'I had a panic attack in this shop last time I was here' is an example of a fact, as is 'the police reported that there have been over fifty accidents on this road in the last year' or 'Isi told me she had been sleeping with Luke'.

Step 3

Next, think about the evidence against your most upsetting thought. If you're prone to a particular thinking error, you can include that here.

To help you gather evidence against your most upsetting thought, ask yourself the following questions:

- Does this thought fall into the category of a thinking error? If so, which one?

- What evidence is there that does not support this thought?

- If you rated your belief in the thought as under 100 per cent, it shows an element of doubt. What is that doubt?

- Are there any things that you might be ignoring because you think they are not important, even though they would actually work against this thought?

- What happened last time you were in a situation like this?

- What experiences have you had that would indicate that this thought is not necessarily true?

Other useful questions to ask:
- Is there another way of looking at this situation?

- What is the worst thing that could happen even if this thought is true?

- If the thought is true, will it still matter in five years' time?

- How might someone else think about this situation?

- If you were not experiencing depression/anxiety/stress/anger/low self-esteem, would you believe this thought?

Table 17.2: Nine-column Thought Diary

Date	Situation	Emotion Rate intensity 0–100%	Thought Rate belief 0–100% and circle the most upsetting thought	Evidence for the most upsetting thought	Evidence against the most upsetting thought	Alternative thought and rate belief in it	Re-rate belief in upsetting thought and intensity of emotion	What to do next

Step 4

You now need to think of an alternative explanation for the event and rate your belief in it. As we saw in her Thought Diary above, Bea's alternative thought is: 'Considering the amount of traffic and the fact that Rob had an important meeting towards the end of the working day, it is most likely that he has been delayed and that he has forgotten to take his phone off silent.'

Thinking of an alternative thought is not always easy to do, and if you have a supporter, they may be able to help with this, but it is still doable on your own. What is most important here is that the alternative thought is believable to you. CBT is not about groundless 'positive thinking' but about being realistic. It is absolutely critical that the alternative thought is credible and consistent with what is going on in your life right now. The key question you need to consider is: taking into account the evidence for and against the thought, can you come up with a more realistic and helpful alternative thought?

Step 5

Well done for getting this far! You are nearing the end of this exercise. Having come up with a more realistic alternative thought, what you need to do next is to re-rate your belief in the upsetting thought and also the intensity of the emotion associated with the thought. Have they changed?

If your ratings have gone down, then that's great. You now have a proven method of evaluating the thoughts that are causing you emotional distress. If they have not changed for the better, then that is important too. Why do you think they haven't? Where did you get stuck? Was it that the original thought was too intense and it was just not possible to gather the evidence to help you think in a different way? If this is the case, practise the technique with a less intense thought and then build up to evaluating your most intense and difficult thoughts. Above all, don't be disheartened: after all, you've probably thought and felt this way for many years. Thinking in a different way is bound to require practice.

Let's look at how Dez used these techniques to work through his angry thought while he was driving (Table 17.3).

Dez's Thought Diary

Table 17.3: Dez's nine-column thought diary

Date	Situation	Emotion Rate intensity 0–100%	Thought Rate belief 0–100% and circle the most upsetting thought	Evidence for the most upsetting thought	Evidence against the most upsetting thought	Alternative thought and rate belief in it	Re-rate belief in upsetting thought and intensity of emotion	What to do next
Fri 2nd	Driving home from work. Caught up in traffic and car cut in meaning I had to brake sharply.	Anger (100%) Rage (100%)	He did that on purpose. (90%) What an idiot (100%) I could have crashed. (80%)	He chose to cut in in front of my car rather than anyone else's.	He actually doesn't know me at all so it is unlikely he has any opinion of me. There was a bit of a gap between my car and the lorry in front so it was probably the easiest gap to go for.	As I like to leave a stopping distance between me and the car in front, I may always be vulnerable to people cutting in. When people cut in it's not to do with me personally.	He thinks I'm a soft touch. (50%) Anger (50%) Rage (40%)	Put on my favourite song and calm my breathing down by breathing more slowly. Tell myself he's the idiot not me.

I must have 'mug' written on my forehead! (80%) **He thinks I'm a soft touch (100%)**	He flashed his hazard lights and waved in the mirror to thank me for letting him in. It happens to other drivers too and they are no more a soft touch than me. This won't matter in five years' time. I am taking this too personally.	Taking it personally only makes me angry and upset for hours. It's not worth ruining my day for someone who seems to be in too much of a hurry. Besides, I can never really know what the other driver is thinking. He's probably just so focused on getting home that he isn't thinking about me or other drivers.

What if your negative thought is actually true? It is important to remember that our automatic thoughts are not *always* wrong! They can be true, false or partly true. For example, the thoughts 'Anna doesn't like me' or 'I have no friends' might be true. If this is the case, problem-solving might be a better approach to take.

Step 6

The final step is all about what you *do* in the given situation. This is a vitally important stage. If you do not behave any differently, then evaluating your thoughts will have less of an impact on your mood. If, however, you can combine thinking differently with *behaving* differently, then you are firmly on the path to recovery.

Continue to practise evaluating your own interpretations

Gathering evidence to evaluate your interpretations of events and help reduce your distressing emotions is a fundamental part of effective CBT. For this reason, we would like you to spend the next week or so practising this. Use the blank forms in the Appendix to help you to do so.

At the end of each day, take a few moments to reflect on how things are going with your evaluations. What is going well and what requires more effort or some help? If you are getting stuck, use problem-solving to help you (for advice on problem-solving techniques, see Chapter 12). As before, you will find evaluation most helpful if you can do it at the time of the event or as close to the time as possible. It is also important that you write things down rather than just doing the exercises in your head: that way you become much more aware of the steps in the process, and can book back on them later as needed.

Summary

Once again, use the space below to write down key points from this chapter. What did you find most helpful, or most encouraging? What, in your view, was most important? Is there anything that you want to find out more about in the Further Resources section?

1. _____

   _____

2. _____

   _____

3. _____

   _____

4. _____

   _____

18 Behavioural experiments

Before we begin ...

Start the chapter by rating your current mood on the scale in Figure 18.1.

-5	-4	-3	-2	-1	0	+1	+2	+3	+4	+5

Negative   Neutral   Positive
mood   mood

Figure 18.1: Mood scale

If you are returning to this book after a break of a few days or more, take a moment to record your mood and anxiety (and whatever else you are recording, such as worry, anger, stress and self-esteem) and plot them on the graphs on pp. 420–39. Keeping track of your mood can help you review progress. Have there been any changes? If so, why do you think that might be? If not, can you think of any reasons?

It may also be helpful to review your problem statements (see Chapter 10, p. 135) and, re-rate those using the 0–100 problem-severity scale. Have there been any changes? Finally, review your SMART goals (see Chapter 10, p. 139) and make a note of any progress that you have made towards reaching them.

Table 18.1: Quiz

Question: What do the following quotes all have in common?

'One must learn by doing the thing. For though you think you know it, you have no certainty until you try.'

Sophocles

'What we have to learn to do, we learn by doing.'

Aristotle

'The knowledge of the world is only to be acquired in the world, and not in a closet.'

Philip Dormer Stanhope, Lord Chesterfield

'There are two modes of knowledge: through argument and through experience. Argument brings conclusions and compels us to concede them, but it does not cause certainty nor remove doubts that the mind may rest in truth, unless this is provided by experience.'

Friar Roger Bacon

Answer: They are all saying the same thing.

These quotes are all from wise people who have drawn the identical conclusion: it is all very well to talk about something, but it is only by taking action that learning takes place. This includes learning about the reality of your thinking, and learning about the impact of your behaviour. It means that to change the way you are feeling, it can be necessary to change the way you behave in certain situations.

By now, we hope that you've identified your unhelpful thinking and any of the thinking errors that you may be making. The preceding chapters will have helped you to think about the evidence for and against your original thoughts, and to arrive at new, alternative perspectives. While this is good in the short term, it is probably not going to be enough to help you change in the long term. What you need to do now is to learn whether your original way of thinking really is a better reflection of reality than your alternative new perspective. To do that you need to *experience* the impact that different types of thinking have on your emotions, and the impact that behaving differently can have on the way you think and feel. In this chapter we will guide you through this process.

Testing your thoughts via experience

In CBT we often use analogies and metaphors to illustrate a point. We might say, for example, that getting used to doing an activity differently can be like putting on a new pair of shoes: it can feel uncomfortable at first but the feeling soon wears off.

One of our favourite analogies was presented by Professor Paul Salkovskis at Bath University. In this story, a young lad has his first day of work experience in the builder's yard. The builders decide to play a trick on him and the foreman tells the boy that his first job is very important. The job is to hold up the brick wall that the builders have built. It is several bricks high and long at this point, and the boy puts his hands either side of the wall at the start of the day. The wall does not fall down. As the day wears on, the boy needs the toilet, but he doesn't let go of the wall. He has been told to hold it up and it is a very important job, after all. He wants to do well. It occurs to him that it may not fall down, but he simply cannot afford to take the risk, no matter what the discomfort and inconvenience. At lunchtime the foreman asks him to carry on for another few hours, even though the boy's arms ache now and he is hungry (and still needs the toilet). The lad does as he's asked. At the end of the day, the foreman praises the lad and tells him that he would be really grateful if he could hold up the wall all night while the other builders go home.

Here's a simple question for you: what does the young lad need to do to find out that the wall will not fall down if he lets go? He may know rationally that the wall will not fall down, and a kind passer-by could tell him (like the person supporting you may try to convince you), but there is only one way to find out that would be completely convincing to him. He needs to take the chance, let go and find out for himself that the wall will not collapse.

What does this story have to do with you? If you suffer from emotional difficulties, you may perceive that you are taking enormous risks when you try out new ways of behaving. It could be that 'the wall falling down' for you is that something terrible will happen to you or your loved ones (for instance, Bea may worry that something bad will happen to Gus if she is not there all the time, so she 'holds up the wall' by always being there or keeping her mobile phone with her when she does have to go out). Though it is hard to try things differently and to take chances, behavioural experiments can help provide the evidence you need to find out that your worst fears will not come true.

Your response to this idea may well be: 'what if my worst fears *do* come true though?' Don't worry: that's a normal reaction. And that's why it's important not to start your behavioural experiments by testing your worst thoughts with the biggest risks attached. Instead, it's best to begin with experiments that don't have such high stakes, to build your confidence towards testing out your worst thoughts.

Behavioural experiments are the ideal tool to test the validity of your fears, because it is only by taking action that learning takes place. In this chapter, we will introduce you to a number of different such experiments, and their stages, and show you how to put them into action for your own problems.

What is a 'behavioural experiment'?

A behavioural experiment is a planned activity that involves you changing your behaviour and seeing what happens in terms of the situation, your feelings, your bodily sensations and your thoughts.

Behavioural experiments have high 'evidential value', which means that the evidence they provide is personally meaningful, relevant and memorable, and so can help change your perspective in the short and long term. They can help you to 'believe in your heart' information that you know rationally in your head.

Behavioural experiments:

- Are there to help you test whether your interpretation of a given situation is accurate.

- Help you to decide whether the alternative perspective you arrived at by weighing up the evidence using Thought Diaries (see Chapter 17) is accurate and fits with reality.

- Are very valuable in helping you compare and contrast thoughts and behaviours to see whether different ways of thinking and behaving are helpful.

- Help you obtain information about what happens when you behave differently.

- Give you the experience of behaving differently and seeing the impact that has on your thoughts, feelings, bodily sensations, the situation and your life and relationships.

Types of behavioural experiment

There are two main types of behavioural experiment

1. Observational experiment

This type of experiment is designed to help you obtain information and it might include you watching people or situations, conducting surveys or gathering information from experts or the internet.

A useful observational experiment for someone like Pearl, for example, might be to find out about the differing ways in which people are affected by Alzheimer's disease. Pearl was inclined to attribute all of her husband's erratic behaviour to his illness, failing to recall that he was rather eccentric before he became ill. In light of the new information she has gathered from the Alzheimer's Society and their doctor about Alzheimer's disease, Pearl is now in a position to interpret her husband's behaviour, and how it makes her feel, in a different way.

An example of a very useful observational experiment for people who have unwanted intrusive thoughts (thoughts that pop into one's mind that are unplanned and unwanted) is to ask other people about the unwanted thoughts, images and impulses that they experience. The vast majority of us have such experiences and asking each other about them can be invaluable in helping us to see that our experiences are normal.

2. Active experiment

This type of experiment usually involves testing the accuracy of your original interpretations and/or the new perspective that you have arrived at through your Thought Diaries. A common behavioural experiment consists of dropping a safety behaviour (see p. 53) and then seeing what happens. Another comprises acting 'as if' you believed an alternative new perspective (even if you don't) and observing the consequences. Bea, for example, tried out a new way of behaving to test whether her anxious thoughts were accurate. She acted as if nothing bad would happen to anyone close to her if she went out shopping for an hour without taking her mobile phone. By doing this, she challenged her fears about what would happen to her son Gus if she wasn't around. At first she was anxious but her anxiety slowly lessened and because she discovered that nothing bad happened while she was away, this gave her confidence to go out for a little longer next time.

The stages of a behavioural experiment

Behavioural experiments follow an eight-stage process.

1. Identify what thought or belief might be causing the problem to persist and rate the extent to which you believe it to be true

The problem might also be a behaviour, in which case you can rate your belief in the importance of that behaviour. Having spent some time on your problem statement and Thought Diaries, you should by now have a good idea of what might be causing your problem to persist. For Leon, it was staying in bed a lot of the day and avoiding friends; for Leah, it was doing nothing but work all the time; for Ash, it was avoiding using his bike; meanwhile Dez's difficulties were persisting because of his belief that life was unfair and unjust.

It may be difficult to pinpoint just one belief, thought or behaviour that might be causing the problem to persist. If that is the case, choose one that you have already looked at using a Thought Diary (see p. 250).

The difference between a thought and a belief is that we can have thousands of thoughts pop into our minds – many we won't notice or remember but some can be troublesome. Beliefs are at a rather deeper level and can be rigid and inflexible. Thoughts are generally easier to change than beliefs.

2. Brainstorm ideas for an experiment to test the thought/belief/behaviour

Using the form below, brainstorm ideas for your experiment. Circle the one that you choose as the best option. There is no single right one. Choose the one that seems most likely to work for you. If you have a supporter, you might find it helpful to discuss ideas together. If not, the examples of Leah, Bea, Dez and Penny below might help, and the different kinds of experiment are discussed in more detail later in this chapter. Think about what you would be able to do if you did not have the problem: how would you act? This is a good starting point for thinking of a behavioural experiment.

3. Make specific predictions about the outcome and devise a method to record it

Making predictions about what you think will happen and writing them down is important. People with depression and low mood tend to recall situations with a rather negative slant, so recording thoughts, feelings, bodily sensations and behaviours at the time of doing the experiment can be particularly helpful.

Recording is also fundamental to keeping the experiment scientific and objective, which as you may remember are key elements of CBT. See examples below for Leah, Bea, Dez and Penny.

4. Anticipate problems and brainstorm solutions

People often find that the behavioural experiment they've chosen is too difficult. It is important, therefore, that the experiment is designed so that you don't tackle the most difficult scenario first. Even though such experiments are not formally graded or ranked in terms of difficulty in the same way as graded exposure (see Chapter 13), it is important that the experiment is manageable so that you will actually obtain useful information and feel a sense of accomplishment.

You will find examples of the problems and solutions facing Leah, Bea, Dez and Penny below. (If you worked through Chapter 12 on problem-solving, you'll have practised anticipating problems and brainstorming solutions, which should help a lot.)

5. Carry out the behavioural experiment, then describe the behavioural experiment you actually carried out

As far as possible, carry out the behavioural experiment as planned. It's important to tackle your behavioural experiment on a day that you are feeling strong and ready to take on a challenge. If you have been up all night with a crying baby or you have a terrible hangover, then today might not be the right day for the experiment. After all, there is always another day. If, however, you find you are simply putting it off, then it is probably worth planning the experiment for a particular time and date in the next couple of days.

Make a note of exactly what you did, which may be different from what you originally planned. For instance, you may have planned to travel to town on a train at rush hour but this felt like too big a step so you might have got on an earlier train that was less busy.

6. Describe what happened (i.e. the results). Were your predictions accurate? What did you observe?

Make a note of exactly what happened. Did it turn out as expected or were there some surprises? Write down what you observed and what sense you made of this. For instance you may have predicted that people would stare at you if you felt hot and sweaty in a busy café, but you might observe that nobody really looks at you. The sense you might make of this is that your worries were unfounded and that nobody is particularly paying attention to what others are doing.

7. Re-rate your conviction in the thought/belief or your belief in the importance of the behaviour

You might respond to your experiment in a variety of ways. Perhaps the results aren't what you expected and that makes you change your thinking. For instance, you may have predicted that someone you had not seen for a while would say no if you asked them to meet up for a coffee, but they said yes. Maybe the results are more ambiguous and indicate that your thought or belief might not necessarily be true, or that you need not necessarily be dependent on the behaviour that you tested. For instance, you might have predicted that something untoward might happen and your family would be trying to get hold of you if you did not take your mobile phone with you, but you return to find out that this was not the case. It might be that the results lead you to be even more convinced that your thought, belief or behaviour is justified. Whichever it is, this is an important discovery, and your original ratings need to be reviewed in light of this.

8. Devise an alternative thought/belief/behaviour that can be tested as a follow-on behavioural experiment

The next step is to decide how to take forward what you have learned, and this will probably involve devising another experiment. You may want to repeat your experiment so that you can obtain more information (or 'data') to ensure that your previous results are correct. Alternatively, you might want to investigate another related thought/belief/behaviour that has not already been tested or for which the results of the experiment were inconclusive. The next steps taken by Leah (survey), Bea (dropped safety behaviours), Dez (contrasted old and new behaviours) and Penny (acting as if) are shown in Tables 18.2–18.5.

Table 18.2: A survey: Leah

Leah was asked to do a presentation to her boss and other colleagues at work. She was incredibly anxious about it and believed that she was out of control and that nobody else would get nervous in her position.

1. Thought/belief/behaviour to be tested and strength of conviction

I am pathetic for being anxious about this presentation. *Nobody else gets anxious about this kind of thing.* Strength of conviction: 95 per cent.

2. Ideas for experiment to test the thought/belief/behaviour. Underline the best one

- *Ask up to ten people I know if they get anxious doing presentations.*

- Look at people doing presentations on YouTube and see if any of them look nervous.

3. Specific predictions about what will happen and how you will record the outcome:

Prediction 1: Everyone will say that they don't get nervous doing presentations.

Prediction 2: Everyone will say that they wouldn't feel anxious doing the presentation that I have to do to my boss and colleagues.

Recording the outcome: I will write a list of questions and record each person's response on a separate sheet. I will collate them all and summarize them at the end of the experiment.

4. Anticipated problems and potential solutions

Possible problem: I might not get the opportunity to ask as many people as I would like due to limited time.

Potential solution: I suppose it doesn't really matter as long as I get all the responses before I do the presentation, but I should try to get as many as possible because it might help. I could set time aside at the weekend to give this some attention rather than going to the gym.

Possible problem: People might not be available or might not want to get involved in the survey.

Potential solution: I could probably think of a 'reserve' list of people in case the ones I have in mind aren't available. I think that most people will actually be OK about doing it, as the questions aren't terribly intrusive.

5. Describe the experiment you carried out

I wrote out the questions that I would ask everyone. The six questions were:

1. Would you get anxious at the prospect of giving a presentation to your boss and colleagues about a project you'd been working on?

2. If yes, how anxious do you think you would be? Rate your anxiety from 0 (none) to 10 (very intense).

3. Do you think you would feel anxious preparing for the presentation (describe)?

4. If yes, how anxious do you think you would be? Rate your anxiety from 0 (none) to 10 (very intense).

5. Do you think you would feel anxious delivering the presentation (describe)?

6. If yes, how anxious do you think you would be? Rate your anxiety from 0 (none) to 10 (very intense).

6. Describe what happened

I managed to do the survey with eight people.

- Seven of them said that they would feel a bit anxious at the prospect of giving a presentation to their boss and colleagues. One said that she wouldn't feel anxious because it would be her project so she would know it inside out.

- Of the seven that said they would be anxious, the anxiety varied from 4–8. The other person rated 0.

- Four out of the eight felt that they would get a bit anxious when preparing the presentation.

- Of the four that said they would be anxious, the anxiety varied from 2–7. The other four rated 0.

- Seven of the eight said they would feel anxious delivering the presentation.

- Of the seven that said they would be anxious, the anxiety varied from 5–10. The other person rated 1.

I was shocked at this. I made a point of asking people that I consider to be really confident, so I didn't expect any of them to be anxious at all. I just assumed that everyone would take this kind of thing in their stride. I suppose it makes me feel a bit more human and not quite as pathetic as I did before. It hasn't changed my anxiety about giving a presentation, but it has changed the way I view myself in relation to my anxiety.

7. Re-rate your conviction

Nobody else gets anxious about this kind of thing. Strength of conviction: 20 per cent.

8. Revised thought/belief/behaviour that can be tested

I am anxious about my presentation but this is normal. Other people would feel the same. That is good to know as my boss and colleagues are likely to be sympathetic if my nerves show a bit. Perhaps I should keep a record of my anxiety levels when preparing and delivering the presentation to see if I fall within the 'normal' range of my friends.

Table: 18.3: Dropping safety behaviours: Bea

Bea does not feel able to go anywhere without her mobile phone in case anything happens to anyone in the family, especially Gus, her youngest son who has mild learning difficulties, and Lily, her granddaughter who has a heart condition. She thinks if she is anywhere with a poor signal she has to leave as quickly as possible in case she is needed by someone, and that she can't do any activity that means leaving her mobile behind or turning it off – like going swimming or to the cinema. She always has her phone charging overnight to be sure it won't run out of battery when she is out.

1. Thought/belief/behaviour to be tested and strength of conviction

I need to be available at all times otherwise I am a bad mother/grandmother. Strength of conviction: 100 per cent.

2. Ideas for experiment to test the thought/belief/behaviour. Circle the best one

- Go out without my mobile phone for the day.

- Switch off my mobile phone for the day.

- <u>Go out with my phone in my back pocket and switched off for a shorter period (maybe an hour).</u>

- Ask people who I think are good mothers or grandmothers if they go out without their phone or if they are available 24/7.

3. Specific predictions about what will happen and how you will record the outcome

If I go out without my mobile phone I will miss an important call from one of the kids. I will be anxious all the time I am out. I will never get over it if anything bad happens. I will keep a note of my anxiety levels on an hourly basis.

4. Anticipated problems and potential solutions

Possible problem: That my anxiety gets so high that I just don't attempt the experiment.

Potential solution: Not sure how to solve this. Maybe just go out for a shorter time.

Possible problem: That something worrying happens to one of the family on the day before so that I don't feel able to do it.

Potential solution: Rearrange for another day when things at home are calm.

5. Describe the experiment you carried out

I went out shopping to the local supermarket with my phone in my bag but switched off. I was away about one hour ten minutes.

6. Describe what happened

I couldn't go out without a phone at first. I took the phone with me but kept it switched off. I went in the morning when it would be quiet and I knew I could get back quickly. I was even more anxious than I thought I would be. I managed thirty minutes but then switched on the phone to check for messages. There were none so I turned it back off again. My anxiety went down once I had checked the phone and the second half of the hour was a bit easier.

I tried the experiment again a few days later and managed to keep the phone switched off for the whole time. My anxiety wasn't quite as bad as the first time. I ended up being out longer than I'd planned because I bumped into a friend. I hadn't seen her for ages so we caught up a bit. Afterwards, I realized that when I was speaking to her my anxiety wasn't so bad, probably because I was distracted. Nothing bad happened while I was out.

I had a third go at the experiment except this time I left my phone at home. When I got back I found I'd missed a call. I was devastated and was shaking when I rang the voicemail to get the message. It was Will, my middle son, asking if I wanted to come over for lunch with Gus at the weekend. I was relieved. Overall, I found being out without my phone very stressful but actually missing the call and hearing the message wasn't nearly as bad as I thought it might be. Obviously nothing bad happened, but if something had then I am sure it would have been different. I think it will take some practice but it is worth persevering.

7. Re-rate your conviction

I need to be available at all times otherwise I am a bad mother/grandmother. Strength of conviction: 80 per cent.

8. Revised thought/belief/behaviour that can be tested

If I go out without my phone it is unlikely I will miss an important call. If I do, then I will pick up a message when I get back and respond right away. My anxiety hasn't been so bad the more I have tried to do this, so I reckon it will continue to get easier if I keep going. Next I'm going to go swimming with my friend and not take my phone. Little by little I think I will be able to build up my confidence.

Table 18.4: Contrasting old and new behaviours: Dez

Dez wants to try to behave differently when faced with traffic jams. Rather than making rude gestures and shouting at people when he is driving, he is going to try counting to ten and playing his favourite upbeat song on his sound system.

1. _Thought_/belief/behaviour to be tested and strength of conviction

If I just let someone cut in front of me when I am driving, without reacting, then I'll end up being furious for hours and just won't be able to let it go. Strength of conviction: 100 per cent.

2. Ideas for experiment to test the thought/belief/behaviour. Circle the best one:

- Next time someone cuts in, don't react. Instead, count to ten and put on one of my favourite happy songs.

- <u>Do the same as the above but contrast it directly with responding in my usual way – I could keep track of how furious I am in both situations.</u>

- Next time someone cuts in, laugh aloud and tell myself they are useless drivers and will probably have an accident one day – HA HA HA.

3. Specific predictions about what will happen and how you will record the outcome

I will be so incensed by someone cutting in that I won't be able to help myself from reacting. If I don't respond I will stay angry for the rest of the day and go home in a really bad mood and take it out on Corrie. I will be just as angry by not reacting as I will be by reacting; it won't make a difference.

To record the outcome, I will keep a diary of exactly what I do each time and rate my levels of bodily tension and feelings of anger.

4. Anticipated problems and potential solutions

Potential problem: Someone cutting in on me might not happen over the next few weeks.

Possible solution: Try to ensure that I travel at rush hour, and on the motorway, because it's more likely to happen then.

Potential problem: I might not stop myself in time and react right away.

Possible solution: If I do that then I will just need to do my best to limit the reaction. Less of a reaction is better than nothing. I can pop on my music as quickly as possible to try to change my mood.

5. Describe the experiment you carried out

It didn't happen for the first couple of days and then on my way home on Friday night, sure enough someone cut in. I was just about to toot my horn and then I remembered and counted slowly to ten (through gritted teeth), put my song on and did a relaxation exercise as I could feel the tension starting to build in my shoulders.

6. Describe what happened

It was strange because I kind of got into the music and started thinking about going out with Corrie later, so by the time I got home the driver cutting in on me was pretty much gone from my mind. I was really surprised at how well it went. Looking back on my day it had been really quite positive: the sales figures for this month were released and they were the best they'd been in six months so I'd left in a good mood. On Monday, someone else cut in on me but this time I deliberately didn't try to control my anger. I just let it go. I was still fuming by the time I got home. The best part of it was I had two similar incidents that happened reasonably close together so I could compare my reactions. I didn't expect there to be such a marked difference in the way I felt on the two occasions.

7. Re-rate your conviction

If I just let someone cut in without reacting then I'll end up being furious for hours and just won't be able to let it go. Strength of conviction: 65 per cent.

8. Revised thought/belief/behaviour that can be tested

My conviction in the original thought probably hasn't shifted as much as I would like because I was in such a good mood on the Friday, and I'm not sure how much influence that had on the outcome. I might not be so successful if it was a normal day or I'd had a bad day at the office. I think I need to do this a few more times before I can draw any firm conclusions. I aim to not react the next five times an incident like this happens, and I will take stock then. Meanwhile I will continue practising my relaxation techniques because I think they might have helped a bit too.

Table 18.5: Acting 'as if': Penny

Penny has problems with self-confidence and low self-esteem. She is dissatisfied with a number of aspects of her life and decided that one of the areas that she will work on is becoming more confident when doing things by herself. She is therefore going to try an acting 'as if' experiment where she is going to go to a café and shopping on her own and act as if she is confident about herself.

1. <u>Thought</u>/belief/behaviour to be tested and strength of conviction

If I act like I am self-confident it won't make any difference to how I feel inside. Strength of conviction: 90 per cent.

2. Ideas for experiment to test the thought/belief/behaviour. Circle the best one

Go for a coffee on my own to the local café and act confidently despite being by myself.

<u>Go to the shops acting very confident when I pay for shopping – chatting, etc. – and rate how I feel inside. Do the same things again acting very unconfident and rate my feelings.</u>

3. Specific predictions about what will happen and how you will record the outcome:

If I act as if I am confident I will not feel like myself. People won't find it believable. It won't make me feel any better.

I will record my level of discomfort while doing it; I will also make notes about how people respond and rate my mood before and after.

4. Anticipated problems and potential solutions

Potential problem: I have a confidence crisis and don't follow through.

Possible solution: This is a possibility but if I choose the right time I should be able to go for it. I can go early on Saturday morning before it gets too busy. If I don't follow through then I need to reschedule for another time and try again.

5. Describe the experiment you carried out

I went to three shops in total. I was really nervous in the first one but tried to act confident and chatted a bit to the woman serving me, who was really friendly and commented on the top I was buying. That went well, so I felt more confident going into the next shop. The second shop was a bit busier so the sales assistant didn't have much time to chat, but she was friendly enough. The next shop I went in I bought a lipstick but went to the counter in a really unconfident way. I rated how I felt inside all three times, my level of discomfort and how people reacted to me in the behavioural experiments worksheet.

6. Describe what happened

I was anxious in the first shop but it gave me a buzz when I came out. The second one felt better and I felt really good. In the third shop I didn't feel good at all and people reacted differently. In the first two shops the assistants were really responsive and friendly whereas I don't know what the third one looked like as I didn't even look at her. I was surprised at how acting as if I was confident did make a difference to how I felt and how other people responded to me. My initial discomfort wasn't as bad as I thought it would be. Also my mood ratings were better after the first two times, but not the third. They were 6, 6 and 4.

7. Re-rate your conviction

If I act like I am self-confident it won't make any difference to how I feel inside. Strength of conviction: 40 per cent.

8. Revised thought/belief/behaviour that can be tested

What I think I've learned is that changing what I did changed how I felt, as well as how others behaved towards me. Although acting as if I'm self-confident seemed to make a difference in this situation, I think I would need to try it in other situations to be really convinced that it works. Perhaps I shall try going into the café next.

Surveys: Designing your own observational behavioural experiment

These can be very helpful in obtaining information about what other people may think or experience, or how other people react. A great deal of low mood, depression, stress, anxiety, anger and low self-esteem results from assumptions about how others view us. Finding out what someone else thinks can be tricky, but conducting an anonymous survey is often a good option.

Surveys are designed to gather information about what people think and how they behave. To help, they have to be highly personalized and therefore relevant to the uniqueness of your own difficulties. In fact, no two surveys are ever quite the same. Surveys can be used to find out what people might do or think in particular situations, and can be used to gain information about the extent of particular behaviours in other people. Take Hannah in case illustration 8, who has low self-esteem. To try to compensate for her view of herself as a bad, worthless person, she set herself very high standards for achievement and success. Over time, she lost sight of what normal standards for achievement and success were. Read her story below to see how she used this strategy to help tackle her problems.

Case illustration 8: Hannah

Hannah is a forty-three-year-old mother of four. People joked that she was 'obsessional' about her house and indeed she was very house-proud. She had raised her children not to make a mess, to take toys out one at a time and to put their toys away immediately after playing with them. She ironed all the children's clothes and her own clothes, bed sheets, underwear, towels and sports clothes. Needless to say, ironing took up a great deal of her time but she enjoyed seeing her children looking neatly presented. She believed that there was 'a place for everything and everything in its place'. She had functioned well like this for many years but she was too tired in the evening to give her partner much time or attention. Their relationship was under stress and she had no interest in intimacy. She was unable to entertain friends in the house or allow her children to have friends over because of the amount of work it would entail for her to tidy up. Her sister complained that she could not relax when she came to visit out of fear of putting something away in the wrong place. Hannah recognized that her need for orderliness and tidiness in the home was above the norm but she believed that it was only slightly greater than that of other people. She also believed that most people thought that she was in control of her life because of her tidy home and the appearance of her children, and she valued this.

Hannah's best friend suggested that perhaps most people do not actually iron their underwear or bed sheets, and that actually many people would think she was out of control due to her excessive need for tidiness. They agreed that together they would construct a survey to find out what other people did in terms of ironing and what they thought of people (not specifically Hannah) who had a tidy home and appearance.

The results of the survey of eight of their friends were surprising to both Hannah and her best friend. Three out of eight of

Hannah's friends did actually iron their underwear and two of the eight ironed bed sheets. Two of the eight said that an extremely tidy home and appearance led them to think that the person 'had nothing better to do' or should 'get a life'; four out of eight said that they did not think anything in particular about whether someone was in control of their life or not because they had a tidy home and appearance; and two out of eight said that they thought a tidy home and appearance meant the person was organized.

Discussing these results, it became clear that there was a range of reactions. It was common among Hannah's friends to iron underwear but not bed sheets and this was interesting information for Hannah about what was reasonable and what was perhaps not. The range of reactions to someone who was excessively tidy led Hannah to re-evaluate some of her motivation for tidiness and need for tidiness and control, irrespective of what other people think.

Survey examples

Think back to the suggestion on p. 21 that particular emotions are linked to particular thoughts (for example, that feelings of anger are associated with a sense of injustice and unfairness, feelings of anxiety are linked to perceived danger, and feeling low and depressed is commonly associated with loss). Surveys can provide a kind of 'reality check' by helping us find out not just how people behave but also how they think and feel and the links between all three.

Surveys can also help us discover that people's reactions often vary – and that can lead to us trying out a new way of behaving (see 'active experiments', later in this chapter). For example, the results of Hannah's survey gave her the confidence to stop ironing her bed sheets. In Table 18.6 there are some examples of surveys designed to gauge a variety of emotional reactions and their associated thoughts and behaviours:

Table 18.6: Example surveys

Emotional reaction	Question 1	Question 2	Question 3	Question 4
Anger	When someone does something that makes you angry what do you think?	How angry does it make you?	How long do you feel angry for?	How do you control your anger?
Anxiety	How often do you feel anxious and how intense is it?	What situations make you anxious?	What happens to your body when you feel anxious?	How do you manage your anxiety?
Low mood/depression	How often do you feel very low?	What do you do when you feel low e.g. do you go to bed? Why do you do this?	Do you criticize yourself for feeling low? Please explain your answer.	What are the best ways you have found to manage your mood when you feel low?
Stress	What makes you stressed?	How often do you shout when you are stressed?	Does shouting make you feel guilty?	What are your top tips for managing stress?
Low self-esteem	What do you think of people who refuse to take a compliment?	What do you think of boastful people?	If someone works very hard at work, what do you think of them?	What kinds of things make you criticize yourself?

What to do with the information from surveys

You may have information from any number of people. Three people is probably the minimum to be useful and ten is really the maximum that can be obtained without too much work, depending on whether you are using email or conducting the survey in person. Here's what to do once you have carried out your survey:

1. Collect the responses

Having constructed your survey, you need to collect the responses. Depending on your type of survey, you will have information about what other people think and do, and how they manage particular situations. If you can, create a summary table or graph to make the information that you've collected as clear as possible.

2. Analyse the responses

The responses to the survey are likely to contain some surprises. It may be, for example, that most people feel fleeting anger when someone does something that irritates them, but that they soon start thinking about something else (such as the football results or what is for dinner). They may manage their anger by telling themselves that 'the world is full of idiots like that', or they may count to ten to calm themselves down. What you usually find is a *range* of responses. Some people will get very angry and some will not give matters a second thought. Some have complex ways of managing anger and others distract themselves until the anger passes.

Surveys help to check reality and can directly challenge all-or-nothing thinking. They often lead on to more active behavioural experiments.

Reality check

The survey is a 'reality' check on how other people think and behave. You now know what is 'normal' and what other people think and do in situations that for you are causing low mood, anger, low self-esteem, anxiety or stress. Now that you have this information about other people's thoughts, emotions and behaviours, you may be better able to re-evaluate your own reaction.

All-or-nothing thinking

What often emerges from a survey is that there is no consensus, no 'right and wrong' and that the answers are not 'all-or-nothing'. Some people think one way and others think another. Some believe that a particular behaviour is necessary for success while others do not. The range of responses should help show that beliefs, behaviour and life itself are complicated, and that rather than there being a right and wrong way, there is a middle ground.

Active behavioural experiments

The information from the survey will, we hope, inspire you to reassess your interpretations of particular situations. For example, your survey may have indicated that people often manage their anxiety by talking to a friend. You may have been reluctant to talk to a friend for fear that you will be a burden or boring. Despite the survey results, you may still doubt whether talking to a friend is helpful or whether they will think badly of you. However, the key to changing beliefs is to gather as much evidence as possible about the reality using a variety of methods, so this may mean moving on to a more active behavioural experiment (i.e. trying out talking to a friend). That way, the old beliefs and behaviours can become unsustainable and a new, more realistic perspective can take root.

Active behavioural experiments

Now we're going to describe a number of active behavioural experiments that can be adapted for all sorts of psychological problems. These experiments typically involve testing thoughts and interpretations by trying out a new way of behaving.

Let's take the example of someone with low mood and anxiety. People with these problems often fear making a mistake and so they tend to check their behaviour repeatedly (the case example of Jeff helps demonstrate this point). They are also checking to make sure they come across to others well, and that they do not look stupid. The first experiment addresses this problem.

Active behavioural experiment to address checking

Case illustration 9 is taken from the self-help guide *Overcoming Perfectionism*, which you can find listed in the Bibliography at the end of the book.

Case illustration 9: Jeff

Jeff was an attractive, friendly and sociable twenty-nine-year-old plumber in a long-term relationship with his girlfriend. He worked for a small plumbing company and was the most senior of the three plumbers that his company employed. He had been with the company since its beginning and was very motivated to make the business a success. He worked extremely hard, and covered the shifts that the other two plumbers did not want (Saturday nights, evenings, weekends). He felt it was his responsibility to cover these shifts as he was the most senior of the three. He also dealt with the financial side of his plumbing work (billing customers and processing their payments, etc.). At the time of deciding to work on his problems he was extremely agitated about the possibility of having given a customer the wrong change. He had contacted the customer, who had told him not to worry (the sum was minimal), but Jeff could not get out of his mind the fact that he had made a mistake over something as important as returning change to a customer. He replayed the scene of handing over the change again and again, trying to focus on the coins to check whether he was providing the wrong amount. He also replayed the conversation with the customer again and again in his mind, trying to detect whether the customer was genuine when he said 'not to worry' or if the customer's tone implied that he thought that Jeff was a criminal and had taken the money on purpose.

Since this incident, Jeff had repeatedly checked all aspects of his plumbing work – in particular that taps are closed. He had begun to phone clients to check that all was OK with both the plumbing and financial arrangements on the pretext of conducting 'customer service'. He would then replay those conversations in his mind in an attempt to detect whether or not his customers were being polite when something really was wrong, or if they were being genuine. His greatest difficulty, however, was with processing the invoices at the end of every job. He checked his calculations, the invoices, and the processing of finances to such an extent that it was adding an extra thirty minutes to each job he completed, which frustrated his customers. He feared he was jeopardizing the business and that it would close because of his checking behaviour.

Jeff's checking involved both his actions (repeatedly checking taps, repeatedly checking his calculations) and his thoughts (replaying the scene). Both of these aspects of checking are common in people with anxiety problems. For people with anxiety in social situations (commonly referred to as social anxiety disorder or social phobia), repeatedly going over a social event is known as a 'post-mortem' or 'post-event processing'. This type of checking can cause a great deal of agitation. For Jeff, checking was having real consequences for his customers (who were having to wait while he checked his monetary calculations at the end of each job). These consequences were then being catastrophized by Jeff, who felt as though the entire business would be jeopardized. It is worth bearing in mind that Jeff was working extremely hard – evenings and weekends – and had very little time off. Being so tired makes it harder to dismiss concerns and worries, and thoughts seem to 'take hold'.

Why was Jeff checking? The answer seems obvious: to make sure he was not making mistakes. However, recent research suggests that repeated checking of this nature does not actually prevent mistakes from being made, nor does it improve memory. What actually happens when you check repeatedly is that it *decreases your confidence* in your memory. In other words, the more you check, the more uncertain you become. Jeff didn't quite believe this so decided to conduct a behavioural experiment to test his belief that repeatedly checking helps him remember.

Jeff's completed behavioural experiment to test the belief that repeated checking helps memory and helps reduce anxiety and worry can be found in Table 18.7.

Table 18.7: Jeff's behavioural experiment

Prediction

If I repeatedly check my calculations, I won't worry so much afterwards and will feel more certain I haven't short-changed someone than if I only check my calculations once.

Experiment

Day 1: Repeatedly check calculations as usual (or even more frequently).

Make note of worry level immediately after checking (0 = no worry, 10 = extreme worry); make note again one hour later.

Make note of certainty that I haven't short-changed someone immediately after checking (0 = not certain; 5 = middle level of certainty; 10 = certain); note again one hour later.

Day 2: Check calculations only once (make same notes as detailed above).

Day 3: Repeatedly check calculations as usual (or even more). Make same notes as those detailed for Day 1.

Day 4: Check calculations only once. Make same notes as those detailed for Day 1.

Day 5: Repeatedly check calculations as usual (or even more). Make same notes as those detailed for Day 1.

Day 6: Check calculations only once. Make same notes as those detailed for Day 1.

Day 7: Review information gathered over previous six days

Results of Jeff's completed experiment

Check repeatedly

	Worry immediately afterwards	Worry after 1 hour	Certainty immediately afterwards	Certainty after 2 hours
Day 1	8	7	1	2
Day 3	9	8	2	1
Day 5	8	7	1	1

Check repeatedly

	Worry immediately afterwards	Worry after 1 hour	Certainty immediately afterwards	Certainty after 2 hours
Day 2	4	4	9	8
Day 4	4	2	9	9
Day 6	4	1	8	9

Interpreting Jeff's results

On the days that Jeff checked repeatedly, his worry levels were high (8 and 9). One hour later, the worry had come down a little, but was still high (7 and 8). On these days, he was really uncertain (1 and 2) whether he had short-changed someone and after one hour he was still unsure. At these times he had a strong urge to phone the customer to check that everything was OK.

On the days that he checked only once, contrary to his predictions, his worry was much lower (4) and one hour later on days four and six had decreased even further. Another real surprise was that he was much more certain (8 and 9) that he had not short-changed anyone on the days when he checked his calculations once, and his certainty remained strong one hour later. He had no urges on these days to call the customer, and he therefore didn't have additional conversations to 'check' in his head

Other checking experiments

Jeff carried out many other checking experiments. He tested his belief that checking conversations in his head made him feel better than not checking, and that phoning clients left him feeling more certain that he had not made a mistake. He did this by comparing how anxious and how certain he felt when checking conversations in his head to how he felt when not checking them, and when phoning clients compared to not phoning them. Jeff discovered that excessive checking was leading to him becoming more uncertain about his decision-making and experiencing greater anxiety as a result. Making this discovery helped Jeff feel more confident about reducing some of his checking.

Active behavioural experiment to address avoidance

Follow this next case illustration to see an example of a behavioural experiment being used to tackle avoidance.

Case illustration 10: Callie

Callie was a thirty-eight-year-old woman working in Human Resources in a university. She had not intended to work in Human Resources but had instead wanted to be an author, after graduating with a first class degree in English. She had actually written most of a novel, which was almost complete. She had shown drafts of it to friends and family who were universal in their praise, and she had contacted a publishing agent in the past, who told her to send a draft when it was finished. The publishing agent had said this approximately five years ago and although Callie had done a little more work on it since then, she had not quite been able to complete it. She had not looked at it for the last three years, although she thought about the ending every day. Her family felt this was a terrible waste of her potential. She agreed, but was unable to articulate why she could not complete the book. Some aspect of her avoidance was a fear that the book would be rejected by the publishers, although she acknowledged that this happened all the time to other people. Another aspect was that she could not find an ending that 'felt right' and that all the endings in her head (and some attempts on paper) felt inadequate. She felt that she was a failure and pathetic for being unable to complete the book and send it off to the agent.

Callie's completed active experiments to address avoidance

Prediction

Callie had various predictions that could be tested using behavioural experiments. The first was that no ending she could write would 'feel right'. Related to this, she predicted that the feeling

---

of it 'not being right' would prey on her mind for a long time, causing distress. The third was that her book would be rejected.

Experiments

Callie conducted a series of behavioural experiments in order to help her build up to being able to complete her book and then test the prediction that her book would be rejected.

Callie's first experiments focused on the issue of 'not feeling right'. This feeling wasn't just restricted to the book but occurred in a variety of situations. She often felt that the reports she submitted at work weren't right and she avoided doing them until the very last minute.

For her first experiment, she completed two reports. One was completed at the very last minute despite her feeling that it wasn't right. The other was completed ahead of time. She had predicted that if she submitted the form earlier, then her discomfort at it not being right would last longer than if she submitted it at the last minute. In actual fact, when she submitted the report ahead of time, she felt a sense of achievement at it not being rushed. Moreover, she didn't think it was either more or less right than the report she submitted right at the deadline. She learned from this that submitting the report ahead of time didn't influence the feelings of 'not rightness' but that it did give her a sense of achievement. It also reduced her worry because she found that the report wasn't hanging over her head.

Callie conducted further behavioural experiments to find out what influenced her feelings about her work being 'not right'. Did tiredness, mood or circumstances influence this feeling? She predicted that the feeling would remain constant all day. Then she conducted an experiment to see how long it actually did last. The behavioural experiment she conducted to test her feeling here was very simple: she simply monitored her feelings of 'not rightness' and found that it waxed and waned throughout the day depending on what she was doing. After doing more than six experiments (submitting reports completed ahead of time and at the last minute, when she was tired and in various mood states including when she was feeling down, when she was irritated, when she was anxious), she agreed to write a single ending for the book, despite acknowledging that it wouldn't be 'right'.

She sent it off to the publishing agent and it was rejected with little explanation, but Callie was remarkably resilient, saying that she felt she now had the capacity to finish the book. The experiments had helped build Callie's confidence in the work she produced and her ability to cope when she experienced feelings that it was not quite 'right'. Although she had known rationally that avoidance was not helping, it was her personal experience of conducting very small, specific behavioural experiments that helped her to overcome it.

Designing your own active behavioural experiment

By this stage, and by completing your Thought Diary, you will have gathered information that calls into question some of the ways that you have interpreted particular situations. You will have been able to weigh up the evidence for and against your interpretations, and have perhaps arrived at a new perspective. You will have learned that some of your previous interpretations might not be true, and the surveys will have provided you with valuable information about the way that the world works in reality and what other people think. Using active behavioural experiments, it's now time to test whether your 'helpful' behaviours are actually causing more problems than they solve.

See Table 18.8 for some examples of common thoughts/predictions with example behavioural experiments to get you started:

Now use the Behavioural Experiment Worksheet in Table 18.9 and the thoughts you identified using your nine-column thought diary (p. 250) to design your own active behavioural experiment.

Table 18.8: Example predictions and behavioural experiments

Thought/prediction	Experiment
Thought: I can't face the world. **Prediction:** I will just sit around moping all day if I don't stay in bed (100 per cent belief) and will feel lousy (100 per cent belief).	One day stay in bed all day and rate your mood and what you did that day. The next day force yourself to get dressed even if it's just in a tracksuit and rate your mood and your activities that day. Is the outcome as you predicted?
Thought: I need to ward off bad luck. **Prediction:** If I don't bring my lucky mascot with me, I will be really worried all day (90 per cent belief) and something bad will happen like a panic attack (80 per cent belief).	Deliberately leave your lucky mascot behind when you are popping to the local shops. Is the outcome as you predicted? Build up to testing the prediction in more meaningful/important situations such as going longer distances and/or out for longer periods of time.
Thought: If I let people see the real me, they won't want to be friends with me. **Prediction:** If I say what I think in a discussion, people will not be interested (100 per cent) and won't ask me out again socially (40 per cent).	Express your own views in a discussion with friends or colleagues. Is the outcome as you predicted?
Thought: If I don't assert myself, people will walk all over me. **Prediction:** If I calmly say to someone why I think their behaviour is unfair, they won't listen (90 per cent). If I yell at them, then they will take notice (95 per cent).	Contrast calmly telling someone why you think they are being unfair with yelling at someone. Which one is more effective in making the person take notice?

Table 18.9: Behavioural Experiment Worksheet

1. Thought/belief/behaviour to be tested and strength of conviction
2. Ideas for experiment to test the thought/belief/behaviour. Circle the best one
3. Specific predictions about what will happen and how you will record the outcome
4. Anticipated problems and potential solutions
5. Describe the experiment you carried out
6. Describe what happened
7. Re-rate your conviction
8. Revised thought/belief/behaviour that can be tested

Summary

In the space below, write down some of the things you found most important in this chapter so that you have a reference guide you can refer to later. What was surprising? Was anything particularly reassuring?

1. _____

   _____

2. _____

   _____

3. _____

   _____

4. _____

   _____

19 The bigger picture

Before we begin ...

Start the chapter by rating your current mood on the mood scale in Figure 19.1.

-5	-4	-3	-2	-1	0	+1	+2	+3	+4	+5

Negative mood	Neutral	Positive mood

Figure 19.1: Mood scale

If you are returning to this book after a break of a few days or more, take a moment to record your mood and anxiety (and whatever else you are recording, such as worry, anger, stress and self-esteem) and plot them on the graphs on pp. 420–39. Keeping track of your mood can help you review progress. Have there been any changes? If so, why do you think that might be? If not, can you think of any reasons?

It may also be helpful to review your problem statements (see Chapter 10, p. 135) and, re-rate those using the 0–100 problem-severity scale. Have there been any changes? Finally, review your SMART goals (see Chapter 10, p. 139) and make a note of any progress that you have made towards reaching them.

So far, we have concentrated on understanding your difficulties in the 'here and now', focusing on tried-and-tested strategies that can make a positive difference straight away. In this chapter we will take a look at the bigger picture. In particular, we will analyse where the problems come from and why they've continued.

Why is looking at the bigger picture useful?

Being aware of the bigger picture can help focus your attention on your most relevant problem areas. It helps you to stand back and look at your difficulties as a whole within your life context. It can shed light on why some techniques to combat those problems may be more useful than others. Moreover, it can also help explain why things are not going so well with certain techniques and even predict potential obstacles. Finally, an accurate sense of the bigger picture will make it easier to identify how and when the problem started and, crucially, what is keeping it going.

So far we have looked at the symptoms that you experience and how to tackle them. This is the most important aspect to changing how you are feeling. However, this may not necessarily help you understand the factors underlying *why* you are feeling the way you are. To illustrate this distinction, let's consider a scenario.

Suppose your car will not start. The direct effects of your car not starting will be all sorts of problems such as being late for work or meeting up with friends. These problems represent the 'here and now' of your car not starting. If you take the car to the garage the mechanic may be able to jump-start the car and get it running again right away and you may never experience any further difficulties with it. However, you might feel more confident that the problem would not come back if you looked into the problem a bit further. It would be useful for the mechanic to lift up the bonnet and inspect a little closer in order to find out the real cause of the problem and why it is persisting.

The same principle applies to our own problems. It is important to be able to address the problem in the present and to feel better quickly, but it is also important to look at what is behind the problem so that you can put measures in place to reduce the chances of it coming back again. That is what this chapter is about. Using the analogy of the car, it might be that the root of the problem of the car not starting is a manufacturing issue. In that case, the mechanic may be able to fix certain components and thereby reduce the chances of the problem recurring, but they won't be able to change the actual origins of the manufacturing mistake. Similarly, you may be able to look back at your early life experiences, which you obviously cannot change. However, some of the beliefs about yourself and the world around you that come from those life experiences may be holding you back, and you can certainly work on changing those.

It may be relatively easy to jump-start a car, but it is likely to take more time to get to the root of the vehicle's problem and to tackle the various bits of wiring under the bonnet. Likewise, you may be finding that your own problems are responding well to the techniques you have learned to apply throughout this book, but it might take a bit more delving into your background and beliefs, and how they interconnect with your current symptoms, to make sense of why you have been feeling the way you have.

Remember Leon, who was depressed after his best friend and girlfriend got together behind his back? His symptoms improved rapidly when he tried behavioural activation strategies (see Chapter 11) and when he focused on his thoughts, identifying the unhelpful ones and then evaluating them and coming up with more realistic alternatives (Chapters 15–17). However, without taking the time to look at his relevant experiences and beliefs, he remains vulnerable to depression. Leon's father left home when he was eight years old, long before his best friend and girlfriend got together. He believes that if he puts his trust in others they will let him down. This is an understandable belief in the context of his life experiences and goes a long way towards explaining why he is depressed. It will be important for Leon to address this unhelpful belief in order to ensure that he does not shy away from letting new people into his life. In the next chapter we will describe some of the strategies that Leon can use to address his unhelpful beliefs.

Assumptions, attitudes and beliefs

By now, you're used to identifying and evaluating your negative automatic thoughts. Cast your mind back to the café example in Chapter 15, when we looked at possible thoughts (interpretations) and their role in our emotions, bodily sensations and behaviours. It soon became clear that one situation (i.e, waiting for a friend to arrive) could be interpreted in lots of different ways. How one person makes sense of an event can often be very different to how another individual sees the same event. These interpretations matter, because they influence how we feel (emotions and bodily sensations) and how we behave. And the more we believe our interpretation, the stronger our emotional reaction to the situation is likely to be.

But *why* do people interpret the same situation differently?

The answer lies in our assumptions, attitudes and beliefs. These beliefs are formed from our early experiences but are also supplemented by later life experiences. For example, Ash's beliefs about safety changed when he had his bike accident. Not all of our attitudes and beliefs are bad or unhelpful. They can also be building blocks to help us make sense of the world.

Based on the experiences we have in early life, we develop core beliefs and attitudes about ourselves, others and our world. Three main themes characterize these beliefs:

1. Achievement – the need to succeed.

2. Acceptance – the need to be liked.

3. Control – the need to feel in command of a situation and oneself.

Despite these overarching themes, each person's beliefs will be unique. Once activated, having been triggered by what we call a 'critical incident', these beliefs lead to related automatic thoughts. For instance, someone who believes that they are a failure may have this belief activated by failing a driving test. Once the belief is activated, they will have even more thoughts of failure in different circumstances.

In order to start developing the 'bigger picture' of your difficulties, we need to look at some of the attitudes, assumptions and beliefs that might be underpinning your negative automatic thoughts. We are particularly interested in attitudes and assumptions which are those expressed using 'if … then …' and 'should'. For example: '*If* I am in control of everything around me *then* nothing bad will happen', '*If* I let people know the real me *then* they won't like me', 'I *should* always put others first', 'I *should* always strive for the best'.

Working at this level will help you to become less vulnerable to the problem you are experiencing. This will not necessarily be a quick process, but it's likely to be worth the effort as it can make a big difference to your overall understanding of your difficulties. Remember, your beliefs are likely to have been around for a long time and are therefore probably strongly held.

As well as being rigid, beliefs can sometimes be quite extreme. In the past they have probably been very useful, and because of that they can be difficult to disregard. For example, imagine a child growing up amongst siblings with parents who reward academic achievement with affection and favour the child who produces the best academic results. The child may develop the attitude: 'If I am not the best at everything I do then I am unlovable.' This attitude may have served that child well in childhood as he worked hard at school and was therefore able to gain affection from his parents. As an adult, however, it may have been less helpful to continue to live by this rule: colleagues may find it difficult to work with someone so fiercely competitive and friends may get frustrated with such a serious, win-at-all-costs attitude.

Long-standing beliefs and attitudes can get in the way of us functioning at our optimum level and can be difficult to change through normal day-to-day life. This is primarily because we tend to live by our beliefs as if they were facts, and never really stop to question them. When the conditions of the belief are not met, we often feel distressed. For example, if a person believes it is important to be liked by everyone, it is probably going to be distressing to discover that someone does not like them. Likewise, if a person who believes that they must succeed at everything finds themselves faced with failure of some kind, whether perceived or real, this is likely to cause enormous upset. To gain an understanding of our problems, it can be helpful to try to identify the beliefs that underpin them.

The diagram in Figure 19.2 portrays the CBT approach to how core beliefs (I am/others are/the world is), attitudes (if … then … statements) and thoughts (the automatic ideas and images that pop into mind throughout the day) fit together.

Figure 19.2: How beliefs, attitudes and thoughts are interconnected

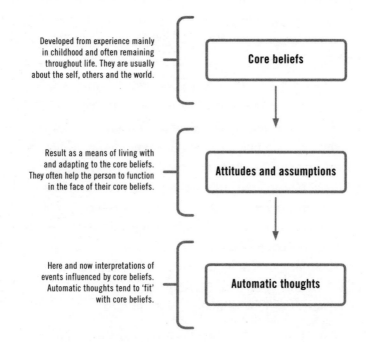

In Figure 19.3 see how these beliefs, attitudes and thoughts fit in the context of a given situation and the impact (reaction).

Figure 19.3: How beliefs, attitudes and thoughts fit in the context of a situation and their impact

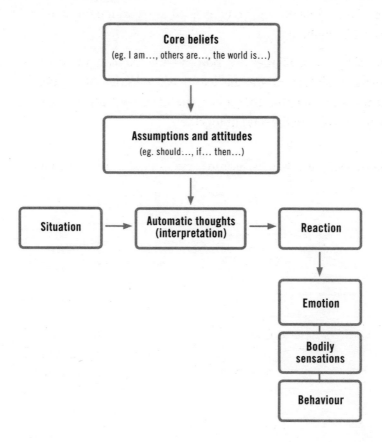

In Figure 19.4 we have provided an example of how these various levels of cognition fit together using an example of someone with a personal belief of being unloveable.

Figure 19.4: Example of how 'I'm unloveable' may be interconnected to attitudes, thoughts and other reactions

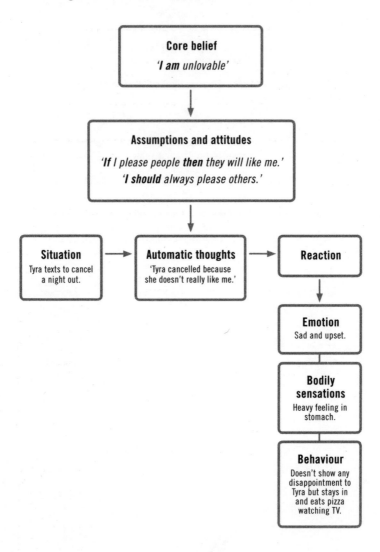

In Figure 19.5 you will see an example of how the various levels of cognition fit together using an example of someone with a personal belief of being vulnerable.

Figure 19.5: Example of how 'I'm vulnerable' may be interconnected to attitudes, thoughts and other reactions

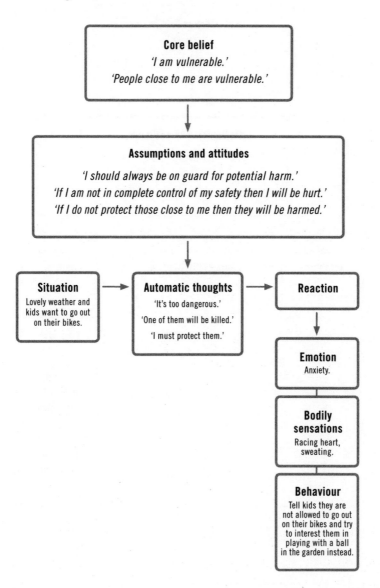

Now try this for yourself in Figure 19.6. Think of a recent time when you were upset, or use a thought from a recent thought diary. You may find it easier to work backwards (i.e. start with the bottom section and move up).

Figure 19.6: How my beliefs, attitudes and thoughts are connected

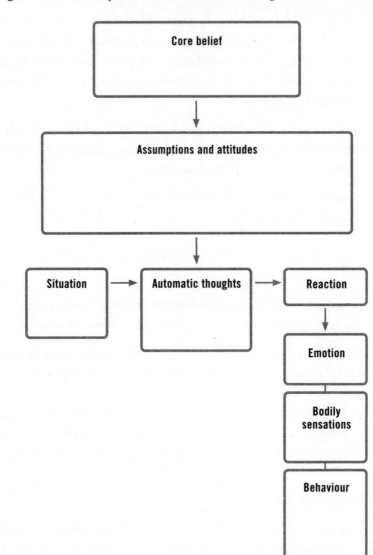

Troubleshooting: Identifying underlying attitudes and beliefs

It is not always easy to work out which attitudes and beliefs underpin our thoughts.

The downward arrow technique

Rather than evaluate your thoughts using the techniques learned in Chapter 17, stay with the negative automatic thought and the emotions that it conjures up. Our main focus is going to be on the thought, though, rather than the feelings. This will help you to examine the attitudes and beliefs that might be behind it.

We are going to use the 'downward arrow technique' – which will help you identify the attitudes and beliefs lurking behind your negative automatic thoughts.

Here are a few questions to ask yourself when you have a negative thought, using the downward arrow technique:

- If you are looking for underlying beliefs about **yourself** you could ask: 'If my thought were true, what does this say about me?'

- If you are looking for your underlying beliefs about **others** you could ask: 'If that were true, what does this say about other people?'

- If you are looking for your underlying beliefs about the **world** you could ask: 'If that were true, what does this say about the world?'

Remember to be careful not to ask 'feeling' questions (e.g. 'how does that make me feel?'), as this will take you off into a different direction – the emotion attached to the thought rather than the underlying belief.

Reread your Thought Diaries

Another strategy you can use to identify your attitudes and beliefs is to look over your Thought Diaries for common themes. For example, Leah found that she had lots of thoughts like 'I can't do this', 'I'm making a mess of this', 'I'll never get this piece of work finished', 'I'll never get it right', 'I'm no good at this'. She noticed that though these thoughts mainly occurred at work, they also happened while she was writing the actual Thought Diaries themselves. Until she reviewed the diaries together she was unaware of any recurring themes. By reviewing her diaries she realized that her core belief about herself was 'I am incompetent'. She expressed this belief as the following assumption: '*If* I don't do everything perfectly *then* it shows I am incompetent'.

Thinking back to your childhood

When Bea was first trying to make sense of her difficulties, she found it useful to think back to her childhood, which is when many of her assumptions and attitudes were first formed. She has very clear memories of the strict family rules she was brought up with. Thinking back, she realized that her current beliefs reflect these rules. For instance, she remembers her mother telling her that it was always best to think the worst of any situation, as any improvement would then be a bonus. If you think this technique might be helpful for you, then ask yourself the following question: 'Does this situation or my reaction to it remind me of anything from my past?'

Building a bigger picture

Attitudes and beliefs play an important part in establishing the bigger picture. Our early life experiences can often lead to the beliefs and attitudes that we end up living our lives by. These beliefs and attitudes can leave us vulnerable to psychological problems, though they may lie dormant until triggered by a specific situation. For instance, a person with a core belief that they are unlovable may not be aware of this belief unless it is triggered by something relevant, say a relationship break-up. It is important to learn how to make rigid beliefs more flexible, otherwise we may remain susceptible to such problems as anxiety, depression or stress.

While it is generally unnecessary to work at core belief level for common emotional problems such as depression, anxiety and stress, this work is often central for people with long-term complex difficulties such as personality disorder. Merely identifying core beliefs in the context of the bigger picture is mostly all that is required with common emotional problems such as depression, anxiety and stress. Core beliefs, attitudes and assumptions are often unproblematic and can lie dormant until

activated by an upsetting and unpleasant event (we call this type of incident a 'critical incident' in CBT). This event will activate the beliefs and
assumption causing the person distress.

What information do you need to build a bigger picture?

Answering the following questions will help you gather the information
you need to build a better understanding of your difficulties, why they
are affecting you now and what is keeping them going.

1. What symptoms do you have (e.g. emotions, thoughts, bodily
   sensations and behaviours)?

2. What triggered the start of your current problems (e.g. Ash's
   bike accident)?

3. What factors might predispose you to developing problems (e.g.
   Pearl has a family history of depression and had experienced
   two previous episodes)?

4. What significant life events have you experienced (e.g. Bea's
   father was fatally injured in an accident at work when she was
   eight)?

5. What are the common themes of your thoughts (e.g. Dez's
   thoughts centre around fairness and entitlement)?

6. What rules, assumptions, attitudes and beliefs do you live
   by (e.g. Penny grew up believing that if she is nice to other
   people they will be nice back and that she should always put
   other people's needs before her own)?

Use this information to put together your own 'bigger picture'. For an
example of a completed 'bigger picture' see Bea's in Figure 19.7.

Example of bigger picture diagram

People often find it helpful to represent their bigger picture using a diagram. Here's an example of how a 'bigger picture' can be illustrated.

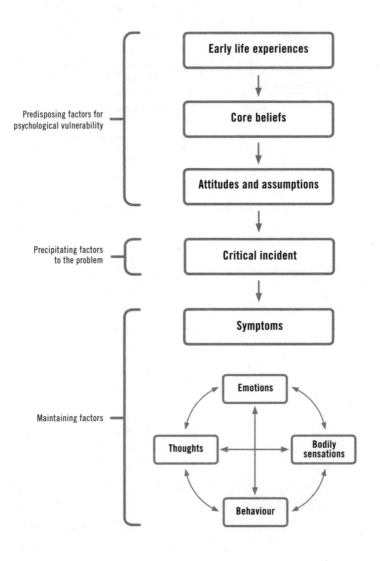

Figure 19.7: Bea's bigger picture diagram

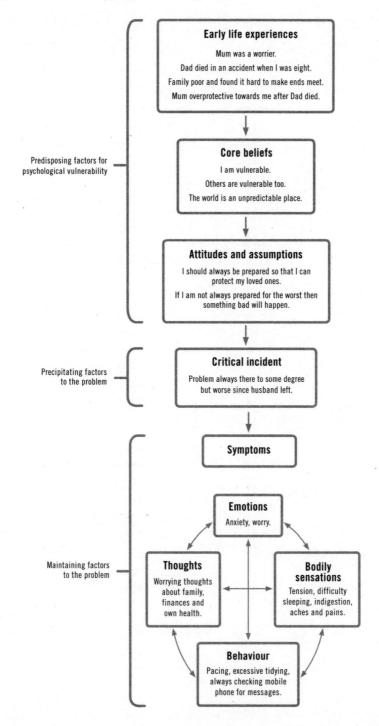

My bigger picture diagram

Now try completing the blank diagram in Figure 19.8. Don't worry if you can't finish it all in one go. It can often take a number of attempts to develop a greater understanding of a given problem. Once you have finished your first attempt, ask yourself the questions in Table 19.1 to see how good a fit your diagram is.

Figure 19.8: My bigger picture diagram

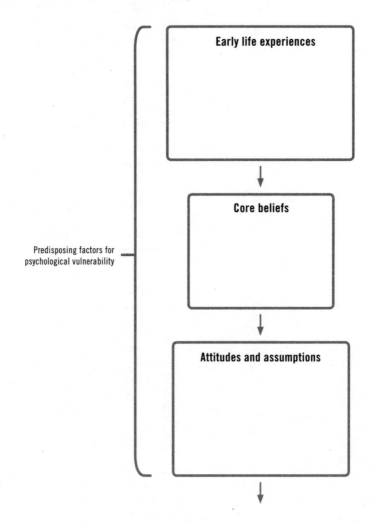

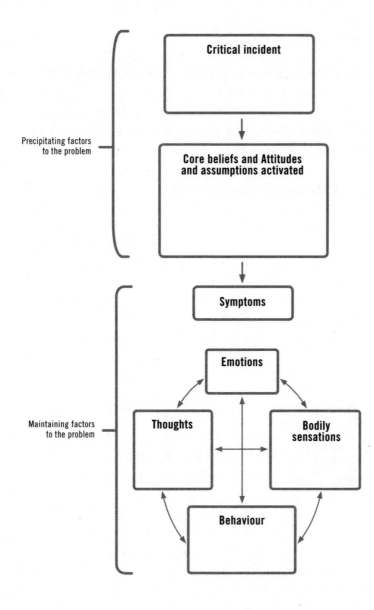

Table 19.1: My bigger picture questionnaire

1. Does the information in your diagram and the links you have made make sense to you?
2. Do any of your early life experiences explain why you might form your core beliefs?
3. Can you see how your attitudes and assumptions were formed?
4. Does the critical incident you have identified make sense in the light of your early experiences, beliefs and attitudes?
5. Do your symptoms fit with the rest of the bigger picture (i.e. do they make sense given the information you have inserted)?

6. *Do you agree with what you see in your bigger picture diagram, or do you have reservations?*

7. *Can you use this bigger picture to guide you to particular treatment strategies? For instance, if one of your symptoms is that you find it difficult to get started, then you might try out some of the behavioural activation strategies, or if a recurring theme is worrying, you might want to focus further on problem-solving strategies.*

8. *Does it help you predict how you might respond to the various treatment strategies and what obstacles might get in the way?*

9. *Are there important issues or symptoms that are left unexplained?*

10. *Can you use your bigger picture to pinpoint potential future difficulties?*

You might find Bea's answers in Table 19.2 helpful in thinking about your own answers.

Table 19.2: Bea's bigger picture questionnaire

1. Does your diagram make sense?   Yes, I can see how each area links to the next.
2. Do any of your early life experiences explain why you would form your core beliefs?   Yes, I think so. My dad dying when I was young and coming from a family of worriers led to me having a sense that I was vulnerable.
3. Does it make sense to you why your attitudes and assumptions were formed?   Yes, being prepared for the worst when you feel vulnerable makes sense.
4. Does the critical incident you have identified make sense in relation to the rest of the bigger picture?   To some extent, yes. However, I feel like I have always been like this so my husband leaving wasn't so much a critical incident but a trigger for my problems getting worse.
5. Do your symptoms fit with the rest of the bigger picture?   Yes, I think so. The recurring theme is the worrying thoughts that make me tense and anxious.
6. Do you actually agree with what you see in your bigger picture diagram or do you have reservations?   I do agree with it but would be happier if my 'critical incident' was clearer as the trigger of it all.

7. Can you use this bigger picture to guide you to particular treatment strategies?

Yes, I think it shows that I need to work on my worrying thoughts and maybe that problem-solving might help too.

8. Does it help you predict how you might respond to the various treatment strategies and what obstacles might get in the way?

I think if anything actually happened to any of my family that would be a massive obstacle for me.

9. Are there important factors that are left unexplained?

I suppose I wonder why my sister seems much more chilled about things, even though she was brought up in just the same way as I was.

10. Can the bigger picture be used to pinpoint potential future difficulties?

I think I am vulnerable to change and anything untoward happening to my children and grandchildren in particular.

Keep your bigger picture somewhere handy so that you can add to it as you make new discoveries about yourself and your difficulties. In the next chapter, you will learn how to use these insights to make lasting change in your life.

Summary

You can use the space below to make your own summary of this chapter, so that when you look back later you will be reminded of what you found most important. You might want to have a think about what was most helpful, encouraging or interesting. Was anything particularly striking? What do you think would be especially useful to remember?

1. _____

_____

2. _____

_____

3. _____

_____

4. _____

_____

20 Making change last

Before we begin ...

Start the chapter by rating your current mood on the scale in Figure 20.1.

-5	-4	-3	-2	-1	0	+1	+2	+3	+4	+5

| Negative | | | | | Neutral | | | | | Positive |
| mood | | | | | | | | | | mood |

Figure 20.1: Mood scale

If you are returning to this book after a break of a few days or more, take a moment to record your mood and anxiety (and whatever else you are recording, such as worry, anger, stress and self-esteem) and plot them on the graphs on pp. 420–39. Keeping track of your mood can help you review progress. Have there been any changes? If so, why do you think that might be? If not, can you think of any reasons?

It may also be helpful to review your problem statements (see Chapter 10, p. 135) and, re-rate those using the 0–100 problem-severity scale. Have there been any changes? Finally, review your SMART goals (see Chapter 10, p. 139) and make a note of any progress that you have made towards reaching them.

In this chapter we are going to look at your attitudes and assumptions in a bit more depth with the purpose of helping you modify them if needed to help make lasting change. By this point we hope you've tried out the various strategies for change. We hope that in the previous chapter you have formed a better understanding of your difficulties by putting together a 'bigger picture'. You will have identified any key unhelpful attitudes and assumptions, or 'if … then …' beliefs, and have begun to see how they link together the various aspects of your bigger picture. If you are now able to identify and evaluate your negative automatic thoughts (see Chapters 16 and 17), understand how your beliefs may be helping to maintain your problems (see Chapter 19), and have noticed some improvement in your symptoms, you are probably ready to start working on modifying these assumptions and attitudes. Part of this will involve looking at how your beliefs can be altered to be more helpful.

For example, someone with the attitude '*If* I ask for help *then* I am inadequate' might benefit from modifying it to something like: 'It's great to be able to deal with problems myself, but I'm only human, so like everybody I know I do need help sometimes.'

Remember that working on beliefs and attitudes can be a long process, because they have almost certainly existed, probably unquestioned, for a very long time. Identifying your 'if … then …' assumptions may have already drawn your attention to just how unhelpful these beliefs actually are. This in itself is likely to help you start the process of change, so you are already on your way there!

If you have a number of attitudes and beliefs you would like to address, it can be difficult deciding which one to prioritize. In previous chapters we have suggested beginning with the easiest problem. However, here the best thing to do is to choose the one you think is most central to your problems. One way to do this is to link back to your bigger picture from Chapter 19. These '*if … then …*' assumptions should make logical sense taking into consideration your early life experiences, the critical incident that has triggered your emotional problems and the symptoms you have been experiencing.

Strategies for addressing unhelpful attitudes and beliefs

There are a variety of strategies that can be used to make attitudes and beliefs more flexible. We'll look now at some of the most helpful ones.

A good place to start is by rating your strength of belief in your assumption or attitude. Do this out of 100, because that way you will have a percentage. Repeat this after each time you use one of the strategies below. Remember: your beliefs and attitudes are probably deeply rooted. This means that it is unlikely that just one technique, tried on one occasion, will be sufficient to modify them. Rather, you might need to use several of the techniques over a number of occasions. On a positive note, remember that these assumptions and attitudes are not facts: they are learned, and therefore they can be changed. And you'll find that some of the skills you've been using to modify your thoughts will be helpful when changing your assumptions and attitudes.

Using the bigger picture diagram you put together in Chapter 19, write your beliefs, assumptions and attitudes in the space below:

_____

_____

_____

_____

From your list, circle the assumption or attitude that you think is the most pertinent to your problems and that you would like to work on. If it takes the 'I should ...' form, try to rewrite it using the 'If .... then ...' form, as it will be easier to work on using this structure. For example, it is easier to see the unhelpfulness of 'If I don't please others then they won't like me' than of 'I should always put others first'.

Weighing up the evidence

Do you remember the 'evidence for and against' technique that we used to evaluate negative automatic thoughts (Chapter 17)? This technique is used in a very similar way when modifying unhelpful beliefs, assumptions and attitudes. Let's look at the example of Leon. He identified the unhelpful assumption perpetuating his problem as the following: '*If* I put my trust in others *then* they will let me down'. He rated his belief in this assumption as 90 per cent, and considers this belief to be central to his difficulties.

In Table 20.1 see what Leon came up with when he thought through the evidence for and against his assumption.

Table 20.1: Weighing up the evidence: Leon

Leon's assumption to be evaluated

If I put my trust in others then they will let me down. (90 per cent conviction that this is true)

What evidence is there that this assumption is true?

I trusted my dad and he left home when I was eight.

I trusted Isi and she had sex with my best friend.

I trusted Perry and he slept with my girlfriend.

What evidence is there that this assumption is not true?

My mum is always there for me.

My brother is always there for me.

I have some good friends who have shown concern for me.

My boss has always been good to me.

Is it true that if you trust another person then that person will always let you down?

I suppose not, because the people I have listed under the question above have not let me down.

If someone lets you down on one occasion does it mean they will necessarily do it again?

That's a tough one as I would probably not have anything more to do with them. I suppose some people have let me down in a small way and have still proven to be trustworthy. My friend Josh once didn't turn up when I was meeting him in town and I was really upset. It turned out though that his car had got a puncture and his phone was out of battery. There are other things like that which have happened to me that I suppose show that people can let you down sometimes, though this doesn't mean they will always do it.

Level of conviction following evaluation

If I put my trust in others then they will let me down. (65 per cent conviction this is true)

On reviewing the evidence for and against his assumption, Leon came up with the following more flexible form of the assumption:

Potential new way of looking at things

Although it can be upsetting when people let you down, it happens sometimes. Most people in my life have not let me down in a big way and if I don't take risks and get to know people then I won't be open to meeting new people, something I want to be able to do. (60 per cent conviction this belief is true)

Weighing up the evidence: Leah

Leah's assumption to be evaluated

If I don't do everything perfectly then it shows I am incompetent. (95 per cent conviction that this is true)

What evidence is there that this assumption is true?

None really but it was something I was brought up believing because my mum did.

What evidence is there that this assumption is not true?

I do make the odd mistake but I don't think that people at work see me as incompetent. In fact people have said the reverse.

Is it true that if people don't do everything perfectly then they are incompetent?

No, I don't suppose so – that sounds extreme but I still think it is important to have an eye for detail and not be sloppy – that would show incompetence in my eyes.

Can you think of someone who you think highly of who does everything perfectly? Include work colleagues, friends, family, people in the public eye.

I think highly of my boss, of Jay, two of my friends in particular and my parents. If I think about it, I know that none of them do absolutely everything perfectly but the one thing they have in common is that they all have high standards so we are all quite similar.

Can you think of someone you know who does not try to do everything perfectly? Do you consider this person to be incompetent?

My friend Sophie definitely doesn't try to do things perfectly, but she is very successful in her job as a university tutor. In fact the teaching team she leads won an award for innovation and teaching excellence!

Level of conviction following evaluation

If I don't do everything perfectly then it shows I am incompetent. (70 per cent conviction this is true)

Potential new way of looking at things

It feels good to do things well but it is impossible to do things 100 per cent perfectly all the time. If I can put less emphasis on perfection, my work and home life will be more enjoyable and it will allow me to try out new things that I might enjoy. (65 per cent conviction this assumption is true)

Using this technique helped Leah start to question her attitudes and assumptions (a process she continued, as we will see below).

Now it is your turn. Start by thinking of useful questions to ask when using the 'evidence for and against' technique for your own beliefs. Answer the questions in Table 20.2. Afterwards, ask whether there's been a change in how strongly you hold your belief.

Table 20.2: Weighing up the evidence for your own belief

1. Belief to be examined and percentage level of conviction
2. What evidence is there that this assumption is true?
3. What evidence is there that this assumption is not true?
4. Is it true that if everyone does X then that means Y?

5. *Is it true that ... ?*

6. *Level of conviction following examination.*

7. *Potential new belief.*

Advantages and disadvantages

As we said earlier, your beliefs have probably proved useful at times throughout your life, but that doesn't necessarily mean that they will always be beneficial. The 'advantages and disadvantages' technique is helpful because it acknowledges the advantages of the belief, while also examining the disadvantages. In so doing, it lets you see the drawbacks of continuing to live by a particular belief.

Here is an example of how Leah used the advantages and disadvantages technique (see Table 20.3). At first she found it easy to think of advantages, and came up with only one disadvantage. Over a couple of weeks, however, she gradually added to the disadvantages list.

Table 20.3: Considering the advantages and disadvantages: Leah

Belief to be examined: If I don't do everything perfectly then it shows I am incompetent. (95 per cent conviction that this is true)	
Advantages of living by this assumption	Disadvantages of living by this assumption
I always try my best. I feel fantastic when things are going well. I've got a good job because of how hard I've worked. I've been complimented on my attention to detail.	I get stressed when producing work, which can affect my sleep, mood and performance. I find it really upsetting when my work is critiqued. I tend to become defensive. I tend to be highly critical of myself and my own performance, which means I am never truly happy with any work I produce. I get down when I have not managed to do something perfectly and that down feeling can last for days. I don't like trying new things in case I can't do them well.
New belief based on advantages and disadvantages: It feels good to do things well but it is impossible to do things 100 per cent perfectly all of the time. If I can put less emphasis on perfection, my work and home life will be more enjoyable and it will allow me to try out new things that I might enjoy.	

As you can see from Leah's list, while there are benefits to living by her rule of perfection, these are heavily outweighed by the disadvantages. Using the exercise above, Leah was able to see that finding a less 'all-or-nothing' and more 'flexible' way of looking at things might support a more functional way of living for her, allowing her to be less perfectionistic.

Once you've identified the advantages and disadvantages of your attitude or assumption, it's time to modify the problematic assumption in such a way that you retain the advantages and minimize the disadvantages. For many people, the advantages and disadvantages technique is an extremely effective strategy for broadening understanding of beliefs and increasing motivation to change.

Take some time to list all the advantages and disadvantages for your belief, assumption or attitude. Think of the good things about it and the problems you experience because of it on a day-to-day basis. Do you avoid certain situations or activities because of a particular attitude? Do you have difficulties dealing with other people because of your beliefs? If the belief you have singled out is not helping you, then the disadvantages should outweigh the advantages. In addition, some of the advantages may not actually stand up to closer examination. You may find it helpful to return to the advantages and spend some time considering how helpful they really are.

List the advantages and disadvantages against your belief in Table 20.4.

Table 20.4: Advantages and disadvantages for your own belief

Belief to be examined:	
Advantages of living by this assumption	**Disadvantages of living by this assumption**
New belief based on advantages and disadvantages:	

Cognitive continuum technique

Assumptions and attitudes tend to be 'all-or-nothing' in nature (e.g. something is either 100 per cent successful or a complete failure). For this reason, what is known as the 'cognitive continuum' (a continuous line with the two polar opposites at each end – perhaps 100 per cent successful to 100 per cent failure) can be a very useful technique to apply in evaluating long-standing beliefs. The technique is also particularly useful for people who label themselves negatively (e.g. 'I am weak', 'I am a complete failure', 'I am worthless', 'I am incompetent') as it helps introduce a grey area to an otherwise polarized black-and-white view.

To show you how this technique works, let's look at one of Penny's beliefs.

Table 20.5: Cognitive continuum: Penny

Step 1

Penny began by defining her belief as clearly as possible. Penny believes that '*If* I am not liked by everyone *then* it means I'm a failure as a person'. This implies that Penny sees herself as being either a 'success' or a 'failure', depending on how popular she is.

Step 2

She then drew a line, representing the 'continuum', and plotted the two extremes of her belief at opposite ends. She then placed a cross, close to the left extreme (100 per cent failure), where she believed she currently fits on the continuum.

___X_____

100 per cent failure   100 per cent success

Step 3

Penny then listed all of the features of being a 'success' in her eyes (e.g. being beautiful, having many friends, having lots of money, having a life partner, having a high-status job).

Step 4

She then drew a continuum for each aspect of being a 'failure', and placed an 'x' to represent the space she felt she occupied on each of the lines, as you can see below:

___X_____

Ugly   Beautiful

_____X_____

No friends   Hundreds of friends

_____X_____

No money   Multi-millionaire

_____X_____

Never had a partner   Always had a partner

_____X_____

No job   High-status job

Step 5

Next Penny placed other people she knows, including friends, family, work colleagues and people in the public eye.

What she discovered was that nobody fell consistently on the right-hand side of the lines. She also discovered that there were people she held in high regard who fell further on the left of some lines than she did.

By using this technique Penny was able to see that there are many more categories than the two she had identified ('success' and 'failure') and that there are varying degrees of being a 'success' and being a 'failure'. As she added each new person, Penny re-evaluated her position on each continuum.

Step 6

At the end of this process, she reconsidered her own place on the original main continuum.

Before using the cognitive continuum technique:

_____X_____

100 per cent failure   100 per cent success

After using the cognitive continuum technique:

_____X_____

100 per cent failure   100 per cent success

My cognitive continuum

Now it's your turn to look at your own beliefs.

1. Define your belief as clearly as possible, using 'If I am ... then ...'.

2. Draw a horizontal line to represent the two extremes of the belief (e.g. success and failure, competent and incompetent, etc.). Place an 'X' where you feel you fall on the scale.

3. Then, as Penny did, break the belief down into its component parts, with a separate line for each of the criteria (for example: success or competence).

4. Place an 'X' to represent where you think you fall on each of these new continua.

5. Place people you know (your colleagues, family, friends or even people in the public eye) on the various continua that you have developed. After each one, reposition yourself on the continua.

6. Once you have finished, go back to the original main continuum: has your judgement of where you sit shifted? And if so, has this repositioning helped modify your belief?

Responsibility pie charts

We often use pie charts in CBT because, like the cognitive continuum technique, they can be particularly useful when working with 'all-or-nothing' beliefs and especially the idea that you are 100 per cent responsible for events.

Here are the steps for using the pie chart strategy:

1. Decide on the belief you want to examine and then rate how strongly you hold that belief.

2. Think of a recent situation that you feel illustrates your belief.

3. Now consider other factors that might have been influential in that situation, no matter how small you think they are.

4. Give each of these factors a percentage rating to show how important you think it is. Then allocate the remaining percentage to the original belief. You will see it's much smaller than your first rating.

This does not mean that you will be absolved of all responsibility: instead it's a great way of standing back to consider the other factors that might also be involved. And that will help you to develop some flexibility in your belief about your level of responsibility.

Let's look at Bea's responsibility pie chart to illustrate this technique.

Bea's responsibility pie chart

1. Bea holds the belief that: '*If* I am not always prepared for the worst *then* something bad will happen'. This makes it sound like she is 100 per cent responsible for everyone around her, but this cannot really be true. There must be other factors involved.

2. Bea selected a recent situation which made her think about her belief. Her son Rob's wife Sadia was supposed to be coming to visit, but fell when getting off the bus and broke her ankle. Bea's existing belief was that she was 100 per cent responsible for Sadia's accident, because the accident would not have happened in the first place if Sadia had not been coming to visit.

3. Bea listed all the other factors that needed to be taken into account:

- Bus stopping short of the kerb.
- Uneven paving slab.
- Sadia not paying attention because she was reading her book.
- Weather conditions – icy.
- Shoes Sadia was wearing: she has fallen in them before.

4. Bea then rated each one of the factors listed above and discovered that the total added up to 85 per cent. This left 15 per cent of the responsibility that she could apportion to her role in the accident.

Bea's responsibility pie chart can be seen in Figure 20.2.

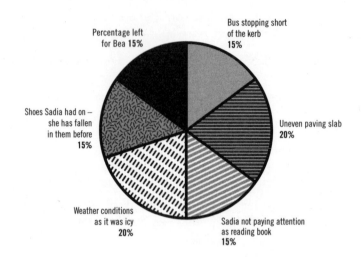

Figure 20.2: Bea's responsibility pie chart

From this, Bea was able to see that she was not 100 per cent responsible for what happened to Sadia.

Given the success she had in applying this strategy to one event, she then decided to try it out with similar events in which she had held herself 100 per cent responsible. She quickly discovered that, as with Sadia's accident, she was never 100 per cent responsible.

Bea found this technique to be beneficial in the short term, because it alleviated some of the sense of responsibility that had been weighing down on her. In the long term, the technique also helped her to start thinking about developing a more flexible form of her 'If ... then ...' belief.

Eventually, she amended her belief to look like this:

'It is important to me that I care for my loved ones but it does not mean that I can take responsibility for everything that happens to them. It is impossible to be prepared for every eventuality and it is not expected of me. By doing this less I won't worry so much and will be better able to enjoy time with and away from my family.'

My responsibility pie chart

If you hold strong beliefs about responsibility then this technique could work for you.

1. Choose an 'If ... then ...' statement that suggests you are 100 per cent responsible for something.

2. Recall a recent situation which made you think about your belief.

3. List all the other factors that needed to be taken into account:

_____

_____

_____

_____

_____

_____

_____

_____

_____

4. Give a percentage score to each one of the factors listed above. Add them up. What percentage does this now suggest you are responsible?

Draw it onto the blank responsibility pie chart in Figure 20.3.

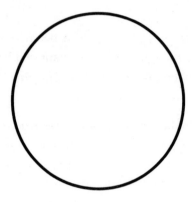

Figure 20.3: My responsibility pie chart

Behavioural experiments

We looked at behavioural experiments in Chapter 18 in relation to working with thoughts. This sort of experiment can also be a powerful tool with which to evaluate beliefs. You may remember that the difference between a thought and a belief is that you can have hundreds, even thousands of thoughts popping into your mind each day, while beliefs are more about the essence of how we view ourselves, others and the world and tend to be strongly held. Acting against an 'if … then …' belief is one of the best ways to help modify it. For example, we know that Penny tries to please others, so during her behavioural experiments she said 'no' sometimes. Leah, on the other hand, who always needed to do everything perfectly, tried making the odd error on purpose. In particular, she submitted to her newspaper a piece containing a blatant spelling error. Dez, meanwhile, who struggled with a sense of justice and fairness, smiled at someone who had cut in when driving.

Do you think this strategy could be useful for you? If so, choose a way of acting against your belief and then try it out. There are a few things to remember in doing this.

- First, in the same way that you use behavioural experiments in order to evaluate thoughts, it is important that before you carry out your experiment you predict the likely outcome. Secondly, you need to record the results.

- Finally, if the prediction does not come true, consider what this means in terms of your 'if … then …' belief. You should then aim to revise the belief in the light of the outcome of your experiment.

Carrying out an experiment like this can feel scary, so try to anticipate and plan for likely problems – for example, unhelpful negative thoughts such as 'the experiment won't work out' or 'I can't risk it'. If you think you might be prone to these kinds of thoughts, it's a good idea to weigh up the evidence for and against before you start, and see whether you can come up with a realistic alternative. Use this strategy for any unhelpful thoughts that might be getting in the way (e.g. 'I will get too anxious', 'I won't do it right', etc.). All these thoughts lend themselves well to examination and evaluation. If you're still uncertain, start by trying out the experiment in your imagination or role-playing it with a friend or your supporter (if you have one).

Acting as if

'Acting as if' is another type of behavioural experiment which works well once you are on the way to modifying a belief. You may remember the technique from Chapter 18 (see pp. 274–6). What you do is act as if the new version of your belief is actually true. See Table 20.6 for Leah's 'acting as if' experiments.

Table 20.6: Acting as if: Leah

Leah tried acting as though she actually subscribed to her new belief: 'It feels good to do things well but it is impossible to do things 100 per cent perfectly all the time. If I can put less emphasis on perfection, my work and home life will be more enjoyable and it will allow me to try out new things that I might enjoy'.

She did so by spending less time checking over her work before it went to the sub-editor, whose job it was to pick up any errors.

What she found was that rarely was anything picked up, and the sub-editor didn't comment on any change in the standard of her work. In fact, on one occasion the sub-editor complimented her on one of her articles – something that was previously a rare occurrence. Leah then listed the evidence in support of her new belief.

She now rates how strongly she believes both the old and new versions of the belief every day. She also keeps a list of other occasions when she has successfully used the 'act as if' technique and is now much more confident in using the strategy.

Once you have used some of the other techniques in this chapter and have established a new version of your belief, do try out 'acting as if'. It can be a bit scary at first but you will quickly start to notice the benefits. As a reminder, you might want to try carrying a flashcard on which you have written the new version of your belief. You could even try using the screensaver on your computer or a prompt on your mobile phone as a handy reminder. Changing the way you behave to fit with your new belief can help to strengthen the belief, which in turn helps make that new behaviour a habit.

Finally

It is worth getting into the habit of regularly rating your conviction in your belief before and after you use any of the techniques explained in this chapter. Once you perceive a shift in your original belief, try to come up with a more flexible form of that belief by retaining the bits that help you and modifying the bits that do not. It is generally best not to change your belief completely, but rather to just shake it up a bit so that it becomes more flexible. This is because the belief was put in place for a purpose and the reason that it is not helpful now is because it is too rigid. Making the belief more flexible is preferable to coming up with a completely new one that may seem less plausible. For instance, if someone's strongly held belief is 'I must be liked by everyone', it would not necessarily be helpful or acceptable to change it to the opposite extreme of 'It doesn't matter about being liked by anyone'. A more flexible and acceptable form of the belief might be something like 'It's nice to be liked but it's not possible to be liked by everyone'. Another person might hold the belief about themselves as being a complete failure but it would seem implausible to change it to the opposite of being a complete success. A middle ground of 'I'm good enough' is much more flexible and likely to be most accurate.

Try rating how strongly you believe the old and new versions of the belief daily, and keep a note to see if this changes over time as you try out more techniques, such as 'acting as if'.

Summary

In the space below, write down any key points or things that you want to remember from this chapter. What was most important? What was particularly helpful?

1. _____

   _____

2. _____

   _____

3. _____

   _____

4. _____

   _____

Part 3

Staying well

21 Staying well

Before we begin ...

Start the chapter by rating your current mood on the scale in Figure 21.1.

-5	-4	-3	-2	-1	0	+1	+2	+3	+4	+5

Negative mood	Neutral	Positive mood

Figure 21.1: Mood scale

If you are returning to this book after a break of a few days or more, take a moment to record your mood and anxiety (and whatever else you are recording, such as worry, anger, stress and self-esteem) and plot them on the graphs on pp. 420–39. Keeping track of your mood can help you review progress. Have there been any changes? If so, why do you think that might be? If not, can you think of any reasons?

It may also be helpful to review your problem statements (see Chapter 10, p. 135) and, re-rate those using the 0–100 problem-severity scale. Have there been any changes? Finally, review your SMART goals (see Chapter 10, p. 139) and make a note of any progress that you have made towards reaching them.

Dealing with setbacks

Our hope is that, by now, you have a better understanding of some of the factors that might be keeping your emotional problems going. We also hope that you have a good idea of how to change how you think and respond to difficult situations. Mostly, we hope that you are feeling better. If, having carefully worked your way through this book, you are still suffering from emotional problems that are interfering with your life, it might be an idea to seek help from your doctor.

If you have made improvements, then that is fantastic. Continue to use the methods you have learned in this book and you should find that they become increasingly instinctive. That will mean that it's less and less likely that you immediately assume you have done something to offend the friend who cancels at the last minute, or that you lash out when someone wrongs you, that you hide away when something makes you feel anxious, or that you feel overwhelmed when things don't go according to plan.

CBT has helped many people overcome their problems, and the majority of those people stay well after such treatment. However, it is also natural that you may experience the occasional setback on your road to recovery: a time when you might experience a deterioration in your mood or other symptoms. For instance, in this chapter we describe the setback experienced by Pearl as her husband's dementia got worse.

What can cause setbacks?

There's a simple answer to this question: life!

Life is full of ups and downs and, depending on how you are feeling, even something small can trigger a setback. Stressful situations can often cause problems: for example, if you were worried about giving a presentation and then it doesn't go well; if you apply for promotion and do not get it; if your job is at risk; if your children are sitting exams; if your partner is stressed at work; if you break your leg and cannot exercise; if you are bullied; if you argue with a good friend; if you become pregnant (whether the pregnancy is planned or unplanned, it brings about a lot of life and hormonal changes which can be difficult to manage); if you or a loved one becomes ill; if your finances are stretched. The list is endless.

What is important is identifying the situations that might lead to a setback and planning how you can deal with these situations before they cause problems. Some setbacks cannot be anticipated and planned for, so it is important to know the warning signs, so that you can identify when a setback might be about to begin and then put in place a plan for how to cope in order that the setback is as short-lived and mild as possible. See Table 21.1 for details of Pearl's setback.

Table 21.1: Setback: Pearl

Pearl interpreted the worsening of her husband's Alzheimer's as: 'I am going to be trapped in this nightmare for years.' She also thought that nobody would want to see John in such a bad state and that he would not want to be remembered this way. She thought she should not put him in a nursing home because that would mean she was neglecting her duty. Additionally, she had promised John that she would take care of him at home and she felt she needed to keep her promise or she would spend the rest of her life feeling guilty.

It was clearly a very tough situation for Pearl. She took care of her husband full-time at home, did not allow anyone other than her daughter to visit and did not go out for weeks at a time. Her own sleeping and eating habits were disrupted and, unsurprisingly, her mood became low.

Once Pearl's mood became low she began to think, 'Here I go again. I'm going to get depressed. I am back to square one. All that CBT was a waste of time; I am back to where I started. What can filling in a few forms do now that John is so ill? Nothing.'

Identifying your setbacks

Take a moment to think what sort of situations have contributed to making your emotional problems worse over the past five years. Write them down in the left-hand column of Table 21.2.

Table 21.2: Identifying potential setbacks

Situation that led to emotional problems in the past	How you reacted to the situation in terms of your thoughts, emotions and behaviour (e.g. effect on mood/anxiety/anger/stress/self-esteem)	Situation that might lead to a setback in future

Now spend some time thinking about how the situation you identified made your emotional problems worse. In particular, try to remember how you reacted to that situation in terms of your thoughts, emotions and behaviour. Then complete the middle column of the table.

Use the final column to identify as many situations as you can think of that might lead to a setback for you over the next five years.

Distinguishing between a lapse and a relapse

In times of trouble, it is easy to forget all you've learned from doing the cognitive behavioural techniques described in this book. However, it is also in such times of trouble that you need these techniques the most. In Table 21.3 is a description of how Pearl managed her difficult situation. What do you think of how she dealt with it?

Table 21.3: How Pearl managed her difficult situation

Pearl realized that her mood was becoming increasingly low again. She did not want to go back to the dark places that she had inhabited for so long before. She took a step back and decided that anything was worth a go. She told herself the following:

'Right, this is a difficult situation but other people have partners with Alzheimer's and don't become depressed. What am I doing differently? What are my thinking errors? Emotional reasoning, catastrophizing and mind reading probably. Just like old times. What did I do before? Oh yes, I filled out my diaries, and tried to look at my thoughts objectively and think about whether there was a different perspective I could then check out with a behavioural experiment. I also tried some routines and activities that I have now lost again, and I problem-solved. The first thought I want to tackle is that I am back to square one. I know in my heart that I am not, and that all I have learned is still with me. I just need to dust it off!'

Clearly, her husband's illness was very stressful, but Pearl's initial reaction – withdrawing and catastrophizing – didn't help her. What did make a difference was Pearl's realization that this was indeed a setback, but that she could do something positive about it by 'dusting off' some of the skills she had learned from her self-help book. She realized that there is a difference between a temporary setback, or 'lapse', and a full-blown relapse (a big and lasting deterioration after a period of recovery). Remembering this will help you maintain the progress you have made so far.

Early warning signs

Most of us experience early warning signs that our mood is in decline or our stress levels are peaking. These can sometimes be a bit unusual. For example, Leah's early warning sign is that she feels quite powerful and able to achieve a great deal. When she feels like this, she stays up later and later to get things done at work and at home. Within a couple of days she has a migraine.

Your early warning signs may be to do with your feelings, e.g. your dip in mood lasts a couple of days rather than a couple of hours, you may feel detached (disconnected from others or even from your emotions), you may not enjoy your usual activities. Irritability is a very common early warning sign of stress, low mood, anxiety, anger and sometimes also low self-esteem.

It could be that your behaviour provides the first sign that you are struggling emotionally as you find yourself unwilling to go out with people, or repeatedly missing something like an exercise class or football training. For some people, their body gives the first clue: for example, their heart may race or they may get hot and sweaty.

Bear in mind that there are no 'right' or 'wrong' early warning signs. As you will see from the descriptions in Tables 21.4–21.8 by Leon, Bea, Dez, Leah and Penny, everybody's experience is different. What is important is that once you experience any signs, you try to deal with the problem as quickly as you can, rather than just hoping that things will get better or assuming that they won't.

Table 21.4: Early warning signs: Leon

Leon, you will remember, had been experiencing depression since breaking up with his girlfriend five months ago. He had become increasingly socially isolated and felt no pleasure or sense of purpose in life. His friendships had suffered, as had his work life. After working his way through Parts 1 and 2 of this book, he feels much better. Here are his early warning signs that things might be going wrong again:

Emotions

Feeling down more of the time.

Thoughts

Thinking more about the break-up again.

Having down thoughts about myself.

Getting suicidal thoughts again.

Bodily sensations

Difficulty sleeping.

Feeling tired all the time.

Not feeling hungry.

Behaviour

Spending more time in bed.

Not keeping on top of the apartment.

Not feeling able to cope with work.

Not seeing friends.

Table 21.5: Early warning signs: Bea

Bea described herself as having always been a worrier, and spent an awful lot of time worrying about her youngest son, Gus, who has a mild learning disability, and her granddaughter, Lily, who has heart problems. Here are her early warning signs for her long-standing problem with anxiety:

Emotions

Feeling anxious and worried more often.

Anxiety and worry lasting longer than just a few minutes.

Feeling more on edge again.

Thoughts

Getting preoccupied by worrying thoughts.

Finding that worrying thoughts are popping into my mind more often.

Bodily sensations

Muscle tension coming back, especially in the back of my neck.

Difficulty getting off to sleep.

Trouble with my stomach.

Behaviour

Having problems putting into practice what I have learned.

Spending more time actively worrying.

Phoning up the kids more to make sure they are OK.

Table 21.6: Early warning signs: Dez

Dez is the fifty-two-year-old man who struggled with his temper. He often felt angry at work or irritated in the car on the way home. These are his early warning signs:

Emotions

More irritable and more anger outbursts.

Thoughts

Thinking again that people are getting at me.

Getting focused again on how unfair and unjust things are and not being able to shake it off.

Bodily sensations

Tension a lot of the time.

Tight chest more often.

Pounding heart.

Behaviour

Being generally more argumentative.

Being more snappy with Corrie.

Getting really angry with other drivers on the way to and from work.

Table 21.7: Early warning signs: Leah

Leah experienced difficulty with stress. This was largely to do with the fact that she thought her job as a reporter for a local newspaper was at risk because of the number of redundancies that had been made in the company. Here are her early warning signs for stress:

Emotions

Stressed.

Uptight.

Anxious.

Down.

Thoughts

Worrying thoughts about my work performance and losing my job.

Getting down on myself for not doing things perfectly.

Worrying Jay might leave me as I am never there for him.

Bodily sensations

Indigestion.

Not sleeping.

Dodgy stomach.

Poor appetite.

Headaches, including migraines.

Behaviour

Over-working.

Not making time for Jay and I to do stuff together.

Not making time to see friends.

Not going to the gym.

Smoking too much.

Staying up late.

Table 21.8: Early warning signs: Penny

Penny's self-esteem was very low. She was bullied from a young age because of her severe eczema and grew up with little confidence in herself. This had been a problem in her adult life and in relationships, and she generally lacked self-belief and a sense of self-worth. Here are her early warning signs:

Emotions

Feeling down about myself.

Thoughts

Worrying about what other people think of me.

Thinking of myself as boring.

Being more self-critical.

Bodily sensations

Not sleeping very well.

Feeling constantly hungry and experiencing an irresistible urge to eat.

Behaviour

Overeating.

Staying in more.

Letting the place get untidy.

Not seeing friends as much.

Not being assertive.

Now we'd like you to have a go at identifying *your own* early warning signs by completing Table 21.9.

Table 21.9: My early warning signs

Emotions

Thoughts

Bodily sensations

Behaviour

The staying well plan

Making a plan of how you intend to stay well will help you to know how to respond to the early warning signs should they start appearing. A staying well plan will also be a summary document for you to look back on and use if and when you experience a setback. Keep it in a safe place that is easily accessible so that you can find it if you need it. It might be an idea also to keep an electronic version on your home computer if you have one.

Ash's Staying Well Plan can be found in Table 21.10.

Table 21.10: Staying well plan: Ash

Since he was knocked off his bike by a car, Ash had been too anxious to even consider riding again. He avoided any mention of cycling, wouldn't listen to the news in case it reminded him of his accident, and had forbidden his children to ride to school as they used to do. He was angry, resentful and depressed about the effect of the accident on his emotions and daily life.

Here is Ash's plan. It includes a comprehensive summary of the original problem, what was keeping it going, and what strategies he used to tackle the problem, as well as a summary of potential setback situations and early warning signs list.

1. Think about how the original problem started

It started very suddenly with the bike accident where I was knocked off my bike by a car.

2. What kept my problem going? Based on your problem statements and your understanding of the connections between your emotions, bodily sensations, behaviour and thoughts, write down what kept your problems going. Clue: think about your interpretation of events/situations/bodily sensations and your response, (e.g. withdrawing).

It was mainly avoidance because I stopped using my bike and stopped the rest of the family using theirs too. I also avoided things on the TV that might upset me and wouldn't talk about the accident.

3. What I have learned so far: My quick reference guide (using the summaries that you have made at the end of each chapter)

Next, Ash wrote down what he had learned from each chapter in order to produce a kind of 'quick reference guide' that he could easily refer to if necessary. He did this by reviewing the summary notes that he had made at the end of each chapter.

Chapter 1: Introduction

- Questions on p. 3 helped me decide that this book may actually help.

- Also good to know that if I am finding it hard to tackle my problem alone then I can ask my GP or someone who can help guide me through it and give me support.

Chapter 2: CBT for emotional problems

- I didn't know anything about CBT, so the main thing for me is that it is known to work for people with my kind of problem.

- Reading the case examples was useful – helped me feel a bit more 'normal'.

- Being able to use the diagram on p. 24 for a recent situation of my own was also helpful.

Chapter 3: Depression

- Doing the questionnaires on pp. 389–408 for the first time was useful.

- It was good to find out more about depression and how this relates to my own experiences.

Chapter 4: Anxiety

- I found out more about anxiety and how to make sense of it. I liked this chapter a lot so if I get uptight about stuff, I should definitely read it again.

Chapter 5: Anger

- This chapter was also relevant as I do have a tendency to lose my temper and I really want to stop doing this because I don't like upsetting the children.

Chapter 6: Self-esteem

- What's happened to me had knocked my self-esteem massively, but I'd not really thought about it this way before. Bit of an eye-opener for me.

Chapter 7: Stress

- I thought I was stressed all the time. Looking back over these last few chapters, I seemed to have everything!

Chapter 8: Symptoms of Anxiety, Depression and Other Common Problems

- Really liked this chapter as it was made really clear that lots of people have symptoms of several problems. I think I was one of those people. Although initially disheartening, learning that this is not uncommon gives me hope that I can help myself.

Chapter 9: Making sense of your problem

- Good to take time to do the questionnaires on pp. 389–408 and the mood scale.

- I know there are more advantages than disadvantages to dealing with the problem but doing the Advantages/Disadvantages exercise on p. 124 really hit home. I've typed it up on my PC screensaver as a reminder, which has proved to be quite handy when I've had a wobbly moment.

Chapter 10: Problem statements and SMART goals

- Really helpful to work on my problem statement: Avoidance of travelling anywhere by bike due to physical symptoms such as racing heart and shaking and a fear that I'll be knocked off again leading me to become increasingly restricted as to how I get to and from work.

- Was also pleased to come up with my four goals:

  1. To cycle to and from work five days a week.

  2. To go cycling with wife Kay and kids most weekends (weather permitting).

  3. To allow kids to cycle to and from school five days a week.

  4. To watch the news at least once a day with minimal upset (i.e. less than 2 on a 0–10 scale of upset).

Chapter 11: Breaking vicious cycles by changing your behaviour

- The key message for me is how important it is to break steps down into manageable smaller tasks. It made me realize that there were a number of smaller steps towards cycling to work again, such as getting my confidence in cycling in quiet areas, at quiet times, etc. first.

Chapter 12: Breaking vicious cycles by solving problems

- I think I realized that I'm generally already quite good at this so that gave me a bit of a confidence boost.

Chapter 13: Facing your fears using graded exposure

- This was a key chapter for me and helped me to get a handle on exactly what I needed to do.

- Doing a hierarchy on p. 198 and thinking through the various steps was very productive.

- Felt great to get started and see that I could do more than one step at a time.

- I realized that as I get closer to the next step it feels more achievable because I've completed the previous ones.

Chapter 14: Managing your anger

- This was also an important chapter for me as I find I am more irritable following the accident.

- I learnt how to relax at times when I am feeling irritable and tetchy with the family.

Chapter 15: Thinking patterns

- Understanding how thoughts influence how we feel and what we do was a big breakthrough.

- I know now that there is more than one type of thought – purposeful thoughts and automatic thoughts (see p. 221) – and that everyone gets them!

- Was struck by this insight on p. 224: Event → Thought/ interpretation → Reactions (emotions, bodily sensations and behaviours).

- Realized that I am prone to catastrophizing and over-generalizing.

Chapter 16: Identifying unhelpful thinking

- Learned to notice and write down my own thoughts.

- Practised noticing the thought behind the emotion – previously I only noticed the way I felt and never really considered what was going through my head.

- Finding out that emotions are usually just one word – never thought of that before.

Chapter 17: Thinking differently

- Saw that I can learn to think differently.

- Realized that my thoughts aren't necessarily facts.

- Will try to be objective when looking at evidence for and against my thoughts.

Chapter 18: Behavioural experiments

- Learned the importance of doing things rather than just thinking about them.

- Interesting to discover the different ways that you can experiment.

Chapter 19: Bigger picture

- I learned why I might have been vulnerable to getting anxious by taking into account my life experiences and my belief systems.

Chapter 20: Making change last

- Worked on making my beliefs more flexible.

- I need to continue reminding myself of my new more flexible beliefs and 'act as if' until they are more automatic.

Chapter 21: Staying Well

- Useful to think through early warning signs.

- Found it really satisfying to draw up this plan of what to do if I have a setback.

- Have written a plan below of what I need to do for the next three months, six months, year and even five years to ensure I continue to make progress. It feels good to plan ahead in a positive way.

Monitoring my mood

- I was a bit sceptical about this at first but I really liked being able to chart my mood and see the improvement over time on the graphs. I did the same with the questionnaires and they have all shown improvement too.

4. Based on the work you have done so far, think about the changes you have made that you want to continue to develop

I have made a huge amount of progress and am now back to cycling to and from work, although I have changed my hours of working so that I avoid rush hour. I am also back cycling at weekends with my family. The kids are cycling to and from school again but not on the old route – I am still a bit too anxious about that, as I worry they might get hit by a car like I was. I made these changes gradually over several weeks and I still get a bit twitchy about it now and again. Overall though I am feeling a lot better. I am confident that, by continuing to tackle my problem like this, my anxieties will lessen.

5. What areas in your life require further attention?

I am still not very good at watching the news without getting enraged and a bit anxious when there's an item about a cycle accident. I also need to work on letting the kids have more freedom to use their bikes and trust that they will use them responsibly. I would like to get to the stage where I can work the hours I used to, which would mean cycling at rush hour.

6. Where do you see yourself in three months' time? What strategies from this book will you continue to keep practising and using in your life to help you get there?

I want to be more confident about letting the kids go out on their bikes and to not get so worked up watching the news. I'd also like to have made some progress in getting closer to cycling at rush hour. Graded exposure has worked really well for me so far, so I think I need to continue using this approach. I also found working on my thinking helpful, so I am going to try to continue that as well.

7. Where do you see yourself in six months' time? What strategies from this book will you continue to keep practising and using in your life to help you get there?

I want to be at the stage where my family and I can do the things we used to do before my accident. I can use the exposure and thought stuff as I need it. I quite like the idea of doing the questionnaires every few weeks just to keep an eye on things and using the mood scale every now and again too.

8. Where do you see yourself in one year's time? What strategies from this book will you continue to keep practising and using in your life to help you get there?

I want to have put the accident and all that followed behind me. If there are any niggling problems then hopefully these tried-and-tested methods will help me. Getting knocked off my bike has been a massive blow to me so maybe I should expect to still be working on some aspects of the problem that might remain.

9. Where do you see yourself in five years' time? What strategies from this book will you continue to keep practising and using in your life to help you get there?

Gosh, I don't often think that far ahead. I like to think that all will be well and I'll have put this problem well and truly behind me. The kids will be really grown up by then and hopefully won't have picked up on any of my anxieties.

10. Based on your work earlier in this chapter, what situations are most likely to lead to a setback and how will you deal with them? It may be that you want to involve other people to help you (e.g. contact your supporter again if you have one) or it may be there are strategies you can use without additional help.

Situation	What I'll do
Seeing news item about someone being knocked off their bike and killed.	I think I would need to get back into working on my thoughts about it and if I was more reluctant to go on the bike then I'd need to do some more exposure.
Me getting knocked off bike again.	I think I would just need to start again with using the exposure techniques and working on my thoughts. It would be harder doing this for a second time.
One of the kids getting knocked off their bikes.	I might need help from a professional if this happened.

11. What are your early warning signs and how will you respond to them?

Early warning signs	What I'll do
Avoiding the news/getting angry at relevant news items.	Use the thought strategies and if avoiding the news again I need to use the hierarchy again to get back into it. I can also ask Kay to help me.
Not letting the kids use their bikes.	This is important as I don't want the kids to become anxious like me. I need to gradually build up to letting them do what they are used to doing and work on my anxious thoughts.
Avoiding using my bike going to and from work.	I would need to check where I am on my hierarchy and hopefully not be too far back. I would need to gradually build up step by step again.

12. Finally, if you had to send a tweet (140 characters, including spaces and punctuation) to the world with one or two key messages about how to overcome emotional problems, what would you tweet?

It hasn't been easy but the benefits have been worth it. I feel like I've got my life back one step at a time. If I can do it you can.

My staying well plan

This plan has been designed as a 'stand alone' document so that if you do experience a setback, you can look at it and remind yourself of some of the most important ways to help yourself. You may wish to copy these pages from the book (or rip them out!) and put them in a noticeable but private place (e.g. on your bedside table). Use the template in Table 21.11 to put together your own staying well plan.

Table 21.11: My staying well plan

1. Think about how your original problem started

| |
| |

2. What kept my problem going? Based on your problem statements and your understanding of the connections between your emotions, bodily sensations, behaviour and thoughts, write down what kept your problems going. Clue: think about your interpretation of events/ situations/bodily sensations and your response, (e.g. withdrawing).

| |
| |

3. What I have learned so far: My quick reference guide (using the summaries that you have made at the end of each chapter)

Chapter 1: Introduction

Chapter 2: Cognitive behavioural approach. Identifying what problems you have

Chapter 3: Depression

Chapter 4: Anxiety

Chapter 5: Anger

Chapter 6: Self-esteem

Chapter 7: Stress

Chapter 8: Symptoms of anxiety, depression and other common problems

Chapter 9: Making sense of your problem

Chapter 10: Problem statements and SMART goals

Chapter 11: Examining activity

Chapter 12: Problem-solving

Chapter 13: Using graded exposure to face your fears

Chapter 14: Managing your anger

Chapter 15: Unhelpful thinking patterns

Chapter 16: Identifying unhelpful thinking

Chapter 17: Thinking differently

Chapter 18: Behavioural experiments

Chapter 19: The bigger picture

Chapter 20: Making change last

Chapter 21: Staying well

Monitoring your mood

You have also been monitoring your mood and anxiety on a regular basis and have plotted them on the chart. Use the box below to write how this might have been helpful to you.

```
┌─────────────────────────────────────────────────────┐
│                                                       │
│                                                       │
│                                                       │
│                                                       │
│                                                       │
│                                                       │
└─────────────────────────────────────────────────────┘
```

4. Based on the work you have done so far, think about the changes you have made that you want to continue to develop.

```
┌─────────────────────────────────────────────────────┐
│                                                       │
│                                                       │
│                                                       │
│                                                       │
│                                                       │
└─────────────────────────────────────────────────────┘
```

5. What areas in your life require further attention?

```
┌─────────────────────────────────────────────────────┐
│                                                       │
│                                                       │
│                                                       │
│                                                       │
│                                                       │
└─────────────────────────────────────────────────────┘
```

6. Where do you see yourself in three months' time? What strategies from this book will you continue to keep practising and using in your life to help you get there?

[   ]

7. Where do you see yourself in six months' time? What strategies from this book will you continue to keep practising and using in your life to help you get there?

[   ]

8. Where do you see yourself in one year's time? What strategies from this book will you continue to keep practising and using in your life to help you get there?

[   ]

9. *Where do you see yourself in five years' time? What strategies from this book will you continue to keep practising and using in your life to help you get there?*

10. *Based on your work earlier in this chapter, what situations are most likely to lead to a setback and how will you deal with them? It may be that you want to involve other people to help you (e.g. contact your supporter again if you have one) or it may be there are strategies you can use without additional help.*

Situations	What I'll do

11. What are your early warning signs and how will you respond to them?

Early warning signs	How I will respond

12. Finally, if you had to send a tweet (140 characters, including spaces and punctuation) to the world with one or two key messages about how to overcome emotional problems, what would you tweet?

What if you are still not feeling well?

We hope that you have benefited from this book. However, you may feel that you need more formal help from a therapist who can offer one-to-one treatment. If this is the case, make an appointment to see your doctor, who will be able to refer you to the right service or advise you on how to self-refer. Don't be disheartened if this book has not helped you as much as you hoped. It is not unusual to need extra support and very many people go on to benefit enormously from seeing a therapist who is able to provide CBT. You might find that you can return to the book during or after therapy to help keep you well.

Our key message to you

Thank you for taking time to read this book and do the exercises. We congratulate you on all the changes you have made and wish you luck with all the changes you still want to make. We hope that this book has helped you become well and that it helps you to stay well.

Summary

It is time for you to make your final summary. As previously, use the space below to write down anything that you found important or especially helpful in this chapter. What was most encouraging? What is the one key message that you will take from this book?

1. _____

_____

2. _____

_____

3. _____

_____

4. _____

_____

References

Chapter 1

1. Office of National Statistics, *Living in Britain: Results from the 2000/1 General Household Survey* (HMSO, 2001); and Office of National Statistics, *Better or Worse: A Longitudinal Study of the Mental Health of Adults Living in Private Households in Great Britain* (HMSO, 2003).

Chapter 3

2. Office of National Statistics, *Living in Britain: Results from the 2000/1 General Household Survey* (HMSO, 2001) and *Better or Worse: A Longitudinal Study of the Mental Health of Adults Living in Private Households in Great Britain* (HMSO, 2003); World Health Organization, *WHO Guide to Mental Health in Primary Care* (The Royal Society of Medicine Press Ltd., 2000).

3. American Psychiatric Association, *Diagnostic and Statistical Manual of Mental Disorders: DSM-5* (American Psychiatric Association, 2013).

Chapter 4

4. Mental Health Foundation, http://www.mentalhealth.org.uk/help-information/mental-health-statistics/men-women/.

5. American Psychiatric Association, *Diagnostic and Statistical Manual of Mental Disorders: DSM-5* (American Psychiatric Association, 2013).

Chapter 5

6. Mental Health Foundation, *Boiling Point: Problem anger and what we can do about it*, 2008.

7. Copyright © 1978/2004 by Raymond W. Novaco. PhD., University of California, Irvine.

Chapter 6

8. José-Vincente Bonet, *Sé amigo de tí mismo* (Editorial Sal Terrae, 1997).

Chapter 7

9. More detailed information on work stress can be found in the HSE's *Stress and Psychological Disorders in Great Britain 2013* report, http://www.hse.gov.uk/statistics/causdis/stress/stress.pdf).

10. This scale can be found in the following articles: S. Cohen, T. Kamarck and R. Mermelstein, 'A global measure of perceived stress', *Journal of Health and Social Behavior*, 24: 4 (1983), 385–96; and S. Cohen and G. Williamson, 'Perceived stress in a probability sample of the United States', in S. Spacapam and S. Oskamp (eds), *The Social Psychology of Health: Claremont Symposium on Applied Social Psychology* (Sage, 1988).

Chapter 8

11. http://www.mentalhealth.org.uk/help-information/mental-health-statistics/men-women/

Chapter 11

12. This activity checklist is similar to one put together by psychologists Patricia Averill and Joy Schmitz in their 'Treatment of dually diagnosed patients using relapse prevention and depression management' workshop presented at the American Psychological Association Annual Convention, Chicago, 1997.

Chapter 12

13. Arther M. Nuzu, Christine Maguth Nezu and Thomas J. D'Zurilla, *Problem-Solving Therapy: A Treatment Manual* (Springer, 2012).

Bibliography

American Psychiatric Association, *Diagnostic and Statistical Manual of Mental Disorders: DSM-5* (American Psychiatric Association, 2013). www.psych.org

Averill, P.M., and J. M. Schmitz, 'Treatment of dually diagnosed patients using relapse prevention and depression management', workshop presented at the American Psychological Association Annual Conference, Chicago, 1997.

Behar, E., O. Alcaine, A. R. Zuellig, and T. D. Borkovec, 'Screening for generalized anxiety disorder using the Penn State Worry Questionnaire: a receiver operating characteristic analysis', *Journal of Behavior Therapy and Experimental Psychiatry*, 34: 1 (2003), 25–43.

Bennett-Levy, James, Gillian Butler, Melanie Fennell, Ann Hackmann, Martina Mueller and David Westbrook, *The Oxford Guide to Behavioural Experiments in Cognitive Therapy* (Oxford University Press, 2004).

Bonet, José-Vincente, *Sé amigo de tí mismo* (Editorial Sal Terrae, 1997).

Cohen, S., and G. Williamson, 'Perceived Stress in a Probability Sample of the United States', in S. Spacapam and S. Oskamp (eds), *The Social Psychology of Health* (Sage, 1988).

Cohen, S., T. Kamarck and R. Mermelstein, 'A global measure of perceived stress', *Journal of Health and Social Behavior*, 24 (1983), 386–96.

Health and Safety Executive, 'Stress and Psychological Disorders in Great Britain' (HSE, 2013) http://www.hse.gov.uk/statistics/causdis/stress.pdf

Improving Access to Psychological Therapies, *The IAPT Data Handbook* (IAPT, June 2011).

Jacobson, Edmund, *Progressive Relaxation* (University of Chicago Press, 1938).

Kroenke, K., R. L. Spitzer and J. B. Williams, 'The PHQ-9: Validity of a brief depression severity measure', *Journal of General Medicine*, 16: 9 (2001), 606–13.

Lazarus, Richard S. and Susan Folkman. *Stress, Appraisal, and Coping* (Springer, 1984).

Lee, Deborah, *The Compassionate Mind Approach to Recovering from Trauma* (Robinson, 2012).

Lejuez, C.W., D. R. Hopko and S. D. Hopko, 'A brief behavioural activation treatment for depression', *Behaviour Modification*, 25 (2001), 255–86.

Marks, I., and A. M. Matthews, 'Brief standard self-rating for phobic patients', *Behaviour Research and Therapy*, 17: 3 (1979), 263–7.

Mundt, J.C., I. M. Marks, M. K. Shear and J. H. Greist, 'The Work and Social Adjustment Scale: A simple measure of impairment in functioning' *British Journal of Psychiatry*, 180 (May 2002), 461–4.

National Institute for Health and Care Excellence, 'Depression in adults with chronic physical health problems: Treatment and management', CG91 (NICE, 2009).

National Institute for Health and Care Excellence, 'Depression in Adults: The treatment and management of depression in adults', CG90 (NICE, 2009).

National Institute for Health and Care Excellence, 'Generalised Anxiety Disorder and Panic Disorder (with or without agoraphobia) in adults: Management in primary, secondary and community care', CG113 (NICE, 2011).

Nuzu, Arther M., Christine Maguth Nezu and Thomas J. D'Zurilla, *Problem-Solving Therapy: A Treatment Manual* (Springer, 2012).

Office for National Statistics, *Psychiatric Morbidity Report* (HMSO, 2001).

Office for National Statistics, *Better or Worse: A longitudinal study of the mental health of adults in Great Britain* (HMSO, 2003).

Ost, L.G., 'Applied relaxation: description of a coping technique and review of controlled studies', *Behaviour Research and Therapy*, 25: 5 (1987), 397–409.

Rosenberg, Morris, *Society and the Adolescent Self-Image* (Princeton University Press, 1965).

Shafran, Roz, Sarah Egan and Tracey Wade, *Overcoming Perfectionism* (Robinson, 2010).

Spitzer, R.L., K. Kroenke and J. B. W. Williams, 'Patient health questionnaire study group. Validity and utility of a self-report version of PRIME-MD: The PHQ primary care study group', *JAMA*, 282 (1999), 1737–44.

Spitzer, R. L., K. Kroenke, J. B. Williams and B. Lowe, 'A brief measure for assessing generalized anxiety disorder: The GAD-7', *Archives of International Medicine*, 166 (2006), 1092–7.

Spitzer, R.L., J. B. W. Williams and K. Kroenke, et al., 'Validity and utility of the Patient Health Questionnaire in assessment of 3000 obstetric-gynaecologic patients: the PRIME-MD Patient Health Questionnaire Obstetrics-Gynaecology Study', *American Journal of Obstetrics and Gynaecology*, 183 (2000), 759–69.

Stott, Richard, Warren Mamsell, Paul Salkovskis, Anna Lavender and Sam Cartwright-Hatton, *Oxford Guide to Metaphors in CBT* (Oxford University Press, 2010).

World Health Organization, *WHO Guide to Mental Health in Primary Care* (The Royal Society of Medicine Press Ltd., 2000).

Further resources

Emergencies

UK resources

Samaritans

This is a twenty-four-hour service for people who are experiencing feelings of distress or despair, including those which may lead to suicide. Volunteers offer support by responding to phone calls, emails and letters. Alternatively, people can drop in to a branch to have a face-to-face meeting. Across the UK you can call Samaritans on 08457 90 90 90. In the Republic of Ireland call 116 123. You can also email Samaritans at **jo@samaritans.org** or write to Chris, PO Box 9090, Stirling, FK8 2SA (Freepost RSRB-KKBY-CYJK).

Mental health emergencies

If a person's mental or emotional state quickly worsens, this can be treated as a mental health emergency or mental health crisis. In this situation, it's important to get help as soon as possible. Call 111 in England to find out where help is available (this is NHS 111, which has replaced NHS Direct). If you feel that you or a person you are with is in immediate danger, call 999.

Urgent care centres provide a variety of services but these vary by area. You may be able to attend such a centre rather than go to the Accident and Emergency Department of your nearest hospital. It is best to phone ahead or call 111 (in England) to find out if the services you require are available at your local urgent care centre.

International resources for emergencies

If you do not live in the UK but feel you may be in danger of harming yourself, go to your local hospital or walk-in clinic, who will be able to help.

Depression

The following website will help you find out more about depression:

http://www.nhs.uk/CONDITIONS/DEPRESSION/Pages/Symptoms. aspx.

A Behavioural Activation Treatment for Depression manual is free to download from: http://web.utk.edu/~dhopko/BATDmanual.pdf.

Self-help books

Paul Gilbert, *Overcoming Depression: A self-help guide using Cognitive Behavioural Techniques* (Robinson, 3rd edn, 2009).

– This book is divided into three parts. The first is about understanding depression, the second is about 'learning how to cope', and the third concerns 'developing supportive relationships with ourselves'. Reviews on Amazon from people who have used the book describe it as 'fantastic'.

Mark Gilson, Arthur Freeman, M. Jane Yates, and Sharon Morgillo Freeman (2009). *Overcoming Depression: A Cognitive Therapy Approach Workbook* (Oxford University Press, 2009).

– This is part of the 'Treatments that Work' series from the United States. This book provides clear guidance on how to become less depressed in a highly accessible and practical format. The accompanying clinician's guide will be of use for those with depression as well as their supporters.

Mark Williams, John Teasdale, Zindel Segal and Jon Kabat-Zinn, *The Mindful Way through Depression: Freeing Yourself from Chronic Unhappiness* (Guilford Press, 2007).

– This award-winning book is written by the leading clinical researchers in 'mindfulness' in the UK, Canada and the United States. Its four parts help the reader understand depression and teach the principles of mindfulness.

UK-based organizations

Depression alliance

This UK charity aims to provide information and support services to those suffering from depression. www.depressionalliance.org

United States-based organizations

The Anxiety and Depression Association of America

Provides a range of information and resources for those suffering from anxiety and depression. www.adaa.org

Anxiety

The following web page will help you to find out more about anxiety:

www.nhs.uk/CONDITIONS/ANXIETY/Pages/Symptoms.aspx.

Self-help books

Michelle G. Craske and David H. Barlow, *Mastery of your Anxiety and Worry: Workbook* (Oxford University Press, 2006).

– This is a classic description that provides step-by-step help for overcoming anxiety and worry. It has an accompanying therapist's guide and is written by the leading clinical researchers in the United States.

Helen Kennerley, *How to Beat Your Fears and Worries* (Robinson, 2011).

Helen Kennerley, *Overcoming Anxiety* (Robinson, 2009).

Kevin Meares and Mark Freeston, *Overcoming Worry* (Robinson, 2008).

Cathy Creswell and Lucy Willetts, *Overcoming Your Child's Fears and Worries* (Robinson, 2007).

Ron Rapee, Ann Wignall, Sue Spence, Vanessa Cobham and Heidi Lyneham, *Helping Your Anxious Child: A Step-by-Step Guide for Parents* (New Harbinger, 2nd edn, 2008).

– These are both fantastic books from the UK and Australia respectively, written by some of the leading clinical researchers in the field of CBT for childhood anxiety. They are highly accessible, practical, and are recommended for all parents whose children are suffering from anxiety.

UK-based organizations

Anxiety UK

The aim of Anxiety UK is to promote the relief and rehabilitation of people suffering from anxiety disorders through information and the provision of self-help services. They also strive to advance awareness of the general public in the causes and conditions of anxiety disorders and associated phobias. www.anxietyuk.org.uk

No Panic

A voluntary charity which helps people who suffer from panic attacks, phobias, obsessive compulsive disorders and other related anxiety disorders. No Panic specializes in self-help through recovery groups and one-to-one mentoring. They conduct their work over the telephone, using cognitive behavioural methods. www.nopanic.org.uk

United States-based organizations

The Anxiety and Depression Association of America

Provides a range of information and resources for those suffering from anxiety and depression. www.adaa.org

Anger

Self-help books

William Davies, *Overcoming Anger and Irritability* (Robinson, 2000).

Stress

Self-help books

Lee Brosan and Gillian Todd, *Overcoming Stress* (Robinson, 2009).

Self-esteem

Self-help books

David Burns, *10 Days to Great Self-Esteem: 10 easy steps to brighten your moods and discovering the joy of everyday living* (Vermilion, 2000).

Melanie Fennell, *Boost Your Confidence: Improving self-esteem step-by-step* (Robinson, 2011).

Melanie Fennell, *Overcoming Low Self-Esteem* (Robinson, 2009).

Mary Welford, *The Compassionate Mind Approach to Building your Self-Confidence* (Robinson, 2012).

Other emotional problems

Self-help books

Lee Baer, *Getting Control: Overcoming your Obsessions, Compulsions and OCD.* (Robinson, 2012).

Gillian Butler, *Overcoming Social Anxiety and Shyness* (Robinson, 2009).

Colin Espie, *Overcoming Insomnia and Sleep Problems* (Robinson, 2012).

Jeremy Gauntlett-Gilbert and Clare Grace, *Overcoming Weight Problems* (Robinson, 2012).

Paul Gilbert, *The Compassionate Mind* (Constable, 2009).

Lynne Henderson, *Improving Social Confidence and Reducing Shyness* (Robinson, 2010).

Claudia Herbert and Ann Wetmore, *Overcoming Traumatic Stress* (Robinson, 2012).

Helen Kennerley, *Overcoming Childhood Trauma* (Robinson, 2012).

Deborah Lee with Sophie James, *The Compassionate Mind Approach to Recovering from Trauma* (Robinson, 2012).

Sue Morris, *Overcoming Grief* (Robinson, 2012).

Roz Shafran, Sarah Egan and Tracey Wade, *Overcoming Perfectionism* (Robinson, 2012).

Derrick Silove and Vijaya Manicavasagar, *Overcoming Panic and Agoraphobia* (Robinson, 2012).

David Veale and Rob Wilson, *Overcoming Obsessive Compulsive Disorder* (Robinson, 2009).

David Veale, Rob Wilson and Alex Clarke, *Overcoming Body Image Problems including Body Dysmorphic Disorder* (Robinson, 2009).

Rob Wilson and David Veale, *Overcoming Health Anxiety* (Robinson, 2009).

UK-based organizations

OCD Action

Provides support and information for people affected by Obsessive Compulsive Disorder. www.ocdaction.org.uk

OCD-UK

Aims to provide information about obsessive compulsive disorder and to support those who suffer from this often debilitating anxiety disorder. www.ocduk.org

Relationship problems

Self-help books

Aaron T. Beck, *Love is Never Enough: How Couples Can Overcome Misunderstandings, Resolve Conflicts and Solve Relationship Problems through Cognitive Therapy* (Penguin, 1989).

– Based on principles of cognitive therapy, this book offers concrete help and advice on relationship problems. It helps to promote clear and straightforward thinking, preventing us from misjudging and miscommunicating in relationships.

Michael Crowe, *Overcoming Relationship Problems* (Robinson, 2012).

– This is a self-help guide, based upon experience in self-help strategies developed at the couples' clinic at the Maudsley Hospital in south London. The book uses a combination of CBT and systemic approaches derived from family therapy. It provides a self-help method to manage the difficulties that can arise in close relationships.

Norman Epstein and Donald H. Baucom, *Enhanced Cognitive-Behavioral Therapy for Couples* (American Psychological Association, 2002).

– The classic guide to CBT for couples. Written for students and clinicians, it is also accessible for those with a personal interest in the topic. It provides plenty of clinical examples and is written by the leading clinical researchers in the field of couples therapy.

Vicki Ford, *Overcoming Sexual Problems* (Robinson, 2010).

Sarah Litvinoff, *The Relate Guide to Better Relationships: Practical Ways to Make Your Love Last* (Vermilion Books, 2008).

– This is a practical steps book that couples can take to keep their love alive long-term.

UK-based organizations

Relate

Offers advice, relationship counselling, sex therapy, workshops, mediation, consultations, and support. They do this by face-to-face meetings, by phone and by email. They can be contacted on 0300 100 1234, or at their website www.relate.org.uk for more information, and to find your local Relate service.

Appendix

Mood scale

Rate your current overall mood on the mood scale below.

-5	-4	-3	-2	-1	0	+1	+2	+3	+4	+5

Negative mood				Neutral					Positive mood

Rate your current overall mood on the mood scale below.

-5	-4	-3	-2	-1	0	+1	+2	+3	+4	+5

Negative mood				Neutral					Positive mood

Rate your current overall mood on the mood scale below.

-5	-4	-3	-2	-1	0	+1	+2	+3	+4	+5

Negative mood				Neutral					Positive mood

Rate your current overall mood on the mood scale below.

-5	-4	-3	-2	-1	0	+1	+2	+3	+4	+5

Negative mood				Neutral					Positive mood

Rate your current overall mood on the mood scale below.

-5	-4	-3	-2	-1	0	+1	+2	+3	+4	+5

Negative mood   Neutral   Positive mood

Rate your current overall mood on the mood scale below.

-5	-4	-3	-2	-1	0	+1	+2	+3	+4	+5

Negative mood   Neutral   Positive mood

Rate your current overall mood on the mood scale below.

-5	-4	-3	-2	-1	0	+1	+2	+3	+4	+5

Negative mood   Neutral   Positive mood

Rate your current overall mood on the mood scale below.

-5	-4	-3	-2	-1	0	+1	+2	+3	+4	+5

Negative mood   Neutral   Positive mood

Rate your current overall mood on the mood scale below.

-5	-4	-3	-2	-1	0	+1	+2	+3	+4	+5

Negative mood   Neutral   Positive mood

Rate your current overall mood on the mood scale below.

-5	-4	-3	-2	-1	0	+1	+2	+3	+4	+5

Negative mood   Neutral   Positive mood

PHQ-9

The PHQ-9 (patient health questionnaire) measures low mood or depression.

Over the last 2 weeks, how often have you been bothered by any of the following problems?		Not at all	Several days	More than half the days	Nearly every day
1	Little interest or pleasure in doing things	0	1	2	3
2	Feeling down, depressed, or hopeless	0	1	2	3
3	Trouble falling or staying asleep, or sleeping too much	0	1	2	3
4	Feeling tired or having little energy	0	1	2	3
5	Poor appetite or overeating	0	1	2	3
6	Feeling bad about yourself — or that you are a failure or have let yourself or your family down	0	1	2	3
7	Trouble concentrating on things such as reading the newspaper or watching television	0	1	2	3
8	Moving or speaking so slowly that other people could have noticed? Or the opposite – being so fidgety or restless that you have been moving around a lot more than usual	0	1	2	3
9	Thoughts that you would be better off dead or of hurting yourself in some way	0	1	2	3
PHQ-9 total score ____					

Scoring PHQ-9

Add up your scores and see where they fall on this index of severity.

0–4   None

5–9   Mild depression

10–14   Moderate depression

15–19   Moderately severe depression

20–27   Severe depression

If you have a score of 10 or above for more than two weeks and/or scoring 3 on question 9, you should visit your doctor.

PHQ-9

The PHQ-9 (patient health questionnaire) measures low mood or depression.

Over the <u>last 2 weeks,</u> how often have you been bothered by any of the following problems?		Not at all	Several days	More than half the days	Nearly every day
1	Little interest or pleasure in doing things	0	1	2	3
2	Feeling down, depressed, or hopeless	0	1	2	3
3	Trouble falling or staying asleep, or sleeping too much	0	1	2	3
4	Feeling tired or having little energy	0	1	2	3
5	Poor appetite or overeating	0	1	2	3
6	Feeling bad about yourself — or that you are a failure or have let yourself or your family down	0	1	2	3
7	Trouble concentrating on things such as reading the newspaper or watching television	0	1	2	3
8	Moving or speaking so slowly that other people could have noticed? Or the opposite – being so fidgety or restless that you have been moving around a lot more than usual	0	1	2	3
9	Thoughts that you would be better off dead or of hurting yourself in some way	0	1	2	3
PHQ-9 total score _____					

Scoring PHQ-9

Add up your scores and see where they fall on this index of severity.

  0–4   None

  5–9   Mild depression

10–14   Moderate depression

15–19   Moderately severe depression

20–27   Severe depression

If you have a score of 10 or above for more than two weeks and/or scoring 3 on question 9, you should visit your doctor.

PHQ-9

The PHQ-9 (patient health questionnaire) measures low mood or depression.

Over the <u>last 2 weeks</u>, how often have you been bothered by any of the following problems?	Not at all	Several days	More than half the days	Nearly every day
1 Little interest or pleasure in doing things	0	1	2	3
2 Feeling down, depressed, or hopeless	0	1	2	3
3 Trouble falling or staying asleep, or sleeping too much	0	1	2	3
4 Feeling tired or having little energy	0	1	2	3
5 Poor appetite or overeating	0	1	2	3
6 Feeling bad about yourself – or that you are a failure or have let yourself or your family down	0	1	2	3
7 Trouble concentrating on things such as reading the newspaper or watching television	0	1	2	3
8 Moving or speaking so slowly that other people could have noticed? Or the opposite – being so fidgety or restless that you have been moving around a lot more than usual	0	1	2	3
9 Thoughts that you would be better off dead or of hurting yourself in some way	0	1	2	3
PHQ-9 total score _____				

Scoring PHQ-9

Add up your scores and see where they fall on this index of severity.

0–4   None

5–9   Mild depression

10–14   Moderate depression

15–19   Moderately severe depression

20–27   Severe depression

If you have a score of 10 or above for more than two weeks and/or scoring 3 on question 9, you should visit your doctor.

GAD-7

The GAD-7 (generalized anxiety disorder questionnaire) measures anxiety levels.

Over the <u>last 2 weeks</u>, how often have you been bothered by any of the following problems?	Not at all	Several days	More than half the days	Nearly every day
1	Feeling nervous, anxious or on edge	0	1	2	3
2	Not being able to stop or control worrying	0	1	2	3
3	Worrying too much about different things	0	1	2	3
4	Trouble relaxing	0	1	2	3
5	Being so restless that it is hard to sit still	0	1	2	3
6	Becoming easily annoyed or irritable	0	1	2	3
7	Feeling afraid, as if something awful might happen	0	1	2	3
GAD-7 total score _____				

Scoring GAD-7

Add up your scores and see where they fall on this index of severity.

0–4   None

5–10   Mild anxiety

11–15   Moderate anxiety

16–21   Severe anxiety

If you have a score of 8 or more you may wish to consider visiting your doctor.

GAD-7

The GAD-7 (generalized anxiety disorder questionnaire) measures anxiety levels.

Over the <u>last 2 weeks</u>, how often have you been bothered by any of the following problems?		Not at all	Several days	More than half the days	Nearly every day
1	Feeling nervous, anxious or on edge	0	1	2	3
2	Not being able to stop or control worrying	0	1	2	3
3	Worrying too much about different things	0	1	2	3
4	Trouble relaxing	0	1	2	3
5	Being so restless that it is hard to sit still	0	1	2	3
6	Becoming easily annoyed or irritable	0	1	2	3
7	Feeling afraid, as if something awful might happen	0	1	2	3
GAD-7 total score _____					

Scoring GAD-7

Add up your scores and see where they fall on this index of severity.

0–4   None

5–10   Mild anxiety

11–15   Moderate anxiety

16–21   Severe anxiety

If you have a score of 8 or more you may wish to consider visiting your doctor.

GAD-7

The GAD-7 (generalized anxiety disorder questionnaire) measures anxiety levels.

Over the <u>last 2 weeks</u>, how often have you been bothered by any of the following problems?		Not at all	Several days	More than half the days	Nearly every day
1	Feeling nervous, anxious or on edge	0	1	2	3
2	Not being able to stop or control worrying	0	1	2	3
3	Worrying too much about different things	0	1	2	3
4	Trouble relaxing	0	1	2	3
5	Being so restless that it is hard to sit still	0	1	2	3
6	Becoming easily annoyed or irritable	0	1	2	3
7	Feeling afraid, as if something awful might happen	0	1	2	3
GAD-7 total score _____					

Scoring GAD-7

Add up your scores and see where they fall on this index of severity.

0–4   None

5–10   Mild anxiety

11–15   Moderate anxiety

16–21   Severe anxiety

If you have a score of 8 or more you may wish to consider visiting your doctor.

Phobia Scales

The Phobia Scales measure very specific anxiety (phobias).

Choose a number from the scale below to show how much you would avoid each of the situations or objects listed below. Then write the number in the box opposite the situation.

0	1	2	3	4	5	6	7	8

Would not avoid it	Slightly avoid it	Definitely avoid it	Markedly avoid it	Always avoid it

Social situations because of a fear of being embarrassed or making a fool of myself. ☐

Certain situations because of a fear of having a panic attack or other distressing symptoms (such as loss of bladder control, vomiting or dizziness). ☐

Certain situations because of a fear of particular objects or activities (such as animals, heights, seeing blood, being in confined spaces, driving or flying). ☐

Scoring the Phobia Scales

These questions help you track the severity of your phobic anxiety. The higher the score, the more severe the anxiety.

Phobia Scales

The Phobia Scales measure very specific anxiety (phobias).

Choose a number from the scale below to show how much you would avoid each of the situations or objects listed below. Then write the number in the box opposite the situation.

0	1	2	3	4	5	6	7	8
Would not avoid it		Slightly avoid it		Definitely avoid it		Markedly avoid it		Always avoid it

Social situations because of a fear of being embarrassed or making a fool of myself. ☐

Certain situations because of a fear of having a panic attack or other distressing symptoms (such as loss of bladder control, vomiting or dizziness). ☐

Certain situations because of a fear of particular objects or activities (such as animals, heights, seeing blood, being in confined spaces, driving or flying). ☐

Scoring the Phobia Scales

These questions help you track the severity of your phobic anxiety. The higher the score, the more severe the anxiety.

Phobia Scales

The Phobia Scales measure very specific anxiety (phobias).

Choose a number from the scale below to show how much you would avoid each of the situations or objects listed below. Then write the number in the box opposite the situation.

0	1	2	3	4	5	6	7	8

Would not avoid it	Slightly avoid it	Definitely avoid it	Markedly avoid it	Always avoid it

Social situations because of a fear of being embarrassed or making a fool of myself. ☐

Certain situations because of a fear of having a panic attack or other distressing symptoms (such as loss of bladder control, vomiting or dizziness). ☐

Certain situations because of a fear of particular objects or activities (such as animals, heights, seeing blood, being in confined spaces, driving or flying). ☐

Scoring the Phobia Scales

These questions help you track the severity of your phobic anxiety. The higher the score, the more severe the anxiety.

Work and Social Adjustment Scale

The Work and Social Adjustment Scale (WASAS) measures the impact of your difficulties on a number of important areas in your life and can be helpful to keep track of improvements in each area.

People's problems sometimes affect their ability to do certain day-to-day tasks in their lives. To rate your problems look at each section and determine on the scale provided how much your problem impairs your ability to carry out the activity.

1. Work

If you are retired or choose not to have a job for reasons unrelated to your problem, please tick N/A (not applicable).

0	1	2	3	4	5	6	7	8	N/A
Not at all		Slightly		Definitely		Markedly		Very severely	☐ I cannot work

2. Home management

Cleaning, tidying, shopping, cooking, looking after home/children, paying bills, etc.

0	1	2	3	4	5	6	7	8
Not at all		Slightly		Definitely		Markedly		Very severely

3. Social leisure activities

With other people, e.g. parties, pubs, outings, entertaining, etc.

0	1	2	3	4	5	6	7	8
Not at all		Slightly		Definitely		Markedly		Very severely

4. Private leisure activities

Done alone, e.g. reading, gardening, sewing, hobbies, walking, etc.

0	1	2	3	4	5	6	7	8
Not at all		Slightly		Definitely		Markedly		Very severely

5. Family and relationships

Forming and maintaining close relationships with others including the people that I live with.

0	1	2	3	4	5	6	7	8
Not at all		Slightly		Definitely		Markedly		Very severely

Total score ☐

Scoring the Work and Social Adjustment Scale (WASAS)

This five-item measure can help you track the impact of your problems on your work, home life, social life, private activities and your relationships.

Work and Social Adjustment Scale

The Work and Social Adjustment Scale (WASAS) measures the impact of your difficulties on a number of important areas in your life and can be helpful to keep track of improvements in each area.

People's problems sometimes affect their ability to do certain day-to-day tasks in their lives. To rate your problems look at each section and determine on the scale provided how much your problem impairs your ability to carry out the activity.

1. Work

If you are retired or choose not to have a job for reasons unrelated to your problem, please tick N/A (not applicable).

0	1	2	3	4	5	6	7	8	N/A
Not at all		Slightly		Definitely		Markedly		Very severely	☐ I cannot work

2. Home management

Cleaning, tidying, shopping, cooking, looking after home/children, paying bills, etc.

0	1	2	3	4	5	6	7	8
Not at all		Slightly		Definitely		Markedly		Very severely

3. Social leisure activities

With other people, e.g. parties, pubs, outings, entertaining, etc.

0	1	2	3	4	5	6	7	8
Not at all		Slightly		Definitely		Markedly		Very severely

4. Private leisure activities

Done alone, e.g. reading, gardening, sewing, hobbies, walking, etc.

0	1	2	3	4	5	6	7	8
Not at all		Slightly		Definitely		Markedly		Very severely

5. Family and relationships

Forming and maintaining close relationships with others including the people that I live with.

0	1	2	3	4	5	6	7	8
Not at all		Slightly		Definitely		Markedly		Very severely

Total score ☐

Scoring the Work and Social Adjustment Scale (WASAS)

This five-item measure can help you track the impact of your problems on your work, home life, social life, private activities and your relationships.

Work and Social Adjustment Scale

The Work and Social Adjustment Scale (WASAS) measures the impact of your difficulties on a number of important areas in your life and can be helpful to keep track of improvements in each area.

People's problems sometimes affect their ability to do certain day-to-day tasks in their lives. To rate your problems look at each section and determine on the scale provided how much your problem impairs your ability to carry out the activity.

1. Work

If you are retired or choose not to have a job for reasons unrelated to your problem, please tick N/A (not applicable).

0	1	2	3	4	5	6	7	8	N/A
Not at all		Slightly		Definitely		Markedly		Very severely	☐ I cannot work

2. Home management

Cleaning, tidying, shopping, cooking, looking after home/children, paying bills, etc.

0	1	2	3	4	5	6	7	8
Not at all		Slightly		Definitely		Markedly		Very severely

3. Social leisure activities

With other people, e.g. parties, pubs, outings, entertaining, etc.

0	1	2	3	4	5	6	7	8
Not at all		Slightly		Definitely		Markedly		Very severely

4. Private leisure activities

Done alone, e.g. reading, gardening, sewing, hobbies, walking, etc.

0	1	2	3	4	5	6	7	8
Not at all		Slightly		Definitely		Markedly		Very severely

5. Family and relationships

Forming and maintaining close relationships with others including the people that I live with.

0	1	2	3	4	5	6	7	8
Not at all		Slightly		Definitely		Markedly		Very severely

Total score ☐

Scoring the Work and Social Adjustment Scale (WASAS)

This five-item measure can help you track the impact of your problems on your work, home life, social life, private activities and your relationships.

Penn State Worry Questionnaire

Name.. Date............

Enter the number that best describes how typical or characteristic each item is of you:

	Statements	Not at all typical	Not very typical	Some-what typical	Fairly typical	Very typical
1	If I don't have enough time to do everything, I don't worry about it.*	1	2	3	4	5
2	My worries overwhelm me.	1	2	3	4	5
3	I don't tend to worry about things.*	1	2	3	4	5
4	Many situations make me worry.	1	2	3	4	5
5	I know I should not worry about things, but I just cannot help it.	1	2	3	4	5
6	When I am under pressure I worry a lot.	1	2	3	4	5
7	I am always worrying about something.	1	2	3	4	5
8	I find it easy to dismiss worrisome thoughts.*	1	2	3	4	5
9	As soon as I finish one task, I start to worry about everything else I have to do.	1	2	3	4	5
10	I never worry about anything.*	1	2	3	4	5

Statements		Not at all typical	Not very typical	Some- what typical	Fairly typical	Very typical
11	When there is nothing more I can do about a concern, I do not worry about it any more.*	1	2	3	4	5
12	I have been a worrier all my life.	1	2	3	4	5
13	I notice that I have been worrying about things.	1	2	3	4	5
14	Once I start worrying, I cannot stop.	1	2	3	4	5
15	I worry all the time.	1	2	3	4	5
16	I worry about projects until they are all done.	1	2	3	4	5
Total (add all the scores together, after reversing*) _____						

How to score the Penn State Worry Questionnaire

Add up your scores for this measure using a scale from 1–5, where:

1 = not at all typical

5 = very typical.

It is important that you 'reverse score' items marked with an * as follows:

Reverse score items 1, 3, 8, 10 and 11:

Very typical of me = 1 (circled 4 on the sheet)

Circled 3 on the sheet = 2

Circled 2 on the sheet = 3

Circled 1 on the sheet = 4

Not at all typical of me = 5 (circled 1 on the sheet).

A score of 45 or more would suggest that worrying is a significant problem.

Dimensions of Anger Reactions II

As accurately as you can, indicate the degree to which the following statements describe your feelings and behaviours. Rate the degree to which each statement applies to you.

1. I often find myself getting angry at people or situations.

0	1	2	3	4
Not at all	A little	Moderately so	Fairly much	Very much

2. When I do get angry, I get really mad.

0	1	2	3	4
Not at all	A little	Moderately so	Fairly much	Very much

3. When I get angry, I stay angry.

0	1	2	3	4
Not at all	A little	Moderately so	Fairly much	Very much

4. When I get angry at someone, I want to hit or strike the person.

0	1	2	3	4
Not at all	A little	Moderately so	Fairly much	Very much

5. My anger interferes with my ability to get my work done.

0	1	2	3	4
Not at all	A little	Moderately so	Fairly much	Very much

6. My anger prevents me from getting along with people as well as I would like to.

0	1	2	3	4
Not at all	A little	Moderately so	Fairly much	Very much

7. My anger has a bad effect on my health.

0	1	2	3	4
Not at all	A little	Moderately so	Fairly much	Very much

Scoring the Dimensions of Anger Reaction II

This scale measures four areas of anger responses (i.e. frequency, intensity, duration, and physical antagonism), and three related to impact on functioning (i.e. adverse effects on social relationships, work, and health). Add up your scores across the seven items. A score of 18 or above would be considered to be in the high range and you may wish to talk to your doctor.

Rosenberg Self-Esteem Scale

	Strongly disagree	Disagree	Agree	Strongly agree
1. I feel that I am a person of worth, at least on an equal plane with others.				
2. I feel that I have a number of good qualities.				
3. All in all, I am inclined to feel that I am a failure.				
4. I am able to do things as well as most other people.				
5. I feel I do not have much to be proud of.				
6. I take a positive attitude towards myself.				
7. On the whole, I am satisfied with myself.				
8. I wish I could have more respect for myself.				
9. I certainly feel useless at times.				
10. At times I think I am no good at all.				

Scoring the Rosenberg Self-Esteem Scale

Add up the scores being careful to reverse score some items as indicated below. The scale ranges from 0–30. A score of under 15 suggests low self-esteem.

Scores are calculated as follows:

For items 1, 2, 4, 6 and 7:

Strongly agree	3
Agree	2
Disagree	1
Strongly disagree	0

For items 3, 5, 8, 9 and 10 (which are reversed):

Strongly agree	0
Agree	1
Disagree	2
Strongly disagree	3

Perceived Stress Scale: 10 items

The questions in this scale ask you about your feelings and thoughts during the last month. In each case, please indicate with a tick how often you felt or thought a certain way.

1. In the last month, how often have you been upset because of something that happened unexpectedly?

0	1	2	3	4
Never	Almost never	Sometimes	Fairly often	Very often

2. In the last month, how often have you felt that you were unable to control the important things in your life?

0	1	2	3	4
Never	Almost never	Sometimes	Fairly often	Very often

3. In the last month, how often have you felt nervous and stressed?

0	1	2	3	4
Never	Almost never	Sometimes	Fairly often	Very often

4. In the last month, how often have you felt confident about your ability to handle your personal problems?

0	1	2	3	4
Never	Almost never	Sometimes	Fairly often	Very often

5. In the last month, how often have you felt that things were going your way?

0	1	2	3	4
Never	Almost never	Sometimes	Fairly often	Very often

6. In the last month, how often have you found that you could not cope with all the things that you had to do?

0	1	2	3	4
Never	Almost never	Sometimes	Fairly often	Very often

7. In the last month, how often have you been able to control irritations in your life?

0	1	2	3	4
Never	Almost never	Sometimes	Fairly often	Very often

8. In the last month, how often have you felt that you were on top of things?

0	1	2	3	4
Never	Almost never	Sometimes	Fairly often	Very often

9. In the last month, how often have you been angered because of things that were outside of your control?

0	1	2	3	4
Never	Almost never	Sometimes	Fairly often	Very often

10. In the last month, how often have you felt difficulties were piling up so high that you could not overcome them?

0	1	2	3	4
Never	Almost never	Sometimes	Fairly often	Very often

Scoring the Perceived Stress Scale: 10 items

- Add up all the negatively stated questions – 1, 2, 3, 6, 9 and 10.
- Then reverse score the positively stated questions – 4, 5, 7 and 8. For these questions:
- $0 = 4$
- $1 = 3$
- $2 = 2$
- $3 = 1$
- $4 = 0$
- Add the two scores together.
- The higher the score, the more stress you are experiencing at that given time.

Perceived Stress Scale: 4 items

The questions in this scale ask you about your feelings and thoughts during the last month. In each case, please indicate with a tick how often you felt or thought a certain way.

1. In the last month, how often have you felt that you were unable to control the important things in your life?

0	1	2	3	4
Never	Almost never	Sometimes	Fairly often	Very often

2. In the last month, how often have you felt confident about your ability to handle your personal problems?

0	1	2	3	4
Never	Almost never	Sometimes	Fairly often	Very often

3. In the last month, how often have you felt that things were going your way?

0	1	2	3	4
Never	Almost never	Sometimes	Fairly often	Very often

4. In the last month, how often have you felt difficulties were piling up so high that you could not overcome them?

0	1	2	3	4
Never	Almost never	Sometimes	Fairly often	Very often

Scoring the Perceived Stress Scale: 4 items

This scale measures the degree to which situations are considered to be stressful. Add up your scores being careful to reverse score some items as indicated below.

Reverse score items 2 and 3:

0 = 4

1 = 3

2 = 2

3 = 1

4 = 0

Monitoring your progress

Use the graphs below to plot your progress over the next few weeks.

Your mood scores on the mood scale

Plot 'scores' on the vertical axis

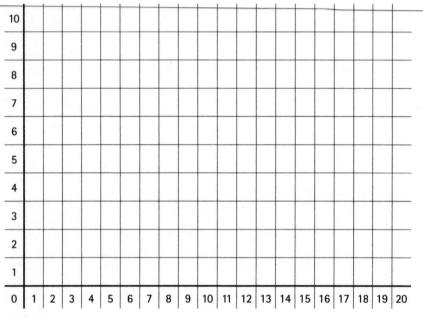

Time/Weeks

Monitoring your progress

Use the graphs below to plot your progress over the next few weeks.

Your mood scores on the mood scale

Plot 'scores' on the vertical axis

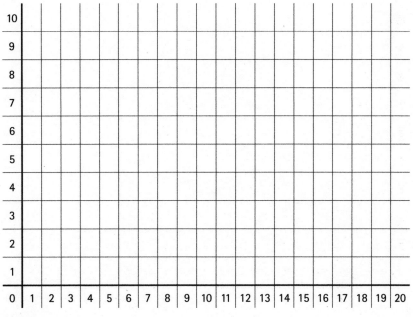

Time/Weeks

Monitoring your progress

Use the graphs below to plot your progress over the next few weeks.

Your mood scores on the mood scale

Plot 'scores' on the vertical axis

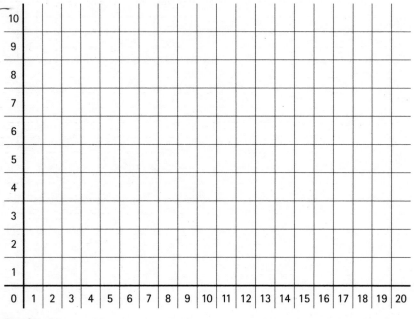

Time/Weeks

PHQ-9 scores

Plot 'scores' on the vertical axis

Time/Weeks

PHQ-9 scores

Plot 'scores' on the vertical axis

30																				
29																				
28																				
27																				
26																				
25																				
24																				
23																				
22																				
21																				
20																				
19																				
18																				
17																				
16																				
15																				
14																				
13																				
12																				
11																				
10																				
9																				
8																				
7																				
6																				
5																				
4																				
3																				
2																				
1																				
0	1	2	3	4	5	6	7	8	9	10	11	12	13	14	15	16	17	18	19	20

Time/Weeks

PHQ-9 scores

Plot 'scores' on the vertical axis

30																				
29																				
28																				
27																				
26																				
25																				
24																				
23																				
22																				
21																				
20																				
19																				
18																				
17																				
16																				
15																				
14																				
13																				
12																				
11																				
10																				
9																				
8																				
7																				
6																				
5																				
4																				
3																				
2																				
1																				
0	1	2	3	4	5	6	7	8	9	10	11	12	13	14	15	16	17	18	19	20

Time/Weeks

GAD-7 scores

Plot 'scores' on the vertical axis

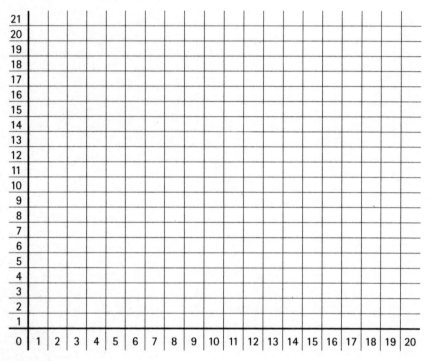

Time/Weeks

GAD-7 scores

Plot 'scores' on the vertical axis

21																				
20																				
19																				
18																				
17																				
16																				
15																				
14																				
13																				
12																				
11																				
10																				
9																				
8																				
7																				
6																				
5																				
4																				
3																				
2																				
1																				
0	1	2	3	4	5	6	7	8	9	10	11	12	13	14	15	16	17	18	19	20

Time/Weeks

GAD-7 scores

Plot 'scores' on the vertical axis

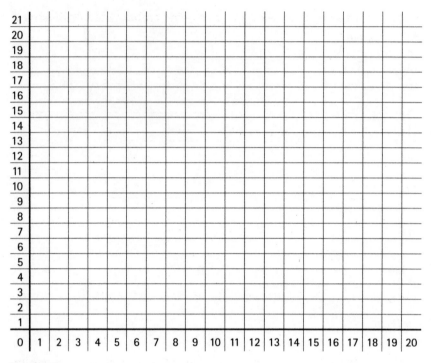

Time/Weeks

Phobia scale scores

Plot 'scores' on the vertical axis

1. Social situations because of a fear of being embarrassed or making a fool of myself.

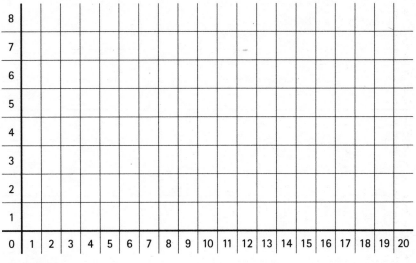

Time/Weeks

2. Certain situations because of a fear of having a panic attack or other distressing symptoms (such as loss of bladder control, vomiting or dizziness).

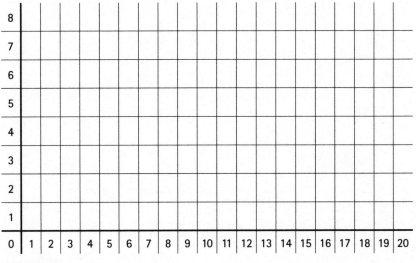

Time/Weeks

3. Certain situations because of a fear of particular objects or activities (such as animals, heights, seeing blood, being in confined spaces, driving or flying).

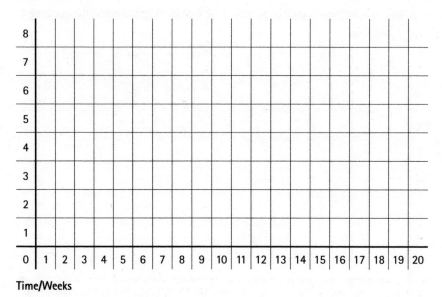

Time/Weeks

Phobia scale scores

Plot 'scores' on the vertical axis

1. Social situations because of a fear of being embarrassed or making a fool of myself.

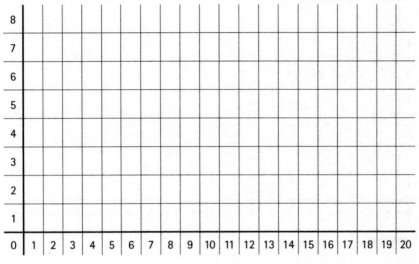

Time/Weeks

2. Certain situations because of a fear of having a panic attack or other distressing symptoms (such as loss of bladder control, vomiting or dizziness).

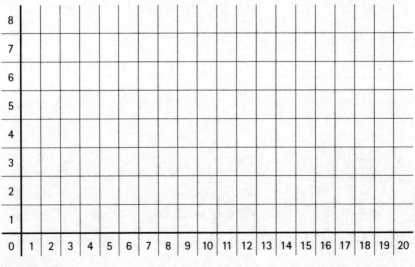

Time/Weeks

3. Certain situations because of a fear of particular objects or activities (such as animals, heights, seeing blood, being in confined spaces, driving or flying).

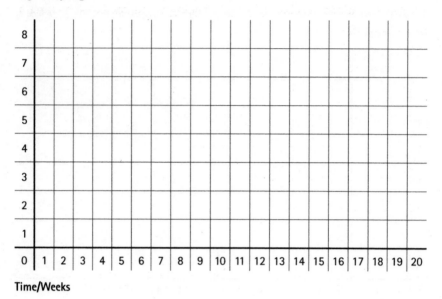

Time/Weeks

Phobia scale scores

Plot 'scores' on the vertical axis

1. Social situations because of a fear of being embarrassed or making a fool of myself.

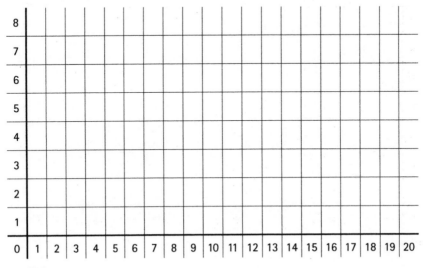

Time/Weeks

2. Certain situations because of a fear of having a panic attack or other distressing symptoms (such as loss of bladder control, vomiting or dizziness).

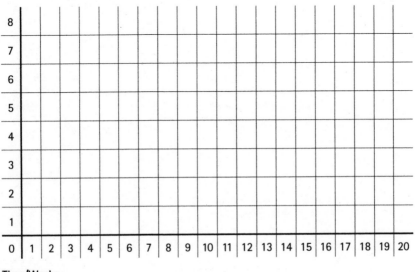

Time/Weeks

3. Certain situations because of a fear of particular objects or activities (such as animals, heights, seeing blood, being in confined spaces, driving or flying).

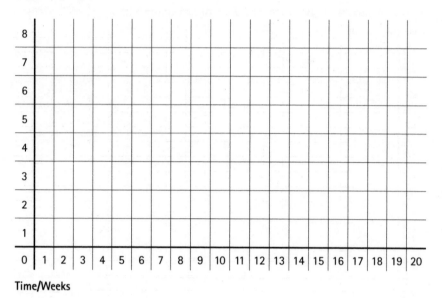

Time/Weeks

Work and Social Adjustment scores

Plot 'scores' on the vertical axis

Time/Weeks

Penn State Worry Questionnaire scores

Plot 'scores' on the vertical axis

40
39
38
37
36
35
34
33
32
31
30
29
28
27
26
25
24
23
22
21
20
19
18
17
16
15
14
13
12
11
10
9
8
7
6
5
4
3
2
1

0 1 2 3 4 5 6 7 8 9 10 11 12 13 14 15 16 17 18 19 20

Time/Weeks

Dimensions of Anger II

Plot 'scores' on the vertical axis

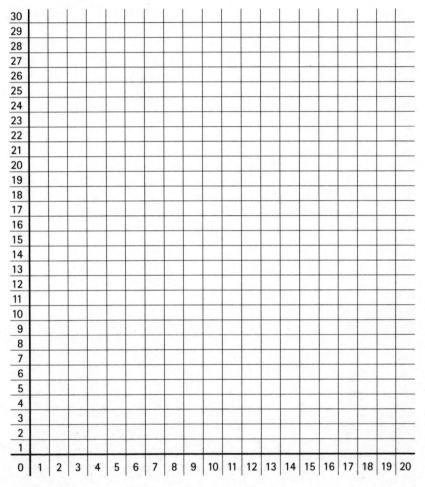

Time/Weeks

Rosenberg Self-Esteem Scale

Plot 'scores' on the vertical axis

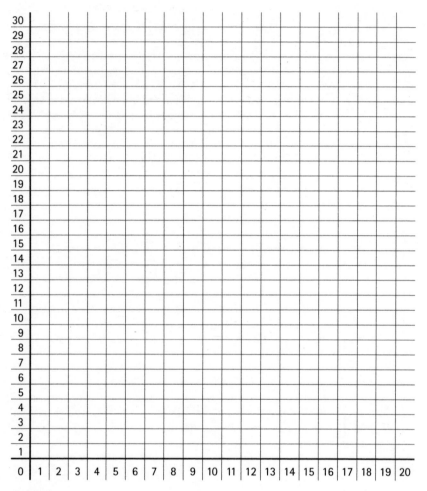

Time/Weeks

Perceived Stress Scale

Plot 'scores' on the vertical axis

Time/Weeks

Symptoms diagram

Situation:

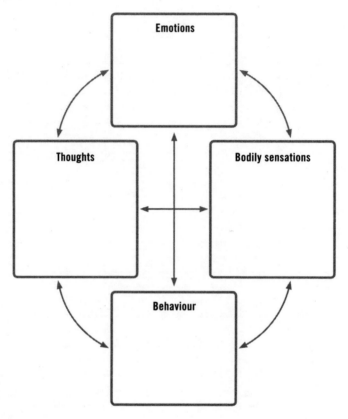

Symptoms diagram

Situation:

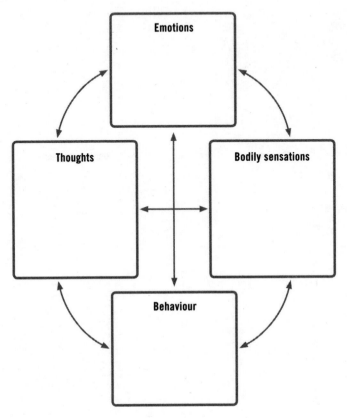

Symptoms diagram

Situation:

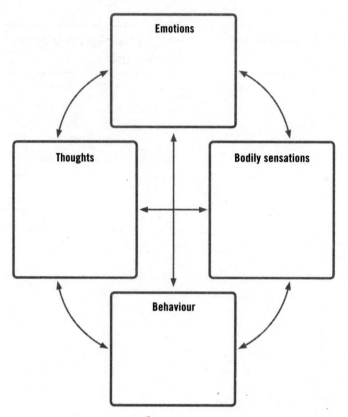

Advantages of changing and disadvantages of staying the same

Advantages of changing	Disadvantages of staying the same

My conclusion:

Problem statement and goals

My problem statement

Symptoms

Trigger	Emotions	Behaviours	Physical	Thoughts	Impact

Problem statement

_____

_____

_____

_____

_____

_____

My personal goals

Goal 1

_____

_____

_____

_____

Goal 2

_____

_____

_____

_____

Goal 3

_____

_____

_____

_____

Goal 4

_____

_____

_____

_____

Behavioural Activation

Daily Activities Worksheet

Time	Activity	Enjoyment (0–10)	Importance (0–10)
5–6 a.m.			
6–7 a.m.			
7–8 a.m.			
8–9 a.m.			
9–10 a.m.			
10–11 a.m.			
11–12 a.m.			
1–2 p.m.			
2–3 p.m.			
3–4 p.m.			

Time	Activity	Enjoyment (0–10)	Importance (0–10)
4–5 p.m.			
5–6 p.m.			
6–7 p.m.			
7–8 p.m.			
8–9 p.m.			
9–10 p.m.			
10–11 p.m.			
11–12 p.m.			
12–1 a.m.			
1–2 a.m.			
2–5 a.m.			
Overall mood for the day (0–10) ___			

Behavioural Activation

Daily Activities Worksheet

Time	Activity	Enjoyment (0–10)	Importance (0–10)
5–6 a.m.			
6–7 a.m.			
7–8 a.m.			
8–9 a.m.			
9–10 a.m.			
10–11 a.m.			
11–12 a.m.			
1–2 p.m.			
2–3 p.m.			
3–4 p.m.			

Time	Activity	Enjoyment (0–10)	Importance (0–10)
4–5 p.m.			
5–6 p.m.			
6–7 p.m.			
7–8 p.m.			
8–9 p.m.			
9–10 p.m.			
10–11 p.m.			
11–12 p.m.			
12–1 a.m.			
1–2 a.m.			
2–5 a.m.			
Overall mood for the day (0–10) ____			

Behavioural Activation

Daily Activities Worksheet

Time	Activity	Enjoyment (0–10)	Importance (0–10)
5–6 a.m.			
6–7 a.m.			
7–8 a.m.			
8–9 a.m.			
9–10 a.m.			
10–11 a.m.			
11–12 a.m.			
1–2 p.m.			
2–3 p.m.			
3–4 p.m.			

Time	Activity	Enjoyment (0–10)	Importance (0–10)
4–5 p.m.			
5–6 p.m.			
6–7 p.m.			
7–8 p.m.			
8–9 p.m.			
9–10 p.m.			
10–11 p.m.			
11–12 p.m.			
12–1 a.m.			
1–2 a.m.			
2–5 a.m.			
Overall mood for the day (0–10) ___			

Activity assessment

What would you like to achieve in each of the following areas?

1. Relationships (forming and maintaining close relationships with others including family, friends and/or romantic partner)
2. Education/career (this could be formal education or self-learning, paid or voluntary employment)
3. Recreation/interests (leisure time, having fun or relaxing, volunteering)
4. Mind/body/spirituality (physical and mental health, religion and/or spirituality)
5. Daily responsibilities (obligations and responsibilities to others and to your belongings. This could include things like cleaning, tidying, shopping, cooking, looking after home/children, paying bills)

Life Areas, Values and Activities Inventory

Life area: Relationships

Value:	Enjoyment (0–10)	Importance (0–10)
Activity 1:		
Activity 2:		
Activity 3:		
Activity 4:		
Activity 5:		

Life area: Education/career

Value:	Enjoyment (0–10)	Importance (0–10)
Activity 1:		
Activity 2:		
Activity 3:		
Activity 4:		
Activity 5:		

Life area: Recreation/interests

Value:	Enjoyment (0–10)	Importance (0–10)
Activity 1:		
Activity 2:		
Activity 3:		
Activity 4:		
Activity 5:		

Life area: Mind/body/spirituality

Value:	Enjoyment (0–10)	Importance (0–10)
Activity 1:		
Activity 2:		
Activity 3:		
Activity 4:		
Activity 5:		

Life area: Daily responsibilities

Value:	Enjoyment (0–10)	Importance (0–10)
Activity 1:		
Activity 2:		
Activity 3:		
Activity 4:		
Activity 5:		

Activity hierarchy

Make a note of the fifteen activities you would most like to achieve, and rate them in order of difficulty from 1 (least difficult) to 15 (most difficult).

Activity	Indicate level of difficulty (1–15)

Problem-solving

1. Specify your problem precisely

....

....

....

....

....

....

....

2. Write down as many possible solutions as you can

1. ....

2. ....

3. ....

4. ....

5. ....

6. ....

7. ....

8. ....

9. ....

10. ....

3. Think through the pros and cons of each solution

Solution 1: ....
....

Pros	Cons

Solution 2: ....
....

Pros	Cons

Solution 3: ....
....

Pros	Cons

Solution 4: ....
....

Pros	Cons

Solution 5: ....
....

Pros	Cons

Solution 6: ....
....

Pros	Cons

Solution 7: ....

....

Pros	Cons

Solution 8: ....

....

Pros	Cons

Solution 9: ....
....

Pros	Cons

Solution 10: ....
....

Pros	Cons

4. Select the best possible solution

Solution: ....
....

5. Plan how to carry out the solution

....
....
....
....
....
....
....
....
....
....
....

6. Put the plan into action

7. Review what happens

....
....
....
....
....
....
....
....
....
....
....

Problem-solving

---

1. Specify your problem precisely

....

....

....

....

....

....

....

---

2. Write down as many possible solutions as you can

1. ....

2. ....

3. ....

4. ....

5. ....

6. ....

7. ....

8. ....

9. ....

10. ....

3. Think through the pros and cons of each solution

Solution 1: ....
....

Pros	Cons

Solution 2: ....
....

Pros	Cons

Solution 3: ....
....

Pros	Cons

Solution 4: ....
....

Pros	Cons

Solution 5: ....
....

Pros	Cons

Solution 6: ....
....

Pros	Cons

Solution 7: ....
....

Pros	Cons

Solution 8: ....
....

Pros	Cons

Solution 9: ....
....

Pros	Cons

Solution 10: ....
....

Pros	Cons

4. Select the best possible solution

Solution: ....
....

5. Plan how to carry out the solution

....
....
....
....
....
....
....
....
....
....
....

6. Put the plan into action

7. Review what happens

....
....
....
....
....
....
....
....
....
....
....

Problem-solving

---

1. Specify your problem precisely

....

....

....

....

....

....

....

---

2. Write down as many possible solutions as you can

1. ....

2. ....

3. ....

4. ....

5. ....

6. ....

7. ....

8. ....

9. ....

10. ....

3. *Think through the pros and cons of each solution*

Solution 1: ....
....

Pros	Cons

Solution 2: ....
....

Pros	Cons

Solution 3: ....
....

Pros	Cons

Solution 4: ....
....

Pros	Cons

Solution 5: ....

....

Pros	Cons

Solution 6: ....

....

Pros	Cons

Solution 7: ....
....

Pros	Cons

Solution 8: ....
....

Pros	Cons

Solution 9: ....
....

Pros	Cons

Solution 10: ....
....

Pros	Cons

4. Select the best possible solution

Solution: ....

....

5. Plan how to carry out the solution

....
....
....
....
....
....
....
....
....
....
....
....

6. Put the plan into action

7. Review what happens

....
....
....
....
....
....
....
....
....
....
....

Graded exposure hierarchy

1. _____

   _____

2. _____

   _____

3. _____

   _____

4. _____

   _____

5. _____

   _____

6. _____

   _____

7. _____

   _____

8. _____

   _____

9. _____

   _____

10. _____

    _____

Exposure Diary

Anxiety scale

0	25	50	75	100
No anxiety	Mild anxiety	Moderate anxiety		Severe anxiety/panic

Date/Time	Activity	Anxiety level (using scale above: 0 = no anxiety, 100 = severe panic anxiety)

Exposure Diary

Anxiety scale

0	25	50	75	100
No anxiety	Mild anxiety	Moderate anxiety		Severe anxiety/panic

Date/Time	Activity	Anxiety level (using scale above: 0 = no anxiety, 100 = severe panic anxiety)

Exposure Diary

Anxiety scale

0	25	50	75	100
No anxiety	Mild anxiety	Moderate anxiety		Severe anxiety/panic

Date/Time	Activity	Anxiety level (using scale above: 0 = no anxiety, 100 = severe panic anxiety)

Identifying my thinking errors diary

Events	Feelings	Thoughts	Possible thinking errors

Identifying my thinking errors diary

Events	Feelings	Thoughts	Possible thinking errors

Identifying my thinking errors diary

Events	Feelings	Thoughts	Possible thinking errors

Four-column Thought Diary

Date	Situation	Emotion	Thought
Include day of week and time of day where relevant	Where were you? What were you doing? Who were you with?	Rate intensity 0–100 per cent	What was going through your head just as you started to feel the emotion? List all thoughts and images. **Rate belief 0–100 per cent and circle the most upsetting thought**

Four-column Thought Diary

Date	Situation	Emotion	Thought
Include day of week and time of day where relevant	Where were you? What were you doing? Who were you with?	**Rate intensity 0–100 per cent**	What was going through your head just as you started to feel the emotion? List all thoughts and images. **Rate belief 0–100 per cent and circle the most upsetting thought**

Four-column Thought Diary

Date	Situation	Emotion	Thought
Include day of week and time of day where relevant	Where were you? What were you doing? Who were you with?	**Rate intensity 0–100 per cent**	What was going through your head just as you started to feel the emotion? List all thoughts and images. **Rate belief 0–100 per cent and circle the most upsetting thought**

Nine-column Thought Diary

Date	Situation	Emotion Rate intensity 0–100%	Thought Rate belief 0–100% and circle the most upsetting thought	Evidence for the most upsetting thought	Evidence against the most upsetting thought	Alternative thought and rate belief in it	Re-rate belief in upsetting thought and intensity of emotion	What to do next

Nine-column Thought Diary

Date	Situation	Emotion Rate intensity 0–100%	Thought Rate belief 0–100% and circle the most upsetting thought	Evidence for the most upsetting thought	Evidence against the most upsetting thought	Alternative thought and rate belief in it	Re–rate belief in upsetting thought and intensity of emotion	What to do next

Nine-column Thought Diary

Date	Situation	Emotion Rate intensity 0–100%	Thought Rate belief 0–100% and circle the most upsetting thought	Evidence for the most upsetting thought	Evidence against the most upsetting thought	Alternative thought and rate belief in it	Re-rate belief in upsetting thought and intensity of emotion	What to do next

Behavioural experiment worksheet

Date:
1. Thought/belief/behaviour to be tested and strength of conviction:
2. Ideas for experiment to test the thought/belief/behaviour. Circle the best one:
3. Specific predictions about what will happen and how you will record the outcome:
4. Anticipated problems and potential solutions:

5. Describe the experiment you carried out:

6. Describe what happened:

7. Re-rate your conviction:

8. Revised thought/belief/behaviour that can be tested:

Behavioural experiment worksheet

Date:
1. Thought/belief/behaviour to be tested and strength of conviction:
2. Ideas for experiment to test the thought/belief/behaviour. Circle the best one:
3. Specific predictions about what will happen and how you will record the outcome:
4. Anticipated problems and potential solutions:

5. Describe the experiment you carried out:

6. Describe what happened:

7. Re-rate your conviction:

8. Revised thought/belief/behaviour that can be tested:

Behavioural experiment worksheet

Date:
1. Thought/belief/behaviour to be tested and strength of conviction:
2. Ideas for experiment to test the thought/belief/behaviour. Circle the best one:
3. Specific predictions about what will happen and how you will record the outcome:
4. Anticipated problems and potential solutions:

5. Describe the experiment you carried out:

6. Describe what happened:

7. Re-rate your conviction:

8. Revised thought/belief/behaviour that can be tested:

Bigger picture/longitudinal formulation

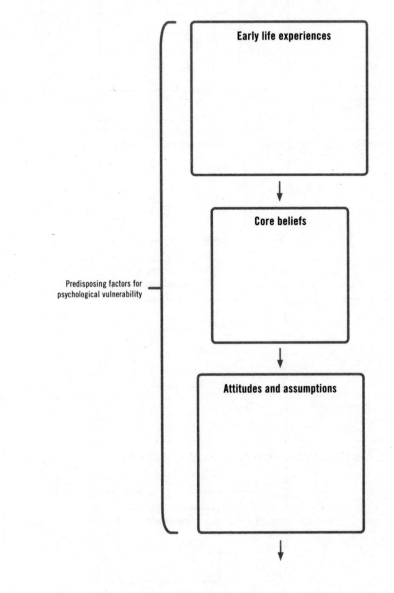

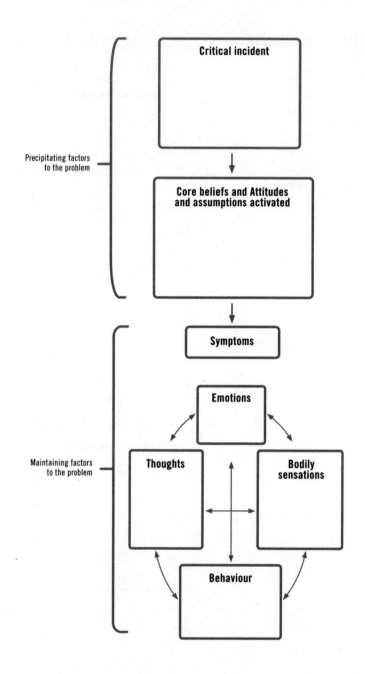

Examining evidence for and against an 'If ... then ...' belief

Belief to be examined (remember to insert percentage level of conviction):
Questions to examine belief:
Level of conviction following examination:
Potential new belief:

Examining evidence for and against an 'If ... then ...' belief

Belief to be examined (remember to insert percentage level of conviction):
Questions to examine belief:
Level of conviction following examination:
Potential new belief:

Examining evidence for and against an 'If ... then ...' belief

Belief to be examined (remember to insert percentage level of conviction):
Questions to examine belief:
Level of conviction following examination:
Potential new belief:

Examining advantages and disadvantages of an 'If ... then ...' belief

Belief to be examined:	
Advantages of living by this assumption	Disadvantages of living by this assumption

New belief based on advantages and disadvantages:

Examining advantages and disadvantages of an 'If ... then ...' belief

Belief to be examined:	
Advantages of living by this assumption	Disadvantages of living by this assumption
New belief based on advantages and disadvantages:	

Examining advantages and disadvantages of an 'If ... then ...' belief

Belief to be examined:	
Advantages of living by this assumption	Disadvantages of living by this assumption
New belief based on advantages and disadvantages:	

Identifying your setbacks

Situation that led to emotional problems in the past	How you reacted to the situation in terms of your thoughts, emotions and behaviour (e.g. effect on mood/anxiety/anger/ stress/self-esteem)	Situation that might lead to a setback in future

Early warning signs

Emotions

Thoughts

Bodily sensations

Behaviour

Staying well plan

1. Think about how your original problem started.

2. What kept my problem going? Based on your problem statements and your understanding of the connections between your emotions, bodily sensations, behaviour and thoughts, write down what kept your problems going. Clue: think about your interpretation of events/situations/bodily sensations and your response, (e.g. withdrawing).

3. What I have learned so far: My quick reference guide (using the summaries that you have made at the end of each chapter).

Monitoring your mood

You have also been monitoring your mood and anxiety on a regular basis and have plotted them on the chart. Use the box below to write how this might have been helpful to you.

---

4. Based on the work you have done so far, think about the changes you have made that you want to continue to develop.

---

5. What areas in your life require further attention?

6. *Where do you see yourself in three months' time? What strategies from this book will you continue to keep practising and using in your life to help you get there?*

7. *Where do you see yourself in six months' time? What strategies from this book will you continue to keep practising and using in your life to help you get there?*

8. *Where do you see yourself in one year's time? What strategies from this book will you continue to keep practising and using in your life to help you get there?*

9. Where do you see yourself in five years' time? What strategies from this book will you continue to keep practising and using in your life to help you get there?

10. Based on your work earlier, what situations are most likely to lead to a setback and how will you deal with them? It may be that you want to involve other people to help you (e.g. contact your supporter again if you have one) or it may be there are strategies you can use without additional help.

Situation	What I will do

11. *What are your early warning signs and how will you respond to them?*

Early Warning Signs	How I will respond

12. *Finally, if you had to send a tweet (140 characters, including spaces and punctuation) to the world with one or two key messages about how to overcome emotional problems, what would you tweet?*

Index